Concepts at Work

Concepts at Work

*On the Linguistic Infrastructure
of World Politics*

Edited by Piki Ish-Shalom

University of Michigan Press
Ann Arbor

This book is dedicated to Katty Ish-Shalom, my conception of love.

Contents

Digital materials related to this title can be found on the Fulcrum platform via the following citable URL https://doi.org/10.3998/mpub.11719182

And then there is the wonderful staff of the University of Michigan Press: The period choice for a very nice first writer, Danielle Coty, Mary Hashman, and Elizabeth Sherburn Demers. They were both supportive and everything, from the good for a published time and beyond.

Preface

I cradle the book in my arms, unsure exactly how I got here: empirically, not conceptually. Conceptually speaking I am well aware of the importance of the topic, of the political importance of concepts and conceptions, and their role in shaping interactions within and between societies and states. The book is about this importance, and in the following pages it will speak for itself. But, empirically, how almost six years after a workshop co-organized in Jerusalem by me and Roee Kibrik, did I get to cradle this edited volume, especially when I was warned time and again from getting myself involved in editing? The mystery, the empirical mystery, is deep indeed, but I can assure you that the journey was not that torturous, and it was even rewarding because of the support I got along the road from the participants (turned contributors), and the editorial staff of the University of Michigan Press.

Accordingly, my gratitude goes first and foremost to the contributors of the chapters, for their first-rate scholarship, comradeship, and patience throughout the long years of working on the book: Jonas Wolff, Anna Geis, Brent Steele, Luke Campbell, Neta Strunin-Kremer, Philippe Beaulieu-Brossard, Christian Bueger, Felix Berenskötter, Mor Mitrani, Jan Wilkens, and Oliver Kessler. I also want to thank those workshop participants who did not continue with us to the book: Roee Kibrik, Raef Zreik, Deganit Paikowsky, Ariel Zellman, and Christopher Hobson. Each one of them enriched our understandings of concepts at work, and left her/his mark on the published product of the workshop. Of course, the workshop could not have taken place without the great staff of The Leonard Davis Institute for International Relations: Chanoch Wolpe and Michal Barak, for whom I am grateful on countless accounts and events.

And then there is the wonderful staff of the University of Michigan Press, the perfect choice for every academic writer: Danielle Coty, Marcia LaBrenz, and Elizabeth Sherburn Demers. They were both supportive and professional, from the go ahead up to publication and beyond. To this admired list I add two anonymous reviewers, who did a superb job in pointing the merits of the preliminary manuscript, as well as its weak points, pushing all of us, especially me, to strive to excellence. I hope they succeeded, yet if they failed, the fault is totally mine for not heeding all their good advices.

Final thanks go to the two constants in my life: family and birds. On the family side it is to Katty (to whom—my conception of love—I dedicate this book), and our three kids (age is certainly not a constant in their case, and they keep growing and maturing from book to book): Noga, Shahaf, and Inbar. On the birds' side, it is to all those feathered perfections, who keep me energized despite the occasional dreary hours of academic life.

Thank you all,
Piki Ish-Shalom

CHAPTER 1

Introduction

Piki Ish-Shalom

Concepts are meaningful. They are so in two ways: (1) as expressively mental representations of phenomena and (2) because of their social and, no less importantly, political significance and function. Concepts gain mutual strength from these two aspects of their nature because an expressively mental representation of a phenomenon can serve as a roadmap for political action. Thus, our conceptions of concepts generate a range of normative stances and commitments, which often dovetail with political measures. This means that concepts are central to our thinking about the world and our actions in it. A good example of this is the concept of "sovereignty," which has long been understood as the jurisdiction of a state over its domestic affairs and its autonomy from external interference (see Wolff, this volume). But this longevity ended, and at the close of the twentieth century a new understanding emerged of sovereignty having the meaning of responsibility. For a brief moment, many thought and hoped that a new era of international politics had dawned, one dominated by a Responsibility to Protect that would empower active intervention by the international community in situations like Darfur and Kenya.

By not opening the black box of sovereignty and studying what it means and to whom, and by not examining the contestation over its proper meaning, we miss an important aspect of international politics. The understandings and contents that we ascribe to concepts, or as termed here "the conceptions of concepts," are socially and politically meaningful. This insight adds an important dimension to the scholarship of constructivists and other interpretivist fellow travelers. In contrast to positivists and neo-positivists, constructivists stress the role of social meanings as critical components of social knowledge and intersubjectivity and their subsequent importance in constructing social reality (Onuf 1989; Kratochwil 1989). What many mainstream constructivists fail to grasp (see Wiener 2013 for an exception; see also Wilkens and Kessler, this volume) is the fundamental importance of contestation and of the short term in the construction of meanings, knowledge, and hence social reality. Contestation over meanings by and through the medium of concepts (see below) is part of the social construction of social reality. Moreover, although quite often the social constructions of social knowledge and social reality are long-term social processes, they also involve short-term political contestations. The meanings of concepts are both fought over politically and learned and internalized socially. Understood thus, it is more correct to talk about the sociopolitical construction of the sociopolitical world. Politics, broadly construed (see below), is an inherent part of the social world or at least of many public realms of the social world, and international politics is obviously one such realm. In a sense, concepts and their meanings are the data (the entry points) of studying contestation and fully encapsulate the sociopolitical construction of the sociopolitical world.

The ten chapters in this edited volume explore these themes. Each chapter analyzes a different case study of a concept and the conceptual politics surrounding it. Following the reasoning of this volume, and notwithstanding the crucial importance of definitions to the academic endeavor, the contributing authors will not offer a conclusive definition for the concepts they study. Indeed, definitions are expected in order to create a common language with the readership. And definitions help to clarify standpoints and to understand the source of disagreements. However, for chapters that aim to show the essential contestedness of concepts, it does not make much sense to offer a single authoritative definition. The authors will, rather, present and analyze a spectrum of available definitions in an effort to reveal their essential contestedness and analyze their political function—in other words, how the definitions function in certain fields, including the political one.

This introductory chapter explicates what concepts are and explores relevant theoretical perspectives, with particular focus on Reinhart Koselleck's conceptual history, W. B. Gallie's essential contested concepts, Pierre Bourdieu's symbolic power of language, and Antonio Gramsci's ideas on hegemony. Using these four perspectives and how they are endorsed in international relations (IR), I will make a case for the political relevance of concepts, in preparation for the empirical chapters that follow.

Concepts

The supposedly simple observation that concepts are meaningful, and, even more pertinently, that they are representational, broaches a set of important ontological questions regarding the nature of the world and its existence independent of the knower. The idea of the meaningfulness of concepts also raises epistemological questions regarding our ability to know and to access (whether directly or indirectly) the world. Indeed, these are important questions. But unless we adhere to the naive and, at least since Kant, unsustainable belief that we have direct and unmediated access to the world, concepts play a major role in our indirect and mediated knowledge of the world. Epistemologically, as "mental representation(s) of an element or phenomenon of the physical, social, or psychological world" (Davis 2005, 12), concepts have a fundamental mediating role between us as sentient beings and the world. Concepts bound phenomena into categories that we can understand and process and that we can form expectations regarding. Yet, and weaving the ontological and epistemological questions together, in the social world, things do not fall neatly into human-made categories represented by concepts (see also Onuf 1989, 24–25). At best, boundaries of categories and concepts are fuzzy, or, as dubbed by Mathias Albert, Oliver Kessler, and Stephan Stetter regarding boundaries between constructed social orders, boundaries are fragile (2008, 58). Existing social objects are linked by comparable features and set apart by distinctive features. Hence, bounding social objects into categories to be represented by concepts involves making arbitrary delineations between those objects, be they phenomena, processes, or otherwise. Perceptive as he so often was, Friedrich Nietzsche captured this succinctly: "Every concept originates through our equating what is unequal" (1968, 46). And as Sheldon Wolin argued to the same effect, political concepts are not "written into the nature of things but are the legacy accruing from the historical activity of political philosophers", (2004, 6; see also Onuf 1989, 24–25).

We should note what this entails (and which is also in line with scientific realism), namely, that the world's existence does not necessarily depend on us knowing it and that our faculty of knowing the world depends on our cognitive and linguistic tools, which is more in line with phenomenology. Hence, bounding existing social phenomena into categories and concepts shapes our understanding of the world. And following constructivism, our knowledge of the world shapes our expectations of the world and hence how we behave in it so that we can participate in its social construction. Of course, more radical thinkers who are committed to the post-structuralist understanding of the performative function of language would also readily embrace the starting point of this volume: that concepts have a central political role in our world. However, and notwithstanding post-structuralist doubts regarding the out-of-discourse existence of the world, what is at stake here in the mean—ontologically speaking—is not really the existence of the world (which we can embrace, doubt, or reject) but rather its independent existence. By turning our attention to the fundamental role of concepts in the social (or sociopolitical) construction of the world, the haunting question about the "independence" of the world's existence loses its sting. One need not doubt the material or out-of-discourse existence of the world in order to question the "independence" element of the equation. The world may indeed exist, but then its knowers who are part of it also exist, and they and the world construct each other continuously and reciprocally. All analysis of the functioning of concepts as meaningful cannot ignore this two-party equation, or in a more traditional sense: no such analysis can ignore the agent and structural component of the social world. Moreover, conceptual analysis also brings the sensitivities of critical theory into the theoretical equation regarding knowers' (including social science theoreticians) responsibilities for the ramifications of their bounding acts (categorization and conceptualization) in the existing world. In other words, taking concepts seriously can be a bridging theme for the varied post-positivist theoretical frameworks, whether constructivists, critical theorists, post-structuralists, feminists, post-colonialists, or otherwise. This is one task that this volume seeks to achieve, by collecting various empirical cases informed by different theoretical frameworks.

Bounding practices, that is, delineating phenomena into categories to be represented by concepts, have many and varied forms, for example, naming, labeling, tagging, and defining. Each practice operates a little differently, in a different social realm, and with varying degrees of reflexivity. Defining, for example, is the academic bounding practice par excellence, and insofar as the other bounding practices are acts of construction, so is defining an act of social construction through categorizing. In other words, to define is to participate in the sociopolitical construction of sociopolitical reality. Take the concept of war, for example (see also Geis, this volume). In IR, this is one of the main phenomena that is studied and defined. And it is surely a central concept for realist security scholars (Walt 1991, 212) and also other IR scholars who participate in the widening and broadening debate over the concept of security. Each theoretical school has its own understanding of war, its links with other themes and entities, and of course its own definition for war. But one of the most acceptable and popular definitions of war is the definition of the Correlates of War project, which uses the figure of 1,000 deaths as an arbitrary heuristic boundary[1] differentiating between events with 1,000 dead, which are classed as war, and events with a mere 999 deaths, which are not. The definition's arbitrariness is indeed heuristic, and as such it is helpful. The heuristic merit of definitions is what led Giovanni Sartori (1970) to stress the positivistic scientific role of concepts in theory construction. Unless phenomena are categorized and named, they cannot be used in our methodologies. For how can we count, compare, trace processes, analyze discourses, and what have you, without bounding abstract and boundless phenomena into categories and then concepts? But, then again, there is nothing exogenously obvious about this conceptual (and sometimes measurable) boundary, a conclusion that questions the positivistic route of Sartori and offers added support for the observation made here that boundaries between concepts and categories are not objective in any material positivist sense but rather the result of bounding practices, which are acts of social construction (see also Dezalay and Garth 1996, 15).

It is in this sense that concepts are representations and for that matter imperfect expressive representations and acts of social construction. They are expressive representations that can exist at the mental subjective level and/or the linguistic intersubjective level (Berenskoetter 2017, 155). On the mental subjective level, they are understood as cognitive properties of the mind. Concepts can be learned and be imprinted in our cognitive system and perhaps even leave physiological traces in the brain. As such, they are expressively representational. It is on the second (linguistic intersubjective) level, which sees concepts as part of the linguistic structures associated with Wittgenstein's language games, that concepts reach beyond individual subjects and their physical brains and assume an intersubjective quality, and thus also social significance and political function. In the intersubjective sphere, concepts are communicated and exist linguistically in a way that enables them to be politically meaningful and serve as political roadmaps. As William Connolly observed, "For to adopt without revision the concepts prevailing in a polity is to accept terms of discourse loaded in favor of established practices" (1974, 2). Alternatively, concepts can undermine the political status quo, for example, by supporting revisionist conceptions.

Consider, for example, the two conceptions of liberty—negative liberty and positive liberty—popularized by Isaiah Berlin (1969). I am here using John Rawls's (1999, 5) definition of conceptions as different meanings attached to a concept. Each of these two conceptions supports a different political agenda. "Negative liberty" prioritizes a protection against the arbitrary interventions of the state or other entity. It is a libertarian conception supporting a neoliberal platform. "Positive liberty," on the other hand, heralds the sociopolitical conditions that allow people to live a meaningful life and freely pursue preferences shaped by their own mind and will. This conception lies at the heart of the welfare state. Berlin viewed the positive conception with suspicion and even scorn. What we learn from Berlin is that each conception is ideologically embedded and can motivate politically. But there is a second lesson to be learned, relating to the importance of the relations between concepts and contexts, or as Felix Berenskoetter puts it, "how the concept is situated in a particular context and shapes (our understanding of) the latter" (2017, 160; see also Bueger, this volume). In the case of Berlin's conceptions, the political and historical context of his normative evaluation of the two conceptions of liberty is extremely important. The context was the Cold War and the power struggle between the United States and the USSR. In that struggle, the United States was regarded as the true herald of liberty while the USSR was seen as the communist usurper of liberty that imposed preferences and views on its citizens and pretended they were the products of free will (Cherniss 2013; Müller 2008). Notwithstanding post-structuralist doubts about human agency and subjectivity, concepts are the brainchild of human agents. But they are also products of their eras and contexts. Even a sophisticated historian of ideas like Isaiah Berlin could not escape his time and fashion a context-free conception of liberty.

This influence of time means that concepts cannot be constant entities. Concepts and conceptions change over time. This historical dynamism is the subject of Reinhart Koselleck's conceptual history (*begriffsge-*

schichte) that studies how the meanings of concepts change diachronically (Berenskoetter 2017; see also Wolff, Geis, this volume). Koselleck presents a historical analysis of what he terms "basic concepts," which are those concepts that play "an inescapable, irreplaceable part of the political and social vocabulary" (1996, 64–65). For Koselleck, basic concepts "combine manifold experiences and expectations in such a way that they become indispensable to any formulation of the most urgent issues of a given time" (64). As Christopher Hobson wrote,

> The pivotal role of basic concepts ensures that they play a fundamental part in the constitution and reconstitution of the social world. In so far as these concepts shape the perceptions and actions of agents, conceptual shifts do not merely reflect material changes, they actively inform such transformations by constituting actors, shaping behavior and helping to remake material structures. (2015, 35)

Thus, diachronic analysis focuses on the social and political aspects of concepts. Furthermore, and related to our issue, basic concepts for Koselleck tend to be contested, because they are basic (and thus open to different interpretation), rendering them amenable to attempts by different actors to monopolize their meaning (Koselleck 1996, 65). Koselleck and his students do not therefore suffice with diachronic analysis but also offer a synchronic analysis focusing on how concepts are understood and challenged and how their meaning consequently changes (Hobson 2015, 34). Thus, concepts are meaningful in being both representations and the shapers and movers of political behavior.

Conceptual Politics and Contestation

Koselleck's insights take us a long way toward understanding the historical contexts in which meanings of concepts change and assume their political function. But as he emphasizes, concepts play an important political role and not just because of their historical contexts; their political significance and function also stem from the manifold experiences and varied expectations associated with them. This then is the multiplicity we find at the center of W. B. Gallie's framework of essentially contested concepts (1956). Because concepts are subjective and intersubjective mental representations, they are inherently vague, ambiguous, and fuzzy (Davis 2005, 5–6). Also, and as Gallie stresses, they are not just vague and fuzzy but also characteristically and essentially contested (1956). Gallie's understanding of the essential contestedness of concepts can be boiled down to three main criteria for determining whether a concept is essentially contested. First, to be essentially contested, a concept must have several alternative legitimate and reasonable meanings—or, as stated in Rawlsian terminology, there must be several possible conceptions of the concept. Second, there need to be irresolvable (actual or impending) disagreements over the appropriate meaning of the concept. Third, when becoming actual, the disagreements must be important enough for certain interlocutors to become politicized, that is, making the concepts essentially contested (Ish-Shalom 2010, 2011; see also Onuf 1989, 2). The contestation over concepts and conceptions is one of the main themes of this volume.

Contestation is a core feature of politics (Wiener 2014), as it is part of the public (and quite often conflictual) effort to allocate resources—material, ideal, and symbolic. The very fact that political concepts meet the three conditions of contestedness makes them a central element of the political act. William Connolly makes this perfectly clear:

> The concepts of politics do not simply provide a lens through which to observe a process that is independent of them. . . . [T]hey are themselves part of that political life—they help to constitute it, to make it what it is. It follows that changes in those concepts, once accepted by a significant number of participants, contribute to changes in political life itself. It follows further that proposals for revision in some dimensions of our concepts carry similar import for political practice. (1974, 180)

The meanings attributed to concepts, as mental representations of the world, are the linguistic media through which people understand the world. In other words, the conceptualization of concepts through bounding practices involves conceptualizing the world around us, fashioning an understanding of the world and how to act in it to achieve our goals. Thus, politics involves a constant effort to conceptualize political concepts and attach them with meanings; this effort is the political par excellence. Attaching meaning to concepts is not a neutral act, as it commits them and renders them useful vehicles of persuasion. As such it is not effortless. It usually takes place in the context of political opposition, making it an act of contestation. The attachment of meaning to concepts is thus at the heart of conceptual politics, as Christopher Hobson and Milja Kurki elaborate: "*the ways in which contested concepts—like democracy—are interpreted, used, and fought over by actors, and how certain meanings and definitions come to influence real world phenomena*" (2011 3; italics in the original). By fulfilling the three conditions of essential contestedness, political concepts become a key aspect of political action. The meanings of concepts (the concepts' conceptions) as mental representations of the world and its phenomena are the linguistic media that allow us to understand the world. Or, to rephrase this: conceptualizing concepts means conceptualizing the world around us, fashioning an understanding of the world *and* ways to act in the world to achieve our goals.

One obvious example of conceptualization is the concept of security, which is usually seen as linked to an objective and material status of being secure or not being secure. But no less and perhaps even more importantly, security is related to such powerful feelings as hope and fear—the expectations and hopes of security and the fear of its lack. These subjective and, more importantly, intersubjective conditions of security are a key to the theoretical analysis of securitization. One of the main lessons that securitization theory offers is that issues are understood and treated as matters of security when they are successfully conceptualized as such matters—that is, when, so to speak, they are dressed up conceptually as security. A successful securitization process needs a relevant agent (usually one accredited as authoritative in security matters), who marshals speech acts to portray a potential threat as an existential threat, a matter of security. The illocutionary force of the locutionary speech acts (its intent) revolves around the effectiveness of the concept of security in framing the mind, and the perlocutionary act results in securitizing the matter at hand, fixating it as security and thus exempting it from the regular day-to-day democratic contestation. The process of securitization is the embodiment of the political power and function of concepts. Securitization draws from theories of performativity, originating with J. L. Austin's (1976) ordinary language philosophy. According to performativity, the distinction between the meaning of a word and its use collapses, because to utter a word is, under certain circumstances, to act and participate in the construction of the social world (MacKenzie 2006, 265).

There are other powerful examples of conceptualization, such as democracy: what is democracy, its proper domains, the principles and norms that should guide and be advanced by it, and, finally, what counts as reasonable, effective, legitimate, and permissible in supporting and even promoting democratization abroad? These are questions of fundamental normative and policy importance. The answers to these questions, which relate to the conceptions embraced by citizens and state leaders, affect states' behavior in the international arena, their goals and interests, and the policies they adopt to secure their aims and interests. Politics, including international politics, can therefore mean a continuous effort toward conceptualizing political concepts and attaching to them meaning; this effort is the *political* par excellence.

At first glance there is nothing problematic about saying, "This effort is the political par excellence." Some may contest it empirically, theoretically, or normatively, but mostly they would at least see it as a reasonable and more likely comprehensible assertion. But the perspective of conceptual politics embraced here and the argument regarding the essential contestedness of concepts raise a peculiar and circular conceptual point. "Political" is a concept itself. It represents a category bounded quite mechanically from other human and social activities. As such the boundaries of the political can be questioned. Indeed and not surprisingly, the boundary question of the political stands at the intersections of many important normative and ideological issues. Socialism questions the strict boundary between the political and economics defended by many liberals; the feminist assertion that the personal is the political is another such critical and subversive move; the liberal endeavor to separate religion from state represents yet another project of bounding politics, and, like many other bounding practices, at times it comes up against the stormy rocks of contemporary democracies; and the attempts to separate the political from the moral may be a noble enterprise, but they are limited when we try to advance a more moral politics, for example, through political theory. Similarly, Hans Morgenthau's attempt to define and delineate politics based strictly on one variable, in this case the kind of interest involved, may be admirable and surely follows the Sartorian logic, but it is fated to collide with the complexities of reality. It is academically admirable because without bounding the political, without defining it, we can hardly expect to advance in understanding reality. Yet, inherently, bounding the political involves moral commitments and is bound to collide with the complexities of the reality that the definers seek to study and understand. Like the above example of the definition of war, the definition of politics is an act of social construction; however, it raises an even more fundamental problem. A circular logic is involved in defining politics: the political must be defined, but defining it involves engaging in conceptual politics, which in its turn relies on understanding what politics is, which requires bounding the political, and so on. We understand from this that sometimes we have no alternative but to give heuristics its due respect, combined with a healthy dash of skepticism and reflexivity. This dual sensitivity and reflexivity regarding the need and drawbacks of bounding into categories and concepts is what scholars of concepts cultivate and is what appears in this volume.

I turn now to two theoretical perspectives—Pierre Bourdieu's sociological perspective and Antonio Gramsci's political theory—to illustrate this dual sensitivity. In recent years, Bourdieu's thinking has made quite an inroad into IR theory, especially through constructivism. While his ideas have been mainly used to theorize practices and gained prominence in IR through the "practice turn," Bourdieu also has much to say about language and its symbolic power (see Bueger, this volume). Consequently, the Bourdieusian framework is of immense importance to those perspectives that take concepts seriously. As expected, Bourdieusian IR scholars are in the forefront of propagating reflexive scholarship (see especially Hamati-Ataya 2011) and are sensitive to the fluidity of the boundaries of the political as well as other social realms or, in Bourdieu's terms, fields. For Bourdieu, a field is "a social configuration structured along three main dimensions: relations of power, objects of struggle, and taken-for-granted rules" (Pouliot 2008, 274). Though fields may indeed be the basic unit of human activities, Bourdieusian scholars are well aware of the overlapping of different fields or, in other words, of the fuzziness of social categories. This is clear in the case of the overlap of the political and academic fields, which has ramifications in the real world and hence calls for reflexivity and responsibility of academia (Büger and Villumsen 2007). Moreover, it is probably not accidental that an important volume introducing Bourdieu to IR (Adler-Nissen 2013) is organized around concepts. As the volume's editor, Rebecca Adler-Nissen, asserts when setting out the book's reasoning:

> Instead, this book questions the a priori definition of concepts. Our shared point of departure is that IR scholars often treat concepts as

the foundations on which theoretical or empirical contributions are based, but seldom as objects warranting critical examination in their own rights. The contributors demonstrate how these often abstract units of meaning could be rethought, specified and operationalised differently, opening up different kinds of analysis. (12)

The Bourdieusian contribution made by Adler-Nissen and the volume's authors is a subversive one. It marks a rethinking of the key concepts in IR. It is a political act, or at least an act of academic politics, with reflexivity built in. According to Bourdieu's tripartite notions of field, habitus, and capital, language plays an important role as a symbolic power, which through performative acts can "create a hierarchy which is, generally speaking, favorable to dominant actors" (Pouliot and Mérand 2013, 38).

Note that Bourdieu thinks that language and concepts have symbolic power and that rather than being neutral tools in the construction of social reality they are thoroughly political. To categorize and classify means to construct social facts that can be politically mobilized (Guzzini 2013, 85). Language carries out acts of exclusions and inclusions through concepts. It participates constitutively in the hierarchical structure of the international system. If a state is labeled a rogue or a pariah, exclusionary consequences follow and, in cases like Gaddafi's Libya, punitive measures as well (Adler-Nissen 2013, 4). Language and concepts are also especially political since not everyone is authorized to give names and classifications and not everyone can benefit equally from the performativity of concepts. Stefano Guzzini expresses this well in ascribing a "power of nomination" to the processes of categorization and classification, such that "not everyone is empowered or entitled to call things into being" (2013, 83). And as Vincent Pouliot and Frédéric Mérand rightly contribute to the argument, with reference to the state, "indeed the state, more than any other institution, possesses the power of appointment, of nomination: it codifies, delegates, and guarantees the implementation of schemas of classification, of 'principles of vision and division,' norms, status, or categories" (2013, 39). Politics is involved in the performative acts of concepts, and it is also the outcome of those acts. And it is with this Bourdieusian understanding that Bueger approaches concepts as part of the "practice turn." He sees concepts as used within sets of activities, which are otherwise known as practices. Thus, the study of concepts implies the study of practices in which concepts play a part (see Bueger, this volume). Concepts are co-constitutive in practices.

Bourdieu thinks that concepts have the dual nature of "doer" and "done" and describes the doing and being done to that the conceptualization of concepts entails as acts of social magic involving "the attempt to make things become reality by giving them a name ('nominating' them) and succeeding in the imposition of this new vision and division of social reality" (Guzzini 2013, 88; see also Adler-Nissen 2013, 9). Calling these acts "social magic" points to an important feature of the classification and categorization through concepts, namely, that the actions of the nominating agent, frequently the state, are seen not as political but as natural (Adler-Nissen 2013, 9). Being natural means that they are not political and contestable, for we do not contest what is natural. This very much relates to the Bourdieusian notion that knowledge within the field is doxa, namely, knowledge that is taken for granted (Poulio and Mérand 2013, 30), and as such it is likewise not subject to reflection and dissidence. The doxic nature of knowledge and the masking of categorization and conception as natural are reasons why the Bourdieusian framework is closely related to Gramsci, who focused on these questions in his discussion of hegemony.

Gramsci's conception of hegemony is especially useful for studying conceptual politics, as it is an exploration of subtle power and elusive politics that does not shy away from the subject of agency (Gramsci 1971, 1992, 1996, 2007; for Gramsci's introduction to the study of IR, see Bieler and Morton 2001; Cox 1981; Davidson 2008; Gale 1998; Gill 1990, 1993, 2012; Ish-Shalom 2013; Joseph 2008; Puchala 2005). That is, his perspective does not hesitate to highlight political actors who use their structural power intentionally and purposefully and employ concepts and conceptions as a powerful hegemonizing tool. Gramscian perspectives do not ignore any of the two parts of the equation: agent and structure, knower and knower's world—the world in which the knower knows, conceptualizes, and acts. It is this sensitivity toward agency that distinguishes the Gramscian perspectives from the more Foucauldian perspectives, and although the latter stress the power of language as discourse, they are suspicious of the notion of human agency. Note, however, that agency is itself an essentially contested concept, loaded with moral, political, and theoretical baggage, performing a meaningful role in contestations across different realms or fields.

On this point, this volume inclines toward Gramscian sensitivity. Contestation lies at the heart of politics, and it involves human agency: it involves actors who struggle purposefully to shape aims and pursue them vis-à-vis other actors and a certain context. Conceptual contestation is conducted by human agency through the linguistic *and* political medium of concepts. No meaningful contestation can exist without agency, probably human agency. With this in mind, this volume's contributors have tasked themselves with identifying the human agency at the foundation of conceptual politics and locating political actors past and present who were involved in the empirical cases described and analyzed here. In undertaking this task, they have addressed the following issues: who conceptualizes and for whom; why do they conceptualize; how and under what structural constraints and opportunities do they conceptualize, and what are the outcomes of their conceptualization.

Gramsci considers hegemony a noncoercive instrument of domination, of subtle domination through society (Bates 1975). Thomas Bates defined Gramsci's hegemony as "political leadership based on the consent of the led, a consent which is secured by the diffusion and popularization of the world view of the ruling class" (1975, 352). Hegemony here is a political web of meanings preventing the everypersons from critically reflecting on the social, economic, and political structure into which they are locked. The everyperson is socialized to accede to the structure as a given, as the product of natural laws, and thus into accepting their (even lowly) position in it as almost divinely ordained (Buttigieg 1992, 21; Gramsci 1992, 236). Ian Lustick captured this process of naturalizing politics: "Hegemonic beliefs, as Gramsci put it, appear not as claims about the world but as 'common sense.' Hegemony is politics naturalized to be experienced as culture" (1999, 339).

With these Gramscian insights in mind, Steven Lukes coined the term "third face of power" (2004). In theorizing the term, he challenged the more traditional notions of power, those facets that involve coercive domination. The first face of power (Dahl 1957) focuses on being able to get people to do things they would not otherwise do. The individual's compliance opposes their own freely formed choice. According to this understanding of power, it is the use or threat of force. The second face of power (Bachrach and Baratz 1962) is more subtle and mainly found in complex decision-making systems. In such systems, it is not only the moment of decision that matters but also the setting of contexts and the vetting of agendas in and through which decisions are taken. Though it is subtle and avoids force, the second face of power still opposes freely formed choices.

As such, it involves conflicts and is a form of subtly coercive domination. Lukes sees these two faces of power as too crude and blind to the most subtle face of power: Gramsci's manipulative hegemony. By manipulating people's perceptions of their own interests, the third face of power prevents freely formed choices from being made and totally eliminates conflict from the political arena (see also Barnett and Duvall 2005, 53). A manipulative hegemony helps to achieve domination effectively and without force. By preventing freely formed choice from being made, and in turn conflict, it may seem at first glance that human agency is also dissolved. But this is not the case. There are political actors who empty the social arena of freely formed choices and eliminate conflicts, and they do so purposefully. They use agency, even at the expense of other actors' agency. The third face of power is relevant to conceptual politics as well. Here, actors mobilize social knowledge, concepts, and conceptions, and as in Bourdieu's framework, knowledge, or at least some important parts of it, is doxic, and many rules and conceptions are taken for granted. In other words, conceptions are decontested purposefully and removed from the political sphere of contestation. It is contestation by other means, so to speak, yet at its very core it is conceptual.

Accordingly, concepts and their conceptions are often not consciously or critically reasoned (Ish-Shalom 2013; Joseph 2008). Thus, and moving beyond the Gramscian framework, we can infer three specific tactics of conceptual politics: (1) attaching a single fixated meaning to essentially contested concepts that produces people's unreflexive action; (2) increasing the fuzziness and ambiguity of concepts, which impedes effective challenge and opposition; and (3) combining the first two into a third, which empties the concept of meaning and then, when it is vacuous, uses it as a slogan and cliché for framing the commonsense.

The first tactic is the most explicitly political. It hegemonizes the commonsense by fixating a concept with a single doxic conception. This is a powerful tactic, producing a highly effective political tool. Fixating conceptions ossifies a perspective into dogmas and doxas and diminishes the capacity for fruitful deliberation and critical contemplation. Take democracy, for example. Despite the complexity and contestedness of this political concept (Kurki 2010), in the public arena, it seems quite an ossified concept, evaluated and measured with a fixed set of structural criteria. It is procedurally and structurally defined, being perceived as a regime that fulfills certain procedural and structural criteria, including electoral process, political pluralism, functioning government, and the legal framework of individual rights and freedom of expression, belief, and association. These fixed criteria are propagated by think tanks like Freedom House and Transparency International, which apply them as benchmarks to quantify, compare, and declare all either democracies or nondemocracies (Löwenheim 2008; Steele 2010, 63).

Note the conceptual binary indicated here. Democracy is contrasted with nondemocracy or with dictatorship, autocracy, and so forth. Likewise, war can be contrasted with peace, liberty with domination, and so on. Indeed, conceptual politics can involve the attempt to overrule the fuzziness and fragility of the boundaries of concepts and divide them into binaries, to contrast a fixated concept with its mirror concept, although the boundaries between the two need not be so clear-cut. Thus, the concept of democracy was used politically as a yardstick for deciding who is with "us" or against "us" in the global war on terror declared and pursued by the Bush administration (see also Wolff, this volume; for other conceptual binaries, see Geis, Beaulieu-Brossard, Berenskötter, this volume). This is an example of the political ramifications of ossified concepts and how the meanings of concepts are converted into political action. In the Bush case, political action arose from the perceived strategic necessity of promoting democracy abroad, if necessary at gunpoint.

A second tactic is to keep concepts fuzzy, almost meaningless, and hence useless, for reasoning and dissenting against government policy and challenging the status quo. Often this tactic does not stand alone and is the first step in a third tactic of emptying a concept of meaning and forcing its use in clichés and vacuous concepts or empty signifiers (see Laclau 1996, 36–46; see also Mitrani on Ernesto Laclau, this volume), making it an excellent political slogan that can be used rhetorically to mobilize followers in uncritical and unreflexive support. Again, the concept of "democracy" is a case in point, as it is often used like this publicly and politically. The intricacies and essential contestedness of the concept of democracy as discussed extensively in academia are transmogrified when democracy is uttered politically. The phenomenon of democracy is expressed as a concept whose meaning is taken for granted though it is actually empty and meaningless (despite being politically meaningful). Israeli politicians often boast that Israel is the only democracy in the Middle East and that the Israel Defense Forces is the most moral military fighting force on earth. These assertions are assumed truths in the Israeli commonsense. Regarded as facts by the public, they are neither reflected upon nor questioned—and never challenged. But probing deeper into the conceptual map that allows this framing of the commonsense finds an emptiness of discussion and a vacuous concept that stifles public deliberation and all possible dissent and criticism. A concept of democracy that is emptied of meaning is therefore antagonistic to democracy or at least to certain civic engagements that the more participatory and deliberative understandings of democracy consider its real essence. Democracy thrives on conceptual discussion and contestation, and to shut down its discussion does it no service.

The preceding sentence is explicitly normative and offers the possibility and warranty of an act of conceptual reconstruction. Reconstruction obliges, as we have argued, that attention be paid to both structure and agent, to the world and the knower who lives in it; conceptualizes it; and acts accordingly. Moreover, reconstruction necessitates the Koselleck type of dynamic and historical understanding of concepts: that concepts can and do change within historical and political contexts. The diachronic understanding of concepts sits well with Robert Cox's framing of critical theory as the type of theory that probes and theorizes the historical origins of existing structures (1981). The possibility of contributing to sociopolitical change as envisioned and promulgated by critical theorists is interwoven inherently with an acute historical sensitivity of the kind achieved by Koselleck and his students. Reconstruction is also fed by the theoretical framework of Gallie, who perceptively realized the internal characteristics of concepts that render them essentially contested and hence the political media and resources of relational power. And, of course, Bourdieu's sociology of field and Gramsci's political theory of hegemony are a pair, for combined they offer us a sociopolitical theory of relations of power and domination concealed by doxic knowledge and taken-for-granted rules, in which essentially contested concepts and politically serving conceptions can and do play an important role. Thus, it is evident that jointly the post-positivist theoretical frameworks establish the importance of studying conceptual politics while providing the analytical and normative tools needed for reconstruction.

With this in mind, the following chapters explore the meaningfulness of concepts, in at least one of the two senses mentioned earlier: their meaningfulness as expressively mental representations of phenomena and/or as having political significance and function. This is the shared goal of all the writers in this volume, coming as they do from a variety of post-positivist perspectives. Taking concepts seriously can and should be a bridging theme for post-positivism with its diverse schools and perspectives.

Description of Chapter Topics

The nine chapters (eight chapters plus a summary chapter) that follow present both a theoretical and an empirical exploration of the meaningfulness of concepts. They address both quantitative and qualitative methodologies and present empirical cases from around the world, which they study at different levels of analysis. In the first chapter, Jonas Wolff examines UN General Assembly debates and argues that although self-determination is morally praised *consensually*, it is nonetheless conceptualized *diversely*, so that, politically, each conceptualization serves a specific agenda within the international arena. Liberal-democratic states link self-determination to democracy with the goal of achieving a liberal world order where the promotion of democracy is both permissible and warranted. Conversely, the states of the Global South conceptualize self-determination that delegitimizes the liberal international agenda of democracy promotion and the responsibility to protect, which they see as an agenda undermining their own sovereignty.

The next set of four chapters addresses security-related concepts and mostly presents analyses on the state level. Brent J. Steele and Luke Campbell explore the political functions of the concepts of winning and success in the war context. They focus on the balance between the ambiguity and fixity of concepts as the source of social and political attraction and how, by mobilizing concepts' emotional content, political agents can create concepts that are politically powerful through "affective familiarization." Empirically, they demonstrate their argument with a detailed analysis of the United States' so-called surge strategy in 2006–7 in Iraq. They study the role of public opinion and, to a greater extent, Just War scholars and their conceptual interventions in constructing the Iraq War as a success story, thus legitimizing its continuation. In her chapter, Anna Geis examines the German avoidance of the concept of war and how the use of such deemphasizing descriptions as "stabilization mission" have in fact benefited from the ambiguity of the concept of war and how they have been employed politically to maintain the cherished image of the German army as armed "social workers," not actually killing and being killed in their overseas missions. This persisted at least until the so-called Kunduz airstrike in Afghanistan in September 2009, which triggered intense debate over whether the German mission in Afghanistan was really a "war." Philippe Beaulieu-Brossard examines the unlikely case of the military application of Gilles Deleuze and Félix Guattari's "rhizome" concept. Using textual analysis and ethnographic interviews, Beaulieu-Brossard examines how defense scientists used the rhizome and related concepts to develop a new way of thinking called "design" in an attempt to promote an ongoing reform agenda in the Israel Defense Forces that could be shared with other Western armed forces. This shows that even post-structuralism and postmodernism are not immune to serving politics and military purposes conceptually. In the next chapter, Neta Strunin-Kremer examines the use of vagueness when conceptualizing the concept of cyberattack in Israeli political discourse. Strunin-Kremer suggests that the vagueness in the concept of cyberattack is used to securitize the cyber discourse so that Israel and other democracies can act in cyberspace and ignore that these activities often contradict the values and images they wish to cultivate among their citizens and the international community.

The final set of three chapters moves from security and single-state analysis to concepts generally considered fuzzier and/or less central to international politics. Christian Bueger takes practice theory and the "blue economy" concept to raise an essential question: How do concepts emerge, acquire meaning, and change? His argument suggests that we should note that concepts are responses to concrete problematic situations. Focusing on the Republic of Seychelles, Bueger demonstrates that the concept of blue economy was adopted and promoted internationally in response to concrete problems, thus contributing to the concept's emergence and change. Felix Berenskötter takes the analysis to the bilateral level, offering a critical analysis of the political function of the concept of friendship in the historically loaded relations between Germany and Israel. Whenever Germany criticizes Israel for its policies and practices toward the Palestinians, it immediately offers assurances of friendship to legitimize its critique and stress its sincerity and commitment to Israel's security. In turn, some Israeli politicians use the German declaration of friendship to explain their consent to the German critique. In the final empirical chapter, Mor Mitrani employs quantitative methodology to argue that the international community is basically a concept and a discursive construct that only materializes when agents talk about it, refer to it, and attribute certain values, rules, and virtues to it. Using Ernesto Laclau's notion of an empty signifier, Mitrani demonstrates that the international community is a discursive vessel that is usable instrumentally for political purposes. Calling it an empty signifier does not imply that this discursive vessel's use is just "cheap talk." Rather, the concept serves as a stabilizing concept in international politics, especially in times of crisis.

In their conclusion, Jan Wilkens and Oliver Kessler link the conceptual analyses and framework to the pertinent theoretical literatures of contested norms and reflexivity. They suggest some novel theoretical venues for merging the literatures and further developing them to assist our understanding of the meaningfulness of concepts for the study of international politics. Using the literatures of concepts, norm contestation, and reflexivity, they conclude the volume with a normative call to open up IR to global context and contexts. As they forcefully argue, when analyzing the political use and outcomes of concepts, scholars need to consider the normative basis of a concept. To be able to do that effectively, more scholarly sensitivity should be applied to the resonation of concepts and their bases with the cultural and social background of those actors who use the concepts and those actors who are being affected. In IR, concepts are enacted and act in diverse and global contexts, and thus conceptual contestations, or conceptual international politics, should be studied globally.

Notes

1. The precise and nuanced definition in the Correlates of War is as follows: "An interstate war must have: a) sustained combat, involving b) regular armed forces on both sides and c) 1,000 battle fatalities among all of the system members involved." See Sarkees and Schafer 2000, 125.

References

Adler-Nissen, Rebecca. 2013. "Introduction." In *Bourdieu in International Relations: Rethinking Key Concepts in IR*, ed. Rebecca Adler-Nissen, 1–23. London: Routledge.

Albert, Mathias, Oliver Kessler, and Stephan Stetter. 2008. "On Order and Conflict: International Relations and the 'Communicative Turn.'" *Review of International Studies* 34 (S1): 43–67.

Austin, John L. 1976. *How to Do Things with Words*. Oxford: Oxford University Press.

Bachrach, Peter, and Morton S. Baratz. 1962. "Two Faces of Power." *American Political Science Review* 56 (4): 947–52.

Barnett, Michael, and Raymond Duvall. 2005. "Power in International Politics." *International Organization* 59 (1): 39–75.

Bates, Thomas R. 1975. "Gramsci and the Theory of Hegemony." *Journal of the History of Ideas* 36 (2): 351–66.

Berenskoetter, Felix. 2017. "Approaches to Concept Analysis." *Millennium: Journal of International Studies* 45 (2): 151–73.

Berlin, Isaiah. 1969. "Two Concepts of Liberty." In *Four Essays on Liberty*. London: Oxford University Press.

Bieler, Andreas, and Adam David Morton. 2001. "The Gordian Knot of Agency-Structure in International Relations." *European Journal of International Relations* 7 (1): 5–35.

Büger, Christian, and Trine Villumsen. 2007. "Beyond the Gap: Relevance, Fields of Practice and the Securitizing Consequences of (Democratic Peace) Research." *Journal of International Relations and Development* 10 (4): 417–48.

Buttigieg, Joseph A. 1992. "Introduction." In *Prison Notebooks*, ed. Joseph A. Buttigieg, 1–64. New York: Columbia University Press.

Cherniss, Joshua L. 2013. *A Mind and Its Time: The Development of Isaiah Berlin's Political Thought, 1928–1953*. Oxford: Oxford University Press.

Connolly, William E. 1974. *The Terms of Political Discourse*. Lexington, Mass.: D. C. Heath and Company.

Cox, Robert W. 1981. "Social Forces, States and World Orders: Beyond International Relations Theory." *Millennium: Journal of International Studies* 10 (2): 126–55.

Dahl, Robert A. 1957. "The Concept of Power." *Behavioral Science*, 2 (3): 201–15.

Davidson, Alastair. 2008. "The Uses and Abuses of Gramsci." *Thesis Eleven* 95 (1): 68–94.

Davis, James W. 2005. *Terms of Inquiry: On the Theory and Practice of Political Science*. Baltimore, MD: Johns Hopkins University Press.

Dezalay, Yves, and Bryant G. Garth. 1996. *Dealing in Virtue: International Commercial Arbitration and the Construction of a Transnational Order*. Chicago: University of Chicago Press.

Gale, Fred. 1998. "Cave 'Cave! Hic Dragones': A Neo-Gramscian Deconstruction and Reconstruction of International Regime Theory." *Review of International Political Economy* 5 (2): 252–83.

Gallie, W. B. 1956. "Essentially Contested Concepts." *Proceedings of the Aristotelian Society* 56:167–98.

Gill, Stephen. 1990. *American Hegemony and the Trilateral Commission*. Cambridge: Cambridge University Press.

Gill, Stephen, ed. 1993. *Gramsci, Historical Materialism and International Relations*. Cambridge: Cambridge University Press.

Gill, Stephen, ed. 2012. *Global Crises and the Crisis of Global Leadership*. Cambridge: Cambridge University Press.

Gramsci, Antonio. 1971. *Selections from the Prison Notebooks*. Ed. and trans. Quintin Hoare and Geoffrey Nowell Smith. New York: International Publishers.

Gramsci, Antonio. 1992. *Prison Notebooks*. Vol. 1. Trans. Joseph A. Buttigieg. New York: Columbia University Press.

Gramsci, Antonio. 1996. *Prison Notebooks*. Vol. 2. Trans. Joseph A. Buttigieg. New York: Columbia University Press.

Gramsci, Antonio. 2007. *Prison Notebooks*. Vol. 3. Trans. Joseph A. Buttigieg and Antonio Callari. New York: Columbia University Press.

Gurevitch, Zali. 2001. "Dialectical Dialogue: The Struggle for Speech, Repressive Silence, and the Shift to Multiplicity." *British Journal of Sociology* 52 (1): 87–104.

Guzzini, Stefano. 2013. "Power: Bourdieu's Field Analysis of Relational Capital Misrecognition and Domination." In *Bourdieu in International Relations: Rethinking Key Concepts in IR*, ed. Rebecca Adler-Nissen, 79–92. New York: Routledge.

Hamati-Ataya, Inanna. 2011. "The "Problem of Values" and International Relations Scholarship: From Applied Reflexivity to Reflexivism." *International Studies Review* 13 (2): 259–87.

Heyd, David. 2015. "Solidarity: A Local, Partial and Reflective Emotion." *Diametros* 43:55–64.

Hobson, Christopher. 2015. *The Rise of Democracy: Revolution, War and Transformations in International Politics since 1776*. Edinburgh: Edinburgh University Press.

Hobson, Christopher, and Milja Kurki. 2011. "Introduction: The Conceptual Politics of Democracy Promotion." In *The Conceptual Politics of Democracy Promotion*, ed. Christopher Hobson and Milja Kurki, 1–15. New York: Routledge.

Ish-Shalom, Piki. 2010. "Political Constructivism: The Political Construction of Social Knowledge." In *Arguing Global Governance: Agency, Lifeworld and Shared Reasoning*, ed. Corneliu Bjola and Markus Kornprobst, 231–46. New York: Routledge.

Ish-Shalom, Piki. 2011. "Conceptualizing Democratization and Democratizing Conceptualization: A Virtuous Circle." In *The Conceptual Politics of Democracy Promotion*, ed. Christopher Hobson and Milja Kurki, 38–52. New York: Routledge.

Ish-Shalom, Piki. 2013. *Democratic Peace: A Political Biography*. Ann Arbor: University of Michigan Press.

Joseph, Jonathan. 2008. "Hegemony and the Structure-Agency Problem in International Relations: A Scientific Realist Contribution." *Review of International Studies* 34 (1): 109–28.

Koselleck, Reinhart. 1996. "A Response to Comments on the Geschichtliche Grundbegriffe." In *The Meaning of Historical Terms and Concepts: New Studies on Begriffsgeschichte*, ed. Hartmut Lehmann and Melvin Richter, 59-70. Washington, DC: German Historical Institute.

Kratochwil, Friedrich V. 1989. *Rules, Norms, and Decisions: On the Conditions of Practical and Legal Reasoning in International Relations and Domestic Affairs*. Cambridge: Cambridge University Press.

Kurki, Milja. 2010. "Democracy and Conceptual Contestability: Reconsidering Conceptions of Democracy in Democracy Promotion." *International Studies Review* 12 (3): 362–86.

Laclau, Ernesto. 1996. *Emancipation(s)*. London and New York: Verso.

Löwenheim, Oded. 2008. "Examining the State: A Foucauldian Perspective on International 'Governance Indicators.'" *Third World Quarterly* 29 (2): 255–74.

Lukes, Steven. 2004. *Power: A Radical View*. 2nd ed. Houndmills, Basingstoke: Palgrave Macmillan.

Lustick, Ian S. 1999. "Hegemony and the Riddle of Nationalism." In *Ethnic, Conflict and International Politics in the Middle East,* ed. Leonard Binder, 332–59. Gainsville: University Press of Florida.

MacKenzie, Donald. 2006. *An Engine, Not a Camera: How Financial Models Shape Markets.* Cambridge, MA: MIT Press.

Müller, Jan-Werner. 2008. "Fear and Freedom: On 'Cold War Liberalism.'" *European Journal of Political Theory* 7 (1): 45–64.

Nietzsche, Friedrich. 1968. *The Portable Nietzsche,* edited and translated by Walter Kaufmann. New York: The Viking Press.

Onuf, Nicholas Greenwood. 1989. *World of Our Making: Rules and Rule in Social Theory and International Relations.* Columbia: University of South Carolina Press.

Pouliot, Vincent. 2008. "The Logic of Practicality: A Theory of Practice of Security Communities." *International Organization,* 62 (2): 257–88.

Pouliot, Vincent and Frédéric Mérand. 2013. "Bourdieu's Concepts: Political Sociology in International Relations." In *Bourdieu in International Relations: Rethinking Key Concepts in IR,* ed. Rebecca Adler-Nissen, 24–44. New York: Routledge.

Puchala, Donald J. 2005. "World Hegemony and the United Nations." *International Studies Review* 7 (4): 571–84.

Rawls, John. 1999. *A Theory of Justice.* Rev. ed. Cambridge, MA: Harvard University Press.

Sarkees, Meredith Reid, and Phil Schafer. 2000. "The Correlates of War Data on War: An Update to 1997." *Conflict Management and Peace Science* 18 (1): 123–44.

Sartori, Giovanni. 1970. "Concept Misformation in Comparative Politics." *American Political Science Review* 64 (4): 1033–53.

Steele, Brent J. 2010. "Of 'Witch's Brews' and Scholarly Communities: The Dangers and Promise of Academic Parrhesia." *Cambridge Review of International Affairs* 23 (1): 49–68.

Walt, Stephen M. 1991. "The Renaissance of Security Studies." *International Studies Quarterly* 35 (2): 211–39.

Wiener, Antje. 2014. *A Theory of Contestation.* Berlin: Springer.

Wolin, Sheldon S. 2004. *Politics and Vision: Continuity and Innovation in Western Political Thought.* Princeton: Princeton University Press.

CHAPTER 2

Talking about Self-Determination

*Contested Conceptions and Political
Implications of an Undisputed Concept*

Jonas Wolff

Ever since the Universal Declaration of Human Rights was adopted, the
tension between human rights and state sovereignty has shaped the debates
about global order.[1] Self-determination is a key concept in this regard, as
it constitutes the common normative ground on which both human rights
and sovereignty claims rest: The two international human rights covenants
both start with the right to self-determination, and the reference to collective self-determination morally substantiates the legal claim to sovereignty
(Wolff 2014). In fact, the overall concept of self-determination meets with
virtually uncontested appraisal. Yet, at every point in time, there have been
intense debates between competing conceptions of self-determination that
have different political implications and, thus, serve different political purposes.[2] In the contemporary world, the concept of self-determination is
politically used both to justify a liberal world order that comes with supposedly benevolent intervention in the internal affairs of states *in order to
promote self-determination* and to reject such interference *in order to protect
and enable self-determination.*[3] The conceptual struggle over the "correct"
conception of self-determination, thus, has immediate implications for
international politics.

Against this background, the present chapter analyzes the characteristics, historical evolution, contemporary usages, and political implications

of the concept of self-determination in international relations. The chapter starts by identifying the descriptive core and further characteristics of the (political) concept of self-determination. While this opening section is theoretical in nature, the remaining two sections analyze empirically how the concept at hand has been understood and used in academic as well as political debates. First, I look at competing conceptions of self-determination, both in historical perspective and with a view to contemporary debates. In terms of sources, this section draws on academic literature. Second, I turn to the political implications for contemporary debates in international politics, focusing on the issue of external interference in the name of democracy and human rights.[4] Empirically, this section analyzes debates in the UN General Assembly (UNGA) that address the issue of self-determination in its relation with democracy and human rights, sovereignty, and noninterference, including with a view to the so-called Responsibility to Protect (R2P).

In sum, the analysis shows that the virtually uncontested descriptive core of the concept of self-determination that is inextricably linked with strong normative connotations, on the one hand, enables and drives an infinite struggle between competing conceptions that are embedded in different worldviews and serve different political purposes. On the other hand, however, this same core delimits the range of plausible conceptions and, thereby, also constrains the range of policies that can be justified in terms of the concept. As a consequence, those who argue for external interference in the name of democracy and human rights can hardly ignore the tension between such interference and the (acknowledged) principle of self-determination, while those who categorically reject external interference in the internal affairs of states have a hard time when it comes to so-called crimes against humanity.

The Concept of Self-Determination

When analyzing self-determination as a political concept, we can identify a fairly consensual descriptive core to which competing conceptions of self-determination refer. At the same time, as I will argue in this section, this descriptive concept of self-determination is a normative, undisputedly appraisive concept. In being not only an appraisive and internally complex concept but also a basic as well as a cluster concept, self-determination is also an essentially contested concept.

According to Jeremy Waldron (2010), there are basically two conceptions of self-determination: a territorial one, according to which "the people of a country have the right to work out their own constitutional and political arrangements without interference from the outside," and an identity-based one, according to which "each ethnically or culturally distinct group" should have "charge of its own constitutional and political arrangements" (397–98). The overarching *concept* of self-determination as such is not explicitly defined by Waldron, but it is clear that, in his view, it refers to a situation in which a given group controls—works out and is in charge of—its own constitutional and political arrangements. These two dimensions of control have also been labeled the "*constitutive* aspect" (the working out) and the "*ongoing* aspect" (the being in charge of) of self-determination (Anaya 2004, 104–5; cf. Buchanan 2003, 206).

Different wordings notwithstanding, this seems to be the fairly consensual *descriptive core* of the overarching concept to which existing conceptions refer (cf. Altman and Wellman 2009, 17; McMahan 1996, 5–6). It is also in line with the established political and legal usage at the level of the United Nations. According to the International Human Rights Covenants, for instance, self-determination entails that given entities ("peoples," in this case) "freely determine their political status and freely pursue their economic, social and cultural development."

Self-determination is an appraisive concept in Gallie's sense, meaning "that it signifies or accredits some kind of valued achievement" (1956, 171).[5] In contrast to related concepts, such as the concept of democracy, in the case of self-determination, authors usually make this *positive, normative valuation* explicit by talking, almost always, about the "right to" or the "norm of self-determination." But even without such an explicitly normative prefix, as in the descriptive formulation given above, self-determination refers to something that is generally acknowledged as positive, valuable.

This dual qualification of the concept—as descriptive and yet normative, appraisive—is not contradictory. As Connolly has argued, "*to describe is to characterize a situation from the vantage point of certain interests, purposes, or standards*" (1993, 23; emphasis in original). In this sense, the normative connotations are woven into the descriptive criteria—and cannot be pulled out without fundamentally changing the concept at hand (cf. Connolly 1993, 32). In the case of self-determination, the precise criteria (and how they are to be applied or measured) are heavily contested, as is the normative status of the concept (a norm, a moral right or a legal right). But no one questions the normative assumption that self-determination is something positively valued. In fact, the academic and the political debate about competing conceptions is so intense precisely because everyone takes it for granted that self-determination is something human beings appreciate, long for, or are even entitled to. Therefore, once you accept a specific understanding of self-determination, you can hardly be against it.

The concept of self-determination is, quite evidently, an essentially contested concept as defined by W. B. Gallie (see Ish-Shalom, this volume). In addition to Gallie's criterion of appraisiveness, the two dimensions (constitutive versus ongoing) can be combined and prioritized in different ways, implying that the concept is "internally complex" and "variously describable" (1956, 171–72).[6] This essential contestedness is also due to self-determination's status as a basic concept. Basic concepts, according to Koselleck, have become "an inescapable, irreplaceable part of the political and social vocabulary"; as they combine "manifold experiences and expectations in such a way that they become indispensable to any formulation of the most urgent issues of a given time," they are "highly complex" as well as "always both controversial and contested" (1996, 64; see also Ish-Shalom, Berenskoetter, Geis, this volume).

Furthermore, self-determination is also essentially contested because it is a cluster concept, as defined by Connolly (1993, 149): In order to make the concept of self-determination "intelligible we must display its complex connections with a host of other concepts to which it is related" and elaborate "the broader conceptual system within which it is implicated." In the case of self-determination, the most directly connected concepts are sovereignty and noninterference, on the one hand, and democracy and human rights, on the other. Because these related concepts are themselves contested, and as there are various ways in which they can be related to each other and to self-determination, a broad range of competing conceptions of the cluster concept of self-determination emerge.

Competing Conceptions of Self-Determination

In this section, I briefly review the evolution of the concept of self-determination and the various, in fact competing, conceptions that have been prevalent over the years and their various normative foundations.

In doing so, I suggest that the dominant usage of the concept of self-determination has dramatically changed from the traditional post–World War II context of decolonization to the post–Cold War context of liberal hegemony. Turning to the post-1990 debate about self-determination, I argue that competing conceptions, on the one hand, can be seen as ranging from self-determination as liberal-democratic self-rule to a genuinely collective, communitarian conception of self-determination but that, on the other hand, the differences between these conceptions are rather gradual—as long as they stick to the descriptive core of the concept, that is.

The right of self-determination of peoples, according to David Scott, has "sources in the late eighteenth and nineteenth century principle of popular sovereignty" and was "pivotal to international sovereignty discourse at least since World War I"; however, it is only after World War II that self-determination was transformed "from a political *ideal* . . . into a *legally binding principle* of international conduct, an international legal norm" (2012, 201; emphasis in original). This transformation took place in the context of the process of decolonization, which framed both the political usage of and the academic debate about self-determination (cf. Anghie 2004, 196; Burke 2010, 35–58; Crawford 2006, 107–31). This context not only elevated the legal/normative status of the concept of self-determination but also profoundly shaped the very understanding of the concept. As a consequence, both the constitutive and the ongoing aspects of self-determination were related to the external independence of a given people that is to enjoy self-determination. In constitutive terms, external self-determination was understood as concerning "the international status of a people," basically encompassing "the recognition that each people has the right to constitute itself a nation-state or to integrate into, or federate with, an existing state"; internal self-determination, in turn, meant that peoples, once they have achieved statehood, can "freely choose their own political, economic, and social system" (Senese 1989, 19). In protecting such freedom of choice from external interferences, internal self-determination was seen as "essentially a negative matter," directly related to the right of nonintervention (Emerson 1971, 466). Both external and internal self-determination, thus, essentially referred to decolonization, with the former being "defined as the right to freedom from a former colonial power" and the latter "as independence of the whole state's population from foreign intervention or influence" (Hannum 1990, 49). In his *Political Theory and International Relations*, Charles Beitz even reserved the concept of self-determination for the external dimension, the right of "colonies or other entities under foreign control . . . to independent statehood" (Beitz [1979] 1999, 92–93).

In the post–Cold War debate about the concept, the distinction between external and internal self-determination is still very much alive—but its terms have changed dramatically (cf. Roepstorff 2013). When Beitz, in a more recent piece, distinguishes between "two different senses of self-determination," an "external" and an "internal" one (2009, 336), both refer to what had traditionally been called the "internal dimension." The external meaning of self-determination, now, implies "a state's legal and political autonomy," that is, the negative protection of a state vis-á-vis potential outside intervention; the internal meaning of self-determination, in contrast, concerns "the relationship between a nation or 'people' and its state" and, thus, the question of whether it is really the people that is governing (determining) itself (Beitz 2009, 336; see also Summers 2013, 229).[7] As a consequence, the legal and political debate about self-determination has moved "away from the problem of empire ('external' self-determination) toward the question of the internal political form of regimes holding state power ('internal' self-determination)" (Scott 2012, 223). And, in the academic debate, the increasingly hegemonic response to this question has been that a given people can only be considered as self-determining if the latter is exercised through more or less specifically defined democratic procedures (cf. Beitz 2009, 336; Cassese 1995, 21; Franck 1992, 52).

The main source of conceptual contestation in the current debate about self-determination concerns precisely this last issue. In terms of the descriptive core of the concept outlined above, the question at hand is whether a given group can only be considered to be controlling its own constitutional and political arrangements if it does so via "political institutions that are in some suitably generic sense democratic" (Beitz 2009, 336) or whether such control only deserves the term "self-determination" if it enables the group "to decide whether to have a democracy around here, and if so, what sort of democracy to have" (Waldron 2010, 408). The above conceptual analysis helps briefly identify the main differences between these two competing conceptions: Self-determination is embedded in different ways in different kinds of conceptual systems, or clusters, bringing about different responses to the issues of internal complexity and diverse describability. As will be seen below, these differences are also directly related to competing normative foundations that, in line with the distinction between a liberal and a communitarian approach, emphasize either individual human beings or political communities as the key bearers of rights.

The liberal-democratic conception relates self-determination to the concepts of democracy and human rights, conceptualizes all three in liberal terms, and thereby prioritizes liberal human/democratic rights over self-determination. In doing so, the primary unit (and normative reference) changes from the collectivity that is supposed to control its own constitutional and political arrangements (self-determination) to the individuals who are to enjoy their political and civil rights (cf. Fox and Roth 2000, 10). Self-determination, then, becomes a function of liberal-democratic self-rule—which is merely exercised collectively. The result is what Reisman (2000, 244) calls a "new constitutive, human rights-based conception of popular sovereignty," which equals a corresponding liberal-democratic conception of self-determination (see also Tesón 1992, 54, 92). In terms of the internal complexity of the overall concept, the subordination of (collective) self-determination to (individual rights–based) democracy also leads to an emphasis on the *ongoing* aspect of self-determination at the expense of its *constitutive* aspect: The very establishment of democratic institutions is seen as a precondition for—rather than the (contingent) result of the exercise of—self-determination. The latter is, therefore, described as something that happens in the framework of and through preexisting democratic institutions—and not as something that may also be concerned with their very constitution.

The genuinely collective conception, in contrast, emphasizes the *constitutive* aspect of self-determination. Correspondingly, self-determination is related rather to sovereignty and nonintervention, which remain indispensable conditions for enabling the former (cf. Altman and Wellman 2009, 4; McMahan 1996, 2; Roth 2000a, 14). To the extent that this conception relates self-determination to democracy and human rights, it does so in a way that clearly prioritizes the former: As Altman and Wellman argue, "The inherent value of democratic rule cannot be grounded in individual rights but rather must be based on an irreducibly collective moral right of political self-determination" (2009, 11). At the same time, a given people, in exercising self-determination, "may in fact favour a nondemocratic form of governance" (29) or a substantive conception of democracy that diverges from liberal democracy (Roth 2000a, chap. 4). Self-determination is, therefore, described not as something that happens in and through (liberal) democracy but rather in terms of a broad notion of popular sovereignty that may be exercised in various ways (cf. Fox and Roth 2000, 13; Roth 2000a, 15, 414).

These conceptual differences notwithstanding, at the level of the overall concept, there is no doubt that meaningful self-determination of a given political community that is organized as a state cannot but include self-determination in its external dimension or sense. Sovereignty and nonintervention are, therefore, necessary parts of the conceptual system in which self-determination is embedded. At the same time, however, the descriptive core outlined in the beginning clearly implies that self-determination always refers to a collectivity and not simply to a given regime or government. Governments exercise self-determination only to the extent that they are recognized as representing "the political community," "the people," "the population," or "the popular will." In this sense, the overarching concept of self-determination to which competing conceptions refer imposes certain (if always contested) limits on the range of these very conceptions.[8] This becomes clear when, once again, reviewing the supposedly opposed arguments about self-determination.

On the one hand, Brad Roth, in criticizing the notion of a right to democracy, argues that "an international community that takes the self-determination principle seriously can scarcely impose a specified method of self-government as a condition of according States the very respect and protection that international law purports in the name of national self-determination to provide." Yet, at the same time, he acknowledges that "one can no longer simply accept at face value the claims of autocratic leaders that their leadership is the expression of an unmanifested popular will or indigenous cultural norms, of which the leaders purport themselves to be the authoritative interpreters"; "the link between the people and sovereign power must be empirical" (Roth 2000b, 507). More specifically, Roth argues that there are "some broadly acknowledged limits to what can plausibly be argued to be a manifestation of popular will," such as the "dominance of a minority race" or the "dominance, direct or indirect, by a foreign state" (2000a, 38–39), and adds that "there are some atrocities, such as genocide and slavery, that go to the core of shared humanitarian values, and are recognized as violating peremptory norms of international law (*jus cogens*)" (32; emphasis in original). This last argument points to Michael Walzer's well-known criterion according to which the right to nonintervention implied by the right to self-determination of a given political community does not apply "when the violation of human rights within a set of boundaries is so terrible that it makes talk of community or self-determination seem cynical and irrelevant, that is, in cases of enslavement or massacre" ([1977] 2006, 90).

On the other hand, Thomas Christiano, in his defense of a human right to democracy, argues that this entitlement does not limit the "legitimate right to collective self-determination" because nondemocratic countries usually "do not have legitimate collective self-determination" (2011, 172–73). Yet, he later adds that if there was really "near unanimity for nondemocracy" in a given society, one could argue "that the members of the population of the nondemocratic society are exercising the normative powers attached to their rights to democracy to waive the right to democracy" (175). In the same vein, Altman and Wellman (2009, 27) argue that self-determining nondemocracies not only have to respect basic human rights but must also allow for constitutional referenda, in which citizens would be entitled "to claim or waive democratic governance."[9]

The Conceptual Politics of Self-Determination

In this final section, I discuss some political implications of the conceptual evolution of and the contemporary conceptual struggle over self-determination. The liberal-democratic conceptualization of self-determination has become an important justification for the external promotion of democracy, but this interpretation has met with resistance on the part of many countries from the Global South, as can be seen in debates in the UNGA. While in this context references to the undisputed concept of self-determination are mainly used by those who aim at protecting states against external interference, the descriptive core of the concept imposes constraints on what can be justified as appropriate behavior on all actors who do not dare to openly reject the principle of self-determination.

According to Reinhart Koselleck, "all concepts have two aspects": "On the one hand, they point to something external to them, to the context in which they are used. On the other hand, this reality is perceived in terms of categories provided by language" (1996, 61; see also Hobson and Kurki 2012, 3–4; Ish-Shalom, this volume). In the former sense, the evolution of the concept of self-determination summarized above clearly reflects the shift from a post–World War II context of decolonization, driven by demands for independence and sovereign statehood, to a post–Cold War context, shaped by the liberal hegemony of the Global Northwest. In terms of the latter kind of relationship between concepts and reality, however, it is through the very lens of a changed understanding of self-determination that the apparently new context after the Cold War has been perceived and interpreted. Empirically speaking, it is far from obvious that the main problem constraining collective self-determination in the Global South is nowadays one related to the domestic political regimes in place rather than one of, say, domestic and/or transnational economic structures and/ or global politico-economic power relations. The liberal-democratic reconceptualization of self-determination, to the extent that it succeeded "in politically framing the public commonsense" (Ish-Shalom 2012, 41), has decontested such a contested empirical observation and, thereby, itself contributed to bringing about a specific "reality" of world politics.

From the perspective of the genuinely collective conception, the liberal-democratic redefinition of self-determination is, thus, part and parcel of "a *civilizational* and an *imperial* project that articulates itself in the political idiom of democracy and the acceleration of global 'democracy promotion'" (Scott 2012, 201; emphasis in original). Indeed, because the liberal-democratic conception regards a given government's claim to collective self-determination as contingent on its complying with the procedural requirements of liberal democracy (cf. Crawford 2000, 94–95; Fox 2000, 89), external activities that aim at promoting or even enforcing democracy are no longer seen as undermining but rather as helping realize self-determination: Democracy promotion, in this sense, "does not deny any peoples' right to self-determination; it gives life to that right" (Ackerman and Glennon 2007; cf. Franck 1992; McFaul 2005, 148–49; Reisman 2000). The conceptual analysis of self-determination, thus, helps understand the shifting terms of the political discourse that has underpinned the rise of the democracy-promotion paradigm since 1990, making something meaningful that otherwise could appear to be rather a contradiction in terms: the idea to interfere from the outside to promote internal self-determination (cf. Wolff 2014).

This change in the understanding of self-determination has, of course, been far from uncontested. This can be illustrated by looking at debates in the UNGA that, in one way or another, address the issue of self-determination in its relation with democracy and human rights, on the one hand, and sovereignty and noninterference, on the other.[10] In fact, the debate within the UN over whether the international community, including individual states, should be entitled to promote democracy and human rights around the world (that is, to promote democratic self-determination) or not (to respect the self-determination of the peoples) is characterized by the hegemony of a fairly traditional conception of self-determination as coined in the context of decolonization. Whereas in the academic debate just mentioned the discussion has been increasingly dominated by a liberal-democratic conception of self-determination, the predominant understanding of self-determination as articulated in the UN context remains much closer to the state-centered, communitarian conceptions predominating official documents (the Charta, the human rights covenants, diverse UNGA resolutions). This clearly results from the formal power structure within the UNGA where countries from the Global South, which tend to stick to a rather traditional conception of self-determination, hold an overwhelming majority. In addition, it also reflects the fairly legalistic type of debates within this international organization in which arguments are usually made by referring to existing legal documents.

As a result, those state representatives who hold a liberal-democratic conception of self-determination avoid using the term "self-determination" at all in order to not weaken their emphasis on universal human rights, democracy, and the need for and legitimacy of promoting both from the outside. At the same time, they frequently cannot but accept suggestions to include a reference to the right to self-determination given that it undoubtedly is an established right that is enshrined, not least, in the human rights covenants. And it is this move that the majority of states, which are wary of international interference in the name of democracy and human rights while supporting a traditional conception of self-determination, usually make. Two examples from the period under consideration that illustrate this dynamic of contestation concern the 2005 World Summit Outcome document (A/RES/60/1) and a resolution explicitly dealing with democracy promotion (A/RES/59/201).[11]

The World Summit Outcome, as adopted by the UNGA in September 2015, contains a brief section on democracy that, inter alia, reaffirms "that democracy is a universal value based on the freely expressed will of people to determine their own political, economic, social and cultural systems and their full participation in all aspects of their lives"; adds "that while democracies share common features, there is no single model of democracy"; and emphasizes "the necessity of due respect for sovereignty and the right of self-determination" (A/RES/60/1, 30). Draft versions of the outcome document did, initially, not contain a single reference to either self-determination or sovereignty but, later, gradually introduced respective language, most probably in response to demands from member states from the Global South.[12] Similar revisions also concern the introductory chapter, "Values and principles," in which references to "the sovereign equality of all States," "the right to self-determination," and the right to "noninterference in the internal affairs of States" were added in the process of revising the original draft version (A/RES/60/1, 2; A/59/HLPM/CRP.1/Rev.1, 1). These revisions clearly responded to concerns raised by the Non-Aligned Movement.[13] Interestingly, not even the US government, which pushed for much stronger language on democracy and human rights as well as on R2P, tried to delete references to self-determination.[14]

The same dynamic can be observed with the UNGA resolution "Enhancing the role of regional, subregional and other organizations and arrangements in promoting and consolidating democracy" that was introduced in November 2004 by Peru, Romania, Timor-Leste, and the United States and adopted in December 2004 by the UNGA. Again, the original draft did not contain a single reference to the right to self-determination but focused entirely on a cluster of concepts made up of democracy, freedom, human rights, and good governance (A/C.3/59/L.62). In response to amendments suggested by Cuba (A/C.3/59/L.77), the authors, however, made significant concessions in this regard. In the final version, a preambular paragraph reaffirms "that all peoples have the right to self-determination, by virtue of which they can freely determine their political status and freely pursue their economic, social and cultural development," while an operative paragraph adds "that democracy is based on the freely expressed will of the people to determine their own political, economic, social and cultural systems and their full participation in all aspects of their lives and, in that context, that the promotion and protection of human rights and fundamental freedoms at the national, regional and international levels should be universal and conducted without conditions attached" (A/RES/59/201, 1–2). Given that the latter phrase is directly taken from the Vienna Declaration adopted at the 1993 World Summit on Human Rights, the authors of the draft resolution could hardly reject its inclusion in the text. Interestingly, Cuba nevertheless abstained from the vote, arguing that other parts of the resolution still "stymied the right of peoples to self-determination"; but Egypt, for instance, now decided to vote in favor because the sponsors of the resolution "had included a reference to certain principles and rights, such as the right of self-determination, which implied the right of all peoples to be free and to pursue their destiny in the manner they thought fit."[15]

In this sense, then, the conceptual politics taking place in these UN debates do not really include a struggle over competing conceptions of self-determination but rather processes of normative contestation between those that emphasize self-determination (as they share the hegemonic conception of the concept in the UN context) and those that deliberately try to avoid it. The latter try to promote a competing cluster of concepts that centers on human rights and democracy but omits self-determination (see also Poppe and Wolff 2017). Yet, by invoking human rights, they open the conceptual door to those that want to bring in self-determination to qualify the political implications of the concepts of democracy and human rights.

Those that try to avoid the concept of self-determination do not, however, normatively reject the principle as such but do not dare to say so. Rather, they hold a different conception but know that references to the concept in UN documents will generally be understood in a different sense. A rare example where this is made explicit is the following remark by the United Kingdom on behalf of the European Union and others: In distancing this group from a resolution on the "Universal realization of the right of peoples to self-determination" that, inter alia, reaffirms "that the universal realization of the right of all peoples . . . to self-determination is a fundamental condition for the effective guarantee and observance of human rights and for the preservation and promotion of such rights" (A/RES/60/145, 2), the British representative emphasizes that the right to self-determination "was closely associated with respect for all human rights, democracy and the rule of law" and that "it was incorrect to suggest that self-determination was a precondition for the enjoyment of all human rights" (A/C.3/60/SR.45, 4). By adding the concept of democracy and, more importantly, by rejecting the prioritization of self-determination vis-à-vis human rights, the meaning and the political implications of both self-determination and the entire cluster of concepts are changed significantly. The competing conception of self-determination is best represented by the UNGA resolution "Respect for the principles of national sovereignty and diversity of democratic systems in electoral processes as an important element for the promotion and protection of human rights." This document contains multiple references to self-determination such as the standard reaffirmation of "the right to self-determination, by virtue of which all peoples can freely determine their political status and freely pursue their economic, social and cultural development" (A/RES/60/164, 1). By relating the concepts of democracy and human rights directly to self-determination, national sovereignty and diversity, the resolution justifies explicit arguments against the external promotion of democracy and human rights.[16]

Also for those that evoke self-determination with a view to its traditional understanding, the virtually uncontested core of the concept implies certain constraints. These, in particular, concern resistance against interventions in the case of mass atrocities that—as noted above—can hardly be justified in terms of any plausible conception of self-determination. This, again, can be seen in the 2005 World Summit Outcome document. As mentioned, states from the Global South have been quite successful in qualifying universalist language on democracy and human rights by inserting references to self-determination and related concepts into both the general chapter "Values and Principles" and the section "Democracy." At the same time, such references have remained absent from the section on R2P, where the potential international response to "genocide, war crimes, ethnic cleansing and crimes against humanity" is, thus, *not* qualified by references to self-determination (or sovereignty) (A/RES/60/1, 30).[17]

Conclusion

Both in academic debates and in the context of the UNGA, conceptual struggles over the (il)legitimacy of external interference are structured by a common normative reference point, that is, by the overarching concept of self-determination. On the one hand, those who argue for external interference in the name of democracy and human rights can hardly ignore the tension between such interference and the (acknowledged) principle of self-determination. As a consequence, the attempt to justify coercive regime change in the name of the promotion of (democratic) self-determination has largely failed—an attempt that arguably would have meant stretching the concept beyond reasonable limits (Poppe and Wolff 2013, 387).[18] On the other hand, those who categorically reject external interference in the internal affairs of states have a hard time when it comes to so-called crimes against humanity. In this case, the social fact that such atrocity crimes cannot be justified as in line with the concept of self-determination plausibly helps explain the 2005 UNGA agreement on R2P as well as the quite notable global acceptance of the overall idea behind R2P in spite of fierce disputes regarding its precise meaning and implementation (see Benner et al. 2015, 10).

Conceptual analysis helps make sense of this observation. The virtually uncontested descriptive core of the concept of self-determination that is inextricably linked with strong normative connotations enables and drives an infinite struggle between competing conceptions that are embedded in different worldviews and serve different political purposes. But this same core, by delimiting the range of plausible conceptions, also constrains the range of policies that can be justified in terms of the concept. The concept of self-determination, as any concept, is used and manipulated by interested actors as much as it imposes its hegemonic meaning on the actor that makes use of it.

Notes

1. Research for this chapter was conducted during a visiting stay at Nuffield College, University of Oxford, in 2013. I thank a series of colleagues at Nuffield and, most importantly, Laurence Whitehead; the participants of a workshop at the Hebrew University of Jerusalem in 2015; the editor of this volume, Piki Ish-Shalom; as well as two anonymous reviewers, for comments and suggestions.

2. The distinction between concept and conceptions is often traced back to Gallie (1956, 176) and/or Rawls (1971, 5), while Rawls himself refers to H. L. A. Hart's *The Concept of Law*.

3. Mor Mitrani (this volume) makes a similar observation with a view to the usage of the concept "international community." The underlying logic, however, is different. While in the case at hand there are heated debates about the "correct" conception of self-determination, in Mitrani's case it is the "emptiness" of the concept—international community as an empty signifier—that allows for different kinds of strategic usage of the concept, which itself remains uncontested.

4. This chapter deliberately leaves aside an important issue in the overall debate about self-determination, namely, the difficult question about the proper collectivity ("the people," "the nation," "the political community," etc.) that is to exercise self-determination and the series of subsequent questions of how to identify, define, or delimit the relevant collectivity in any given case. See, for instance, Buchanan (2003, 331–424); Crawford (2006); and Moore (1998).

5. The overall point here is that essentially contested concepts are not merely used

to describe something but at the same time ascribe a positive value to the phenomenon at hand, either because it is judged to be a good thing in and of itself or because it is seen to have positive consequences (Collier et al. 2006, 241). As Collier et al. (2006, 216) argue, Gallie himself only considers appraisiveness in terms of a "*positive* valuation," but it is hard to see why decidedly "*negative* valuation" should be excluded. In this broader sense, then, the criterion of appraisiveness refers to the necessary "normative component" of essentially contested concepts.

6. In the terminology of Collier et al. (2006, 216–22), the remaining of Gallie's seven criteria are openness, reciprocal recognition, exemplars, and progressive competition.

7. It has to be noted, however, that the debate about the secession from, or breakup of, states is still very much concerned with the traditional dimension of external self-determination (cf. Buchanan 2003, 331–424; Crawford 2006; Moore 1998).

8. This, of course, does not mean that it is—logically or politically—impossible to conceptualize self-determination in ways that deliberately break with these limitations. But such a move would mean that the speaker at hand either (mis)uses the concept of self-determination in ways that are inappropriate in terms of the conventional usage of the concept (and, thereby, renders the argument basically incomprehensible for audiences shaped by the conventional understanding) or deliberately tries to fundamentally change the terms of the political discourse, to use Connolly's phrase, with a view to establishing a new overarching concept of self-determination (on this general issue, see Connolly 1993, 32–35).

9. A similar kind of differentiation can be observed in the debate about self-determination in international law (cf. Cassese 1995, 347; Crawford 2006, 334).

10. While this contested cluster of concepts is dealt with in the General Assembly's Third Committee each year (and, throughout the 2000s, in fairly similar terms), I focus on the 59th and 60th General Assembly (2004–5), which included the preparation for and actual holding of the World Summit in September 2005. On the UNGA debates on self-determination and human rights in previous decades, see Burke (2010).

11. Here and subsequently, UN documents are cited by their official symbol. They can be accessed via the United Nations' Official Document System, https://documents.un.org/prod/ods.nsf/home.xsp.

12. See the unofficial draft outcome document presented by UNGA president Jean Ping on 3 June 2005 (available at http://bit.ly/29klL7a) as well as the revised outcome document from 22 July 2005 (A/59HLPM/CRP.1/REV.1). I cannot trace the amendments mentioned to specific member states' interventions, but, in terms of their substance, they respond to concerns usually voiced by members of the Non-Aligned Movement (see, for instance, the documents cited in note 13).

13. For instance, statements and proposals by the Pakistani ambassador (21 June 2005, available at http://bit.ly/29u2Hqz) as well as by the Non-Aligned Movement (1 September 2005, available at http://bit.ly/29u2G5V) explicitly pushed for including references to self-determination (relating this concept with principles such as sovereignty and noninterference).

14. See the more than four hundred revisions of the draft outcome document presented by the United States in August 2005, available at http://bit.ly/29lBiJh.

15. See the brief debate on the (draft) resolution in the UNGA's Third Committee on 24 November 2004 (A/C.3/59/SR.53, 10–2).

16. One paragraph, for instance, calls upon "all States to refrain from financing political parties or other organizations in any other State in a way that is contrary to the principles of the Charter and that undermines the legitimacy of its electoral processes" (A/RES/60/164, 2). Africa, Asia, and Latin America almost unanimously supported the resolution (110 states in total), while the US (together with Australia, Israel, Marshall Islands, Micronesia, and Palau) voted against the text and most European as well as a few African, Asian, and Latin American states abstained (61 in total).

17. This is, of course, not to say that no one tried to constrain the possibility of interference in the name of R2P. In its statement from 21 June 2005 (see above), Pakistan, for instance, argued: "Any endeavor to promote protection of civilians should not become a basis to contravene the principles of non-interference and nonintervention or question the national sovereignty and territorial integrity of States."

18. As Martha Finnemore (2008, 208) has argued with a view to humanitarian intervention, "even those who support broad and active policies of humanitarian action strongly support self-determination."

References

Ackerman, Peter, and Michael J. Glennon. 2007. "The Right Side of the Law." *American Interest* 3 (1): 41–46. https://www.the-american-interest.com/2007/09/01/the-right-side-of-the-law

Altman, Andrew, and Christopher H. Wellman. 2009. *A Liberal Theory of International Justice.* Oxford: Oxford University Press.

Anaya, S. James. 2004. *Indigenous Peoples in International Law.* 2nd ed. Oxford: Oxford University Press.

Anghie, Antony. 2004. *Imperialism, Sovereignty and the Making of International Law.* Cambridge: Cambridge University Press.

Beitz, Charles R. [1979] 1999. *Political Theory and International Relations.* Princeton, NJ: Princeton University Press.

Beitz, Charles R. 2009. "The Moral Standing of States Revisited." *Ethics & International Affairs* 23 (4): 325–47.

Benner, Thorsten et al. 2015. "Effective and Responsible Protection from Atrocity Crimes: Toward Global Action. Findings and Policy Options from an International Research Project on 'Global Norm Evolution and the Responsibility to Protect.'" *GPPI Policy Paper,* April. http://www.globalnorms.net/fileadmin/user_upload/Publications/GlobalNorms_2015_Effective_and_Responsible_R2P.pdf

Buchanan, Allen. 2003. *Justice, Legitimacy, and Self-Determination: Moral Foundations for International Law.* Oxford: Oxford University Press.

Burke, Roland. 2010. *Decolonization and the Evolution of International Human Rights.* Philadelphia: University of Pennsylvania Press.

Cassese, Antonio. 1995. *Self-Determination of Peoples: A Legal Reappraisal.* Cambridge: Cambridge University Press.

Christiano, Thomas. 2011. "An Instrumental Argument for a Human Right to Democracy." *Philosophy & Public Affairs* 39 (2): 142–76.

Collier, David, Fernando Daniel Hidalgo, and Andra Olivia Maciuceanu. 2006. "Essentially Contested Concepts: Debates and Applications." *Journal of Political Ideologies* 11 (3): 211–46.

Connolly, William E. 1993. *The Terms of Political Discourse.* 3rd ed. Princeton, NJ: Princeton University Press.

Crawford, James. 2000. "Democracy and the Body of International Law." In *Democratic Governance and International Law*, ed. Gregory H. Fox and Brad R. Roth, 91–120. Cambridge: Cambridge University Press.

Crawford, James. 2006. *The Creation of States in International Law.* 2nd ed. Oxford: Oxford University Press.

Emerson, Rupert. 1971. "Self-Determination." In *American Journal of International Law* 65 (3): 459–75.

Finnemore, Martha. 2008. "Paradoxes in Humanitarian Intervention." In *Moral Limit and Possibility in World Politics*, ed. Richard M. Price, 197–224. Cambridge: Cambridge University Press.

Fox, Gregory H. 2000. "The Right to Political Participation in International Law." In *Democratic Governance and International Law*, ed. Gregory H. Fox and Brad R. Roth, 48–90. Cambridge: Cambridge University Press.

Fox, Gregory H., and Brad R. Roth. 2000. "Introduction: The Spread of Liberal Democracy and Its Implications for International Law." In *Democratic Governance and International Law*, ed. Gregory H. Fox and Brad R. Roth, 1–22. Cambridge: Cambridge University Press.

Franck, Thomas M. 1992. "The Emerging Right to Democratic Governance." *American Journal of International Law* 86 (1): 46–91.

Gallie, W. B. 1956. "Essentially Contested Concepts." *Proceedings of the Aristotelian Society* 56:167–98.

Hannum, Hurst. 1990. *Autonomy, Sovereignty, and Self-Determination. The Accommodation of Conflicting Rights.* Philadelphia, PA: University of Pennsylvania Press.

Hobson, Christopher, and Milja Kurki. 2012. "Introduction: The Conceptual Politics of Democracy Promotion." In *The Conceptual Politics of Democracy Promotion*, ed. Christopher Hobson and Milja Kurki, 1–15. London: Routledge.

Ish-Shalom, Piki. 2012. "Conceptualizing Democratization and Democratizing Conceptualization: A Virtuous Circle." In *The Conceptual Politics of Democracy Promotion*, ed. Christopher Hobson and Milja Kurki, 38–52. London: Routledge.

Koselleck, Reinhart. 1996. "A Response to Comments on the Geschichtliche Grundbegriffe." In *The Meaning of Historical Terms and Concepts: New Studies on Begriffsgeschichte*, ed. Hartmut Lehmann and Melvin Richter, 59–70. Washington, DC: German Historical Institute.

McFaul, Michael. 2005. "Democracy Promotion as a World Value." *Washington Quarterly* 28 (1): 147–63.

McMahan, Jeff. 1996. "Intervention and Collective Self-Determination." *Ethics & International Affairs* 10 (1): 1–24.

Moore, Margaret, ed. 1998. *National Self-Determination and Secession.* Oxford: Oxford University Press.

Poppe, Annika E., and Jonas Wolff. 2013. "The Normative Challenge of Interaction: Justice Conflicts in Democracy Promotion." *Global Constitutionalism* 2 (3): 373–406.

Poppe, Annika E., and Jonas Wolff. 2017. "The Contested Spaces of Civil Society in a Plural World: Norm Contestation in the Debate about Restrictions on International Civil Society Support." *Contemporary Politics* 23 (4): 469–88.

Rawls, John. 1971. *A Theory of Justice.* Cambridge, MA: Harvard University Press.

Reisman, W. Michael. 2000. "Sovereignty and Human Rights in Contemporary International Law." In *Democratic Governance and International Law*, ed. Gregory H. Fox and Brad R. Roth, 239–58. Cambridge: Cambridge University Press.

Roepstorff, Kristina. 2013. *The Politics of Self-Determination: Beyond the Decolonisation Process.* Abingdon: Routledge.

Roth, Brad R. 2000a. *Governmental Illegitimacy in International Law.* Oxford: Oxford University Press.

Roth, Brad R. 2000b. "Evaluating Democratic Progress." In *Democratic Governance and International Law*, ed. Gregory H. Fox and Brad R. Roth, 493–516. Cambridge: Cambridge University Press.

Scott, David. 2012. "Norms of Self-Determination: Thinking Sovereignty Through." *Middle East Law and Governance* 4 (2–3): 195–224.

Senese, Salvatore. 1989. "External and Internal Self-Determination." *Social Justice* 16 (1): 19–25.

Summers, James. 2013. "The Internal and External Aspects of Self-Determination Reconsidered." In *Statehood and Self-Determination: Reconciling Tradition and Modernity in International Law*, ed. Duncan French, 229–49. Cambridge: Cambridge University Press.

Tesón, Fernando R. 1992. "The Kantian Theory of International Law." *Columbia Law Review* 92 (1): 53–102.

Waldron, Jeremy. 2010. "Two Conceptions of Self-Determination." In *The Philosophy of International Law*, ed. Samantha Besson and John Tasioulas, 397–413. Oxford: Oxford University Press.

Walzer, Michael. [1977] 2006. *Just and Unjust Wars: A Moral Argument with Historical Illustrations.* 4th ed. New York: Basic Books.

Wolff, Jonas. 2014. "The Question of Self-Determination in International Democracy Promotion." *PRIF Working Paper*, no. 19 (March). http://www.hsfk.de/fileadmin/HSFK/hsfk_downloads/PRIF_WP_19.pdf

CHAPTER 3

The Concept of Success in (and of) War

Brent J. Steele
Luke Campbell

> America doesn't have victories anymore, we don't win,
> we don't win at anything.
>
> —Donald Trump, president of the United States (*Daily Mail*, 2016)

The notion of winning or success in war is an important political concept used in some formulations of jus ad bellum and also in hypotheses that predict an increase or decrease in public opinion for wars. Indeed, Anna Geis's chapter in this volume parses the carefully considered German public's opinion on the changing nature of the German military's role in the International Security Assistance Force mission in Afghanistan and the particular unease with the transition from stabilization to counterinsurgency and with it the withering possibility of success. There is very little question that this underexplored, ethereal concept is important in large part because of its social, political, and scholarly scope. This chapter seeks to answer the question of how winning and success in war are conceptualized (or not) and, in a related fashion, what political functions are served by the concept set of winning and success in war. We suggest that certain concepts, and their political functions, are shaped by emotional processes, whereby subjects embody through affective familiarization what the concept means to them. Intellectuals also play a role in imbuing otherwise ambiguous concepts with a sense of "objectivity" and therefore further fasten certain policies while closing off alternatives.

In line with the Gramscian perspective laid out in the introduction, we want to make three assertions up front and defend those throughout this chapter. First, as Cox notes in his iconic article that in part introduced Gramsci to international relations (IR), concepts are necessarily ambiguous. Gramsci saw a concept as "loose and elastic and [it] attains precision only when brought into contact with a particular situation which it helps to explain—a contact which also develops a meaning of the concept" (1983, 162–63). This ambiguity is important because it provides a flexible context for actors to imbue concepts with their meaning, including both those who develop the concept as well as "audiences" who can internalize their meanings individually and even personally—thus, emotionally (see also Strunin-Kremer, Geis, Beulieu-Brossard, this volume).

Second, the role of intellectuals proves important not only in the development of these concepts but also in their "grounding" applications to politics. While intellectuals can assist the sphere of civil society to "act towards an alternative social order at local, regional, and global levels" (Cox 1999, 28), they can also provide a "smoothing" function in the legitimating sphere and further entrench power. Put another way, to promote a counter-hegemonic order proves difficult because such an order has been imbued as "universal in form," as not being contingent on class or nation. Intellectuals who participate in establishing the rigidity and certainty of "laws" of social science, for example, craft further certainty and rigidity in the relations of social beings. Thus, this function of intellectuals vis-à-vis concepts is a reflexive one (Amoureux and Steele 2015), wherein their positions as intellectuals relate to their ability to not only develop but also clarify, protect, and promote concepts as they rub against the subjects they are supposed to "just" explain.

Third, and bringing these two together, we call attention to the balance between them—ambiguity and fixity. We thus emphasize in this chapter the role of social scientists and intellectuals in delivering "elastic" concepts "into particular situations" to help them both develop meaning via social scientific "precision." At the same time, such concepts must also remain ambiguous enough—open enough—so that the ambiguity serves a political function in closing off alternative ways of thinking and acting. As one of us noted in a previous work, "Power is made possible and exists through the ambiguous space" (Steele 2010, 14). Yet this grounding by intellectuals and social scientists is only part of the process we seek to investigate in this chapter. For "winning" and success are no doubt both ambiguous but also powerful signifiers in that there exists an assumed finality and clarity in the concept itself, thereby making it a socially *attractive* concept as well. The necessary social resonance of such a sticky and nebulous concept obtains its use, we argue, through a familiar and structured socially affective process that we describe as "affective familiarization."

The process of affective familiarization brings together two components. First, affect is conceptually derived from the social production of emotions and emotional states explored theoretically in IR scholarship and has been characterized as a phenomenon that encompasses the emotions that propagate from micro levels but then develop into the "social patterns" of collectives (Ross 2013, 3). Familiarization involves both "habit" as a type of action (or inaction) in IR (Hopf 2010) and the sociology of processes of collective memory (Halbwachs 1992; also Bueger, this volume).

We bring this discussion together in four sections. First, we review two literatures on success or winning and war—as it has been treated in deliberations in Just War and as it has been viewed by scholars debating what shapes democratic public opinion for supporting (or not) war. The second section introduces and develops our referent of "affective familiarization" and how it can be utilized to understand in the US case the collective emotional "stakes" of winning wars. The third section then revisits and rereads the scholarship on winning wars, taking special notice of the role of the scholar-intellectual in fostering a politics of "winning" war to justify it. We provide some illustrations from the case of the 2007 "surge" strategy used by the Bush administration to justify and extend the United States' involvement in the Iraq War.

One scholar, Peter Feaver, who had contributed to debates over "winning" wars and their relationship to public opinion, was directly involved in the decision and justification to add additional forces to a war that was deeply unpopular at that time. Professor Feaver, a political science professor at Duke University, took leaves from academia to serve in several administrations, including on the National Security Council with the George W. Bush administration as a "Special Advisor for Strategic Planning and Institutional Reform from 2005–2007." While Ricks (2009) details Feaver's time as an adviser on the surge and the surge's role in shaping the Bush administration's views on both its military and political benefits, our point below is that the concept of "success" that he and his collaborators developed is one that enabled a deployment like the surge. At a time when the Iraq War was incredibly unpopular, Feaver's thesis that public opinion turns around to support wars with a "winning" strategy proved popular for the Bush administration, which had no intentions of pulling out of Iraq (see also Geis on German support for the International Security Assistance Force in Afghanistan, this volume). Our conclusion calls for a reflexive stance for scholars to consider in perpetually disturbing concepts and the politics they perform when left unchallenged.

Success(es) and War

Two related literatures focus on the concept of success or winning. The first arises in the literature on public opinion and war, specifically public opinion regarding support for war as a "dependent" variable being investigated. What, this literature asks, determines or shapes a public's support for a war? Several hypotheses have been examined over the years, but, as noted by John Mueller is his famous 2005 rejoinder in *Foreign Affairs* to those debates, most of these alternative independent variables have been considered less influential upon public opinion. This includes the notion of positive or negative events, an effective (or not) antiwar opposition, an effective (or not) alternative strategy to the war, and whether body bags are shown or not. Thus, most of the disagreement has centered over two competing claims: (1) that public opposition rises in reaction to rising casualties, including deaths, making the public "casualty-averse" (Mueller 2005) or (2) that public opposition rises or falls in relation to the perception that a war can be "won" or "lost," making the public "losing-averse" (Gelpi, Feaver and Reifler 2009; Feaver 2005). The latter hypothesis centralizes "winning" as a concept that is internalized by the public and used to shape and even determine their support for war.

Debates within the Just War tradition constitute the second body of literature that also incorporates "winning" and "success." This is seen through a couple of different specific discussions of Just War. The "reasonable chance for success" condition of jus ad bellum, or what Walzer titles in his magnum opus "war's ends, and the importance of winning" (1977), is one that assumes that a Just War should be fought only when the endgame, the chances for a successful conclusion, is determined. As Heinze and Steele summarize this condition, "A war should not be waged unless there is a reasonable hope that the goals the initiator hopes to achieve (those goals embedded in the just case) can, indeed, be achieved. This prudential criterion serves to essentially ban lethal violence that is known in advance to be futile" (2009, 11).[1]

The problem (but, as we suggest below, the "solution" as well) is that what "success" is becomes difficult to determine. Walzer notes this up front, for "while it is sometimes urgent to win, it is not always clear what winning is" (1977, 110). This has even led some critics of the Just War tradition, like Laura Sjoberg, to suggest that success depends entirely on what processes or outcomes the participant hopes it produces (2009, 168). For some, it may not be the destruction of the opponent's center of military gravity but rather their masculine identity that is considered the "successful" outcome being sought in a war. For others, like the feminist ethicists on war, Sjoberg notes that instead "success" is about creating a just and stable basis for peace. What Sjoberg and other critics seek to point out is precisely the difficulty embedded in success rendered in the former way: winning objectively and success subjectively occupy distinct spaces. Subjective success, rescuing, or upholding masculine identity could be achieved outside of any objective "winning."

On the other hand, while "winning" and victory seem important in Just War, this condition of "success" remains not only elusive but sometimes willfully ignored by certain groups of Just War scholars—though it is a condition that has historically "stacked" the deck against nonstate actors' just use of force and is thus considered both a "conservative" and "restrictive" one (O'Driscoll 2008). Yet it has also been considered in a twenty-first-century context to be in great tension with the other conditions of Just War, "smother[ing] just cause" and other jus *ad bellum* principles, thereby "blocking the possibility of Just War reasoning" (76).[2]

Now, we would admit that both articulations of winning and success in war could be engaging slightly different concepts. They are for sure, we would note, engaging different *timings* or sequences within or before war. The Just War condition of success is supposed to be a priori, whereas the public opinion hypothesis is one articulated usually when a war has already commenced and the evaluation of it by the public is aimed not at the present but the future. Further, this elides the distinctions between the related terms of "winning," "success," and "victory" as we have used them so far. We will return to this distinction momentarily. For now, we note that the tensions or distinctions between success and winning are less a result of how those are measured or conceptualized and more a result of the *political functions* that each concept provides in how one views war, its commencement, its legitimacy, and its continuation.

For instance, the hypothesis on winning to influence public opinion was most famously proffered by Peter Feaver and Christopher Gelpi in a 1999 op-ed appearing in the *Washington Post* following the end of Operation Allied Force. There, they made the famous claim that the public would endure over six thousand US battle deaths to bring democracy to the Congo. Referencing their survey data, the two concluded:

> Collectively, these results suggest that a majority of the American people will accept combat deaths—so long as the mission has the potential to be *successful*. The public can distinguish between suffering defeat and suffering casualties. (Feaver and Gelpi 1999; emphasis added)[3]

Feaver and Gelpi's op-ed can be considered hopeful and inspiring, in that it energizes the agency possible within war—one need not worry about casualties influencing US public opinion if the overall "victory" is still in sight (and notice in the above quote that they use "successful" as their concept). Put another way, and contrary to its supposedly "restrictive" function in jus ad bellum, the concept of success here enables a political function regarding the *continuation* of war. Leaders themselves have more room to fight wars, and the public has a more open mind in supporting wars, if Feaver and Gelpi's thesis is correct. And if that's the case, then our judgment for foreign policy should focus upon either selecting executives who have the strength and will to see out a mission or critically interrogating ones who lose their "stomach" prematurely, as Feaver and Gelpi adjudicated in the case of the Clinton administration and Somalia (1999). Thus, here the winning thesis is *permissive* of further violence—one can turn public opinion around regardless of casualties if a polity implements a successful strategy. The impetus here exists in the decidedly nebulous concept of success and winning, however conceived. If success can be achieved outside of "winning," then there is an inherently attractive element to this politically.

The "success" condition of jus ad bellum, however, is *restrictive* of war. It is one of the more conservative conditions, hence titled a "prudential" condition, for war. The more it is emphasized, the less one emphasizes the moral evaluation of the "evil" being confronted, at least ahead of a conflict.

The point is that if one is to worry about what "success" is, they may delay their actions or not act at all—the Just Warrior may be stuck in a paralysis-by-analysis mode that only serves to be self-defeating if and when the war finally commences. Further, this condition ignores the vitalist possibilities springing from war.

And so it is for those Just Warriors like Nigel Biggar and James Turner Johnson, who supported and continue to use Just War principles to justify the wars of the 2000s. The "success" condition gets in the way of evaluating the other moral benefits of war that should be valorized rather than condemned. The reason stems from a relatively recent insistence that there ought to be a hierarchical categorization to the principles embedded in the *jus ad bellum*: deontological (moral) and supportive (prudential). In this rendering, the deontological principles—just cause, legitimate authority, right intention—occupy a privileged moral position and as such are the distinct purview of states as the only moral arbiter in the international system. As holders of these positions, the representatives of the states then use the prudential categories, success included, to determine if a just war is actually "prudent." However, as Johnson argues, "to determine that a particular use of force is imprudent is not the same as determining that it would be unjust," adding that "not everything that is morally justified is prudent to do" (2005, 19). Thus, the restrictive condition of jus ad bellum has itself become permissive. In fact, and returning to Cox's ambiguity assertion noted in our introduction regarding concepts, sometimes the ambiguity of the success condition is used to justify a pivoting from it toward a more forceful reading justifying the war. We return to his thesis below, but Nigel Biggar in his book *In Defence of War* provides an immediately important illustration of centralizing the ambiguity of the condition to set up his own judgments about war:

> We cannot judge the success or failure of the intervention in Iraq by way of a comprehensive weighing of its actual effects, since these are often indeterminable and incommensurable, always constantly evolving, and attributable to a variety of agents. (2013, 310)

Biggar points out as well that success is a prudential condition that may be difficult to envision not only after but *especially* ahead of time, thus the need to move away from it toward other conditions of the jus ad bellum.

Some other prominent Just War scholars are beginning to take notice of this problematic separation, especially the political usage and potential abuse. In such a separation, wherein supposedly morally superior representatives of the state are left to determine prudence, the "ideal of victory threatens to encourage a dangerous 'eyes on the prize' disposition that discounts respect for constraints in war" (O'Driscoll 2015, 811). O'Driscoll adds, as a caution, that "the threat is evident" (811). But as O'Driscoll notes in another venue about the broader use of Just War and the *positionality* of the scholar vis-à-vis that use, those writing on Just War to "defend" it are not just writing about war but also participating in its use by others. Just War, O'Driscoll contends following from Walzer, "is the language of power":

> Presidents, prime ministers, and generals alike have deployed the concepts and categories of the just war to justify their preferred policies and courses of action. . . . The implication of this for us, as scholars and commentators, is that just war is, so to speak, a colonized language. As such, it cannot provide a pure form of resistance (whatever that would look like). (2014, 212)

But those who write about Just War in this manner described by O'Driscoll are therefore participating within the political contexts in which the conditions and languages of war are being deployed. They are thus no longer on the sidelines "watching" how those concepts work but intervening upon and interacting with actors "out there" as they grapple with those conceptual contexts. And all of them, and us, are part of those not only political but affective contexts. Theorizing and better specifying those contexts represents the purpose of the following section.

Affective Familiarization and Success

> We're soldiers. But we're American soldiers! We've been kicking ass for 200 years! We're ten and one!
>
> —John Winger, played by Bill Murray, in *Stripes* (1981)

The concept of "affective familiarization" has deep roots in sociological theory as well as connections to previous theoretical work in emotions in IR. Elements of "familiarity" are most connected to sociological concepts of collective memory, while affect is conceptually derived from the social production of emotions and emotional states explored theoretically in IR scholarship. Affect is commonly understood to transcend the specific "feeling states" of individuals by enabling understandings of how emotional flows act upon individuals and enact particular sociopolitical norms and behaviors and act as guides and frameworks to capture meaning, structure action, and give agency to identities. The social function of affect is twofold: (1) affect is understood to contribute to the preservation of the moral rules of society and (2) is constructed in such a way as to sustain and endorse cultural systems of belief and value (Harre 1986). Familiarity (or habit) and affect are very closely related in one key aspect: both are more automatic than reflective. This is a key element of extending and complicating the assumed notion of prudence expected to inform the use of force in line with the probability of success.

Habit is practice based and thus characterized by a *lack* of agency and deliberation. This form of action is unreflective, assumed, and lodged in particular expectations about outcomes. Once ingrained, habits are quite difficult to be broken, largely because of the relative comfort they provide. In a way, habit makes action "easier." What is crucial to note is that the logic of habit effectively limits choices; it isn't so much that there is *no choice*; rather, it's just that ingrained, repeated exposure creates certain *unreflective expectations* about subsequent action and attendant outcomes associated with certain action. Hopf (2010) argues that this is a particularly useful way to understand elements of IR, where too much agency and rationality is assumed at the expense of certainty, predictability, and ingrained patterns of behavior.

Another function at work in structuring this concept in line with traditional action is the historical analogical aspect, or "familiarization." Familiarization can be further separated into two representative functions, each of which is a crucial element of connecting familiarity to affect: the past as present and the past as future. Familiarization is a distinct process associated largely with memory, ingrained memories, and the act of misremembering.

In the past as present, familiarization implies an inherent level of "comfort" upon building comparisons and looking back. Comfort, or familiarity, found in the past is granted a type of legitimacy by the very nature of the looking back (Halbwachs 1992). Indeed, the familiarity imparted by certain collective memories can serve important political and cultural needs in addition to satisfying psychological and emotional desires. Rather than popping up as isolated and disjointed "episodes," the reconstruction of events is most often connected to similar spatial and temporal events previously experienced or understood (48). Yet, the historical function of familiarization does not in fact assume that the details inherent in the re-creation of that analogy have to be factually accurate or even to represent the "whole" picture. Misremembering or incomplete analogies, intentional or not, can actually be an important part of the process, as it privileges certain aspects of the analogy that are constitutive of the force the example can have. Thus it is not particularly important that an analogy be critiqued for its incommensurability to a particular reality or *the* way things actually happened so much as that the purpose for which the analogy is enlisted is more fully understood; the more appropriate aim is to uncover what it is that the analogy is *doing*.

The important connection between these two elements is the representation of the past in the present through rhetoric, symbols, monuments, memorials, and comparisons, all of which are meant to have a "ritualization" effect (Connerton 1989). These elements have emotional (affective, more appropriately) connections to the society because they are of a cultural, historical, and ideational sort. Indeed, indelible images, photographic, televised, and represented memorially, combined with key rhetorical "triggers" have the ability to "fix cultural memory, sometimes deceptively, and to extend it beyond the original witness" (Torgovnick 2005, xvii). In this way, particular arguments and narratives detailing the evolution of social history and memory through these particular "technologies of representation" are highly important media through which past and present "loops" of connected understanding take on specific meaning (Torgovnick 2005).[4]

These specific "technologies" are cultural elements of reproduction and representation that connect at a social level, breed elements of inherent and constructed familiarity, and transcend individuals to connect the group temporally and spatially. These representations on display in many socially shared mediums are continually represented and reinforced, indeed sustained beyond what might be considered the limits of rationality, because of the very nature of what they represent; their meanings are of such importance and easily understood emotionally that seemingly little effort is required on the part of those presenting and those receiving to fully digest the historically and affectively "looped" connections made.

If familiarization is about the stories and narratives a society uses to remember and understand particularly momentous events in its past, then these events have analogical power to create expectations for future outcomes as well, presenting the possibility for measuring how "the future will rise to the level of the past" (Noon 2004, 342). Because of the affective conditioning of war and conflict, winning and success become "momentous" and powerful due to their reactive, and almost habitual, associations. Though fanciful, Bill Murray's character illustrates a profoundly important aspect of familiarization and its "ease" of use: war's small-N problem. The ability to present the war "record" in such a way points up the limited number of conflicts and their relative memorial and social impact. One could not only recall the "record" of war outcomes but very likely pinpoint not only the ten victories but almost certainly the one "loss" that blemishes the "record."

Ironic perpetuations of the United States as "back to back world war champions" taps into and reinforces an easily retrievable (habitual) narrative that connects individuals socially through the shared affective familiarity. Most recently, anniversary celebrations marking seventy years since the end of World War II offered an opportunity not only to reflect on that war and revere its memory but also to provide a way to measure the relative success of current military campaigns (Wolfgang 2015).[5] And this is not the first and only time these distinct and telling comparisons have been offered. Throughout his prosecution of the so-called War on Terror (WOT), George W. Bush consistently and intentionally compared the WOT, and specifically its measure of success, to that of the victory achieved in World War II. Nor is this particular phenomenon limited to the United States. Russia's own recent World War II anniversary celebrations raised fears that "war memories were being exploited to justify belligerence towards Ukraine and the West" (Shevchenko 2015).

This connection is therefore increasingly effective particularly when past and future events are directly connected in temporally and spatially similar ways. Specific to the notion of familiarity engaged here, legitimation of action and meaning in those contexts follows distinct patterns that are culturally and historically specific and relies upon prior use of such language and prior dependence of meaning with which such language and attendant symbolism have come to be associated. Indeed, Fierke notes that "the ability to make sense of social action, to imbue it with legitimacy, rests on . . . distinct historical patterns" (2010, 94).

It is especially important to point out here that as far as Just War theory's notion of success is viewed, affective familiarization is a way in which social action is understood in a particular manner. It gives meaning to social action; it provides a frame through which a certain understood meaning can be ascribed to a particular action. Recall that the "prudential" criteria, as currently rendered, of success in Just War theory presents a particular standard of achievability: "Going to war without a reasonable chance of prevailing is imprudent" (Eckert 2014, 64). Recall also that one of the biggest challenges of "sorting out" the prudentialist perspective is that the hierarchical separation of Just War theory's criteria can have the practical effect of shifting success calculations out of prudential considerations of "can win" to culturally, historically, and affectively derived statements of "must win."

Yet it also involves a "forward looking" element—that a future where the collective has to "live" with failure will no doubt be not only a difficult one but a completely different affective environment. It will, therefore, be a "new" familiarity that likely will be much more affectively difficult to grapple with. This temporal extension into both past and future, in the present, would explain (for instance) the continuous attempts by Peter Feaver and Nigel Biggar (noted below) to relitigate the "success" of the Iraq War.

It is crucial to understand that conversations and debates about potential action and its attendant expectations are formed inside and not necessarily exogenously given by the international system or the perceived sociality of state and actor relations (Steele 2008). Further understanding of the way in which socially affective elements of decision-making structure action and effect arguably one of the most important decisions, that of using military force and the means by which the stated measure of success is understood, can transcend beyond the purview of decision makers themselves to scholars and citizens and is thus of profound importance. It is to this purpose we now turn with some illustrations provided by the very scholars whose conceptual interventions into the academic literatures on winning could be utilized for political purposes.

Winning Wars

In the two bodies of literature on "winning" that we discussed in the first section, when it comes to the similarity of how these concepts are utilized in terms of *effects* or (put another way) political positions regarding war, there is more overlap than distinction between the two groups. When it comes to justifying war and particular wars, both the proponents of the "winning" thesis on public opinion (like Peter Feaver) and the critics of the "success" condition in Just War (like Nigel Biggar) surprisingly settle on similar cases *constructed in particular narratives or stories* to note that wars can be "just" if we approach success in a particular way. Both, we note below (see Feaver 2011; Biggar 2013, 308–10), use the "surge" strategy as a way to justify the Iraq War on "success" or "winning" grounds.

These two seemingly different approaches to winning or success in war depend less on a measurable delineation of the concept and are instead conditioned more by affect, emotions, aesthetics, and, for lack of a better phrase, *political construction*, both by the "public" that assesses the war and by the scholars using the concepts themselves. Again, the ambiguity of the concepts themselves—evidenced by the fact that these "careful" scholars use the terms "winning," "success," and "victory" interchangeably—is a particular feature that enables such fixation of the concept. And both sets of scholars are caught up in the hermeneutic circle, not only hypothesizing which criteria should be used to judge a quandary (either why public opinion goes up or down or whether a war can be considered just) but using that criteria to make the case, to *make the judgment themselves and advocate for it to persuade others in turn.*

The concepts themselves are intrinsically (like most concepts—democracy, among others, comes to mind) ambiguous and thus left to be constructed and deployed by the scholars even after they make their cases for the function of winning and success. In the public opinion literature, what "winning" is becomes difficult to delineate and in fact depends upon a variety of emotional, aesthetic, and affective processes. Its political function (of energizing the agency possible within war) deems it an attractive option for policy makers. As John Mueller noted in one of his critiques of the Gelpi and Feaver thesis:

> In their subsequent book, Gelpi and Feaver do acknowledge in a footnote that the numbers in the op-ed were "overly susceptible to misinterpretation" and they then rejigger their analysis of the same poll question and essentially conclude that their figure for Congo was some 6,800 percent too high. The *damage, however, had already been done*, this unfortunate op-ed has been widely cited, applied,

and misinterpreted, particularly in military publications. (2005 243–44; emphasis added)

Further, what winning actually is depends less on its a priori delineation and more on its conceptualization after the fact. Sometimes, it is in re-presentational form, where "winning" remains elusive but "losing" can be captured in an image or a series of images that become encoded in the political community sanctioning and/or judging the war they are involved with. One can think of the Saigon helicopter photo, discussed by one of us as an important cultural marker for the United States thereafter: "What "winning" would have entailed in Vietnam is still unclear to many historians, but what losing looked like was captured in this photo" (Steele 2010, 146).

On the rare occasions where the "winning" thesis proponents do engage what "winning" or at least its opposite means, they still at most only surmise, as well as qualify or condition, their guesses as to what it is that the public is looking at to determine "winning" or losing. In a 2006 *International Security* piece, Reifler, Gelpi, and Feaver suggested that the downtick (at that time) in support for the Iraq War was due to

political deadlock over the drafting of a constitution, a lack of demonstrable progress regarding the efficacy of Iraqi security forces, and the persistence of deadly attacks by insurgents [that] undermined that optimism. Of course, the results of the October 15, 2005, referendum on the Iraqi constitution and the subsequent national election will also need to be factored into the mix. Our model claims that public estimations of the success of those milestones—and the ability of insurgents to react—will further shape public tolerance for the war. (9)

Notice how important such day-to-day "milestones" are, then, to the concept of success. Thus, the ontological space for shaping public opinion gets expanded. It is not just the "strategy" at issue and whether it is a "winning" one or not—it is also how "public estimations of the success of those milestones" get formulated at the time that will shape public "tolerance for the war" as well.

Yet we wish to push further, focusing not only on how concepts function politically but also on why concepts like winning are so attractive for political communities and particular scholars more generally. It is precisely in the concept's ambiguity where it becomes powerfully attractive, where license is provided by scholars using the term for their own political position regarding support for (or opposition to) a particular war.

Thus, success in war as conceptualized by neopositivist scholars Christopher Gelpi and Peter Feaver is increasingly fragile and malleable and, further, not only creates an urgency for leaders to "fix" these meanings but also enables a role for intellectuals to "clarify" how success gets conceptualized as well. As a result, although they are neopositivist scholars living in a dualist world where our concepts are used to understand a world that "exists independently of our knowledge of it" (Jackson 2011, 31), Gelpi and Feaver jump into that world to justify particular policies related to their concept, in the same way as do Just War scholars like James Turner Johnson and Nigel Biggar.

For example, Gelpi and Feaver used their thesis to justify the continuation of the Iraq War in the so-called surge of 2007, and much of this depended upon affect, image, and aesthetics, as it does for an objectively "successful" strategy. The surge strategy was implemented in 2007 as a reaction to the increasing sectarian violence and instability in Iraq that resulted (in large part) from the United States' failed occupation of that country. The surge involved three basic components. First, as the name implied, the quantity of combat troops in Iraq was increased by up to twenty thousand (with an additional ten thousand support personnel). Second, US forces under the new command of General David Petraeus implemented a counterinsurgency strategy that the general had used to effective results during his time earlier in the war commanding the 101st Airborne Division. Third, the strategy was pitched as a "winning" one publicly that privately was sold to the Bush administration *by Feaver* himself as a way to turn public opinion around (Ricks 2009, 41). Although the deployment coincided, eventually, with a decrease in violence, the period also saw "other candidates for that decrease, including the Sunni Awakenings and a broader ethnic homogenization of previously 'mixed' Sunni-Shia areas of Iraq that included, especially, Baghdad" (Steele 2016, 71). Perhaps because debates continued for years after the surge regarding what factors were chiefly responsible for the decrease in violence, Feaver (2011) produced a study published in *International Security* that spent as much space justifying the "surge" strategy as it did the notion that "winning" turned public opinion around after that strategy was implemented. Feaver revisited this argument in a 2015 article where he argued that because (then Democratic presidential candidate) Hillary Clinton had come around on the surge, it, again, could be deemed a "success" (Feaver 2015).[6]

Nigel Biggar, a professor at the University of Oxford, has also weighed in on the "success" of the Iraq War. In a section of his book on the ad bellum condition of "success" and the Iraq War, Biggar argues that one has to have low expectations for what was achieved in Operation Iraqi Freedom. "Full-blown liberal democracy," Biggar tells us, "was always fantastically overambitious." But, "significant regime-*improvement* in Iraq" is where Biggar pivots to

> plant my flag in the position articulated by the spokesman of the group of young professional Iraqis who visited me in Oxford in March 2010. At the end of our meeting, I asked them bluntly, "Should the invasion of 2003 have happened?" Without hesitating, their spokesman responded, "It was good that it happened. It could have been done better. And it isn't over." (2013, 310)

Of course, how success is conceptualized here depends on both space and time. The *spatial* involves asking one or two young professional Iraqis rather than, say, the hundreds of thousands who lost their lives as a result of the violence and chaos of the invasion. The *temporal* conditioning here is that the question is asked in March 2010 rather than, say, in 2014–17, when ISIS took control of the Sunni portions of Iraq that were, by the by, excluded from the Shia-dominated Maliki government enshrined as a result of the "success"ful surge strategy that Biggar and Feaver claim saved the Iraq War. But the narrative process utilized by Biggar also suggests an emotional, affective element—hence, the interest for some of these scholars in the role images play in influencing public opinion on the issue of winning (Gartner and Gelpi 2016) and specifically in how images influence the "emotional states and attitudes" of the public, which, in turn, influence their beliefs on whether "success" or "failure" is occurring on the battlefield. Thus, an important political concept can in turn constitute collective affective states and the types of policies and values associated with them. The result is that attempts to achieve success may instead be more about the *appearance* of success[7]—the emotional appeal of feeling successful that drives the perpetuation of conflict for seemingly political purposes.[8]

Conclusions

We have argued in this chapter that the concept of success in war, treated from initially different angles in both Just War scholarship and the literature on public opinion, is one of the most politicized concepts we have in IR. Far from being a restrictive condition, success, because of its emotive content, also depends not on objective definitions but on a process of affective familiarization that political leaders, and also intellectuals, play a part in formulating.

We have intimated above that affective familiarization is important for political concepts more broadly and at a number of levels and, thus, for further analyzing the ways in which political concepts "travel" into the places and spaces where they resonate and influence broader publics. Thus, we would call attention to the micropolitical spaces that are important "affective contexts" where this familiarization gets not only consumed but circulated, reinforced, and perhaps contested (Solomon and Steele 2017). This type of analysis involves, according to William Connolly, paying attention to "organized combinations of sound, gesture, word, movement and posture through which affectively imbued dispositions, desires and judgments become synthesized" (2002). These spaces include "in and around the dinner table, the church, the movie theater, [and] the union hall." But Connolly also calls our attention to forms of entertainment and popular culture, like "the TV sitcom and talk show, the film," as well as our "classrooms"—spaces that all "set the table for macro-policy initiatives in these domains by rendering large segments of the public receptive or unreceptive to them" (2002).

We have focused so far on the conceptualization of success by intellectuals, largely, but a move toward locating and then specifying the affective familiarization of concepts might stimulate scholars to pay attention to a variety of places and spaces in their studies. Our classrooms are, of course, a place that we pay attention to when it comes to exposing students to the concepts we use as political scientists and IR scholars to study the world "out there." We have to spend a lot of time and, in some cases, creative energy, whether we think about it or not, familiarizing our students with what these oftentimes mysterious and yes, ambiguous, concepts "mean." We might also pay attention to how they formulate their understandings of those concepts in their discussions with their contemporaries and to what influences those conceptualizations and from *where* as well.

Let us note two other everyday contexts where especially the concept of success gets consumed. One is film. We, of course, have a quote by actor Bill Murray's character in *Stripes* about success that opens up our second section. Military and war movies often refer to success in war. In a rare subdued scene in the 1986 Vietnam film *Platoon*, Sergeant Elias tells Private Chris Taylor, as they are looking up at the stars one evening after a battle: "What happened today was just the beginning. We're gonna lose this war." Taylor responds incredulously, "Come on. You really think so? Us?" Elias concludes, "We been kicking other people's asses for so long, I figured it's time we got ours kicked."[9] The point isn't just that movies, and other forms of entertainment and art for that matter, *reflect* these types of attitudes about winning or losing wars. It's that they can also be *productive* of the type of affective familiarization about political concepts that we noted earlier in this chapter. This is why film analysis is used so often by scholars interested in micropolitics, including Connolly (2002) but also Michael Shapiro (2009).

A second context would be the other forms of commemoration about particular wars, and their warriors, that also implicate political concepts in ways we may not recognize. The relatively recent practice of "honor flights" in the United States, where members of the "greatest generation" from World War II are flown from their local airports all over the country on direct flights to Washington, DC, is a case in point. The ceremony of these flights has increased as the generation's numbers decrease every day, with the flights often including a procession of veterans (many in wheelchairs) through airport terminals and often during Memorial Day weekend. No doubt other emotionally imbued concepts like sacrifice and honor are at the forefront of these processions—but it is notable that these flights started in 2004 with the completion of the World War II memorial and thus with the "greatest generation" of that war's veterans[10] rather than the previous one who fought in World War I.

A final point is about the concept of success and winning. It implies a need to pay attention not only to the varied *spaces* where this political concept gets negotiated but to the importance of *time* as well. In most sports, a "win" happens after an opponent is defeated and there is a clear score and a clear *finish* to the contest. But while some wars, like World War II, seemingly had fairly clear temporal "endings," war itself continues on for some time. In a critique of Nigel Biggar's *In Defence of War*, Cian O'Driscoll calls attention to not only the lingering effects of war but the lack of any finality to it, no matter how much "success" there is. O'Driscoll argues that heroic depictions of war and success are

> not the entire story. [They do not] grapple with the reality that, regardless of what a colonel in the Royal Marines or dozens of war memoirs may claim, significant numbers of soldiers are afflicted by rage, regret, and trauma, even long after the fighting has ceased for them. Indeed, the depressing figures for suicides among active duty soldiers and the murder of military spouses, only just coming to light, suggest that there is a hidden history here—an excess that is not treated in Biggar's analysis. (2014, 214)

Thus, it is not only the *ambiguity* of concepts that we want to continue to call scholars' attention to. That indeed has been a focus of our analysis here. But O'Driscoll's metaphor of a concept's *excess* is important as well. Concepts exceed the meanings we have for them, and that excess does more than enable just one particular reading. Excess makes it possible for others to contest the attempts to fix those meanings too. Thus, perpetually destabilizing concepts is perhaps the best role we can embody as scholars when so many others are moving us in the opposite, more fixed, more certain, direction.

Notes

1. Thomas Hurka (2005) subsumes the chances for winning under proportionality as not only important "additional" conditions but interrelated conditions for winning itself.

2. O'Driscoll has an ongoing project focusing specifically on "victory" and its treatment in Just War theory (forthcoming).

3. Notice here that the term used by the two scholars is "successful." This interchangeability with "winning" and victory happens without notice by those public opinion scholars investigating Feaver and Gelpi's thesis.

4. We return to this theme on "where to look" for affective familiarization, and thus the circulation and grappling with political concepts, in our conclusion.

5. What is also notable here is not what is remembered but what is forgotten as well. These commemorations over World War II have been contrasted by the curiously quiet and/or nonexistent centennial commemorations in the United States over its participation in World War I. The United States has, for the most part, been fairly subdued in its own World War I centenary commemorations. This may be because, as Jessica Auchter (2017) notes in a forthcoming contribution on centennial poli-

tics, many US Americans view World War II as the "Good War," which overshadows the country's participation in World War I. It may also be due to the United States' delayed entrance into that war or to the war's ambiguous ending with the country's "return to normalcy" and rejection of participating in the League of Nations.

6. In fact, Feaver used the term "success" five times in this 2015 article.

7. See Gelpi and Gartner, 2016

8. This is especially possible in the articulation of the "key explanatory variable" for proponents of this thesis, that it is based on "the extent to which they [the public] believe that the United States will emerge victorious" (Reifler, Gelpi, and Feaver 2006, 25).

9. See http://www.imdb.com/title/tt0091763/quotes.

10. See https://www.honorflight.org/about-honor-flight-networtk/.

References

Amoureux, Jack, and Brent J. Steele. 2015. *Reflexivity and International Relations: Positionality, Critique, and Practice.* London: Routledge.

Auchter, Jessica. 2017. "The 'Greatness' of the Great War: Commemoration and the Politics of Soldier Dead." *Australian Journal of Politics and History* 63 (3): 345–56.

Biggar, Nigel. 2013. *In Defence of War.* Oxford: Oxford University Press.

Bourdieu, Pierre. 1990. *Logic of Practice.* Palo Alto: Stanford University Press.

Connolly, William. 2002, "Film Technique and Micropolitics." *Theory and Event* 6 (1), doi:10.1353/tae.2002.0003

Connerton, Paul 1989. *How Societies Remember.* Cambridge, UK: Cambridge University Press.

Cox, Robert W. 1983. Gramsci, Hegemony and International Relations: An Essay in Method. *Millennium*, 12(2): 162–75.

Cox, Robert W. 1999. Civil Society at the Turn of the Millenium: Prospects for an Alternative World Order. *Review of international studies*, 25 (1): 3–28.

Durkheim, Emile. 1997. *The Division of Labor in Society. New York:* Free Press.

Eckert, Amy E. 2014. "Introduction." In *The Future of Just War: New Critical Essays*, ed. Caron E. Gentry and Amy E. Eckert. Athens, Ga, University of Georgia Press.

Feaver, Peter D. 2011. "The Right to Be Right: Civil-Military Relations and the Iraq Surge Decision." *International Security* 35 (4): 87–125.

Feaver, Peter D. 2015. "Hillary Clinton and the Inconvenient Facts about the Rise of the Islamic State." *Foreign Policy*, August 15. http://foreignpolicy.com/2015/08/13/clinton-surge-iraq-maliki-obama/

Feaver, Peter D., and Christopher Gelpi. 1999. "A Look at Casualty Aversion: How Many Deaths Are Acceptable? A Surprising Answer." *Washington Post,* November 7. http://www.washingtonpost.com/wp-srv/WPcap/1999–11/07/061r-110799-idx.html

Fierke, Karin. 2010. "Wittgenstein and International Relations." In *Interpretive Dialogues: Continental Philosophy and International Relations Theory,* ed. Cerwyn Moore, 83–94. New York: Routledge.

Gelpi, Christopher, Feaver, Peter. D., & Reifler, Jason. (2009). *Paying the Human Costs of War: American Public Opinion and Casualties in Military Conflicts.* Princeton, NJ: Princeton University Press.

Gartner, Scott S. and Gelpi, Christopher .F., 2016. The affect and effect of images of war on individual opinion and emotions. *International interactions,* 42(1), pp.172–88.

Halbwachs, M. 1992. *On collective memory.* Chicago: University of Chicago Press.

Harré, Rom. 1986. *The social construction of emotions.* London: Blackwell

Heinze, Eric A., and Brent J. Steele. 2009. "Introduction." In *Ethics, Authority and War: Non-state Actors and the Just War Tradition,* ed. Eric A. Heinze and Brent J. Steele, 1–20. New York: Palgrave.

Hopf, Ted A. 2010. "The Logic of Habit in International Relations." *European Journal of International Relations* 16 (4).

Hurka, Thomas. 2005. "Proportionality in the Morality of War." *Philosophy & Public Affairs* 33 (1): 34–66.

Jackson, Patrick T. (2011). *The conduct of inquiry in international relations: Philosophy of science and its implications for the study of world politics.* New York: Routledge.

Johnson, James Turner (2005). *The war to oust Saddam Hussein: just war and the new face of conflict.* New York: Rowman & Littlefield.

Mueller, John. 2005. "The Iraq Syndrome." *Foreign Affairs,* 84 (6).

Noon, David. 2004. "Operation Enduring Analogy: World War II, the War on Terror, and the Uses of Historical Memory." *Rhetoric and Public Affairs* 7 (3): 339–64.

O'Driscoll, Cian. 2008. *The Renegotiation of the Just War Tradition and the Right to War.* Houndsmill, Basingstoke, UK: Palgrave.

O'Driscoll, Cian. 2014. "Tough Reading: Nigel Biggar on Callousness and the Just War." *Soundings: An Interdisciplinary Journal* 97 (2): 207–17.

O'Driscoll, Cian. 2015. "All Costs and in Spite of All Terror? The Victory of Just War." *Review of International Studies* 41 (4): 799–811.

Reifler, Jason, Christopher Gelpi, and Peter Feaver. 2006. "Success Matters: Casualty Sensitivity and the War in Iraq." *International Security* 30 (3): 7–46.

Ricks, Thomas. 2009. *The Gamble.* New York: Penguin.

Ross, Andrew A. G. 2013. *Mixed Emotions: Beyond Fear and Hatred in International Conflict.* Chicago: University of Chicago Press.

Shapiro, Michael. 2009. "Managing Urban Security: City Walls and Urban Metis." *Security Dialogue* 40 (4–5): 443–61.

Shevchenko, Vitaly. 2015. "Russia Awash with Symbols of WW2 Victory." *BBC News,* 8 May.

Sjoberg, Laura. 2009. "Gender, Just War and Non-state Actors." In *Ethics, Authority and War: Non-state Actors and the Just War Tradition,* ed. Eric A. Heinze and Brent J. Steele. New York: Palgrave.

Solomon, Ty, and Brent J. Steele 2017. "Micro-moves in International Relations Theory." *European Journal of International Relations* 23 (2): 267–91.

Steele, Brent J. 2008. *Ontological Security in International Relations: Self-Identity and the IR State.* New York: Routledge.

Steele, Brent J. 2010. *Defacing Power: The Aesthetics of Insecurity in Global Politics.* Ann Arbor: University of Michigan Press.

Steele, Brent J. 2016. "Whistle Disruption: Reflexivity and Documentary Provocation." In *Reflexivity and International Relations*, ed. Jack Amoureaux and Brent J. Steele. New York: Routledge.

Torgovnick, Marianna. 2005. *The war complex: World War II in our time.* Chicago: University of Chicago Press.

Walzer, Michael. 1977. *Just and Unjust Wars.* New York: Basic Books.

Weber, Max. 1968. *Economy and Society.* Vol. 1. New York: Bedminster Press.

Wolfgang, Ben. 2015. "70th Anniversary of VE Day Obama Honors Generations that Saved World." *Washington Times*, 8 May.

CHAPTER 4

The Ambivalence of (Not) Being in a "War"

The "Civilian Power" Germany and the "Stabilization Operation" in Afghanistan

Anna Geis

"War" is one of the "basic concepts" dealt with in conceptual history (Janssen 1982).[1] War plays a central role in our sociopolitical language and our social imaginaries. Images of war are dramatic reminders of our fundamental existential vulnerability as human beings. They tend to dominate collective memory practices of communities that have experienced wars, and they are in general far more "impressive" on the human consciousness than images of peace (Paul 2004). "War" and "peace" have often been used as counter-concepts, denoting opposite conditions, in the history of ideas, in theology, and later on in the social sciences. They also constitute the founding concepts of international relations (Levy 2002).

The notion of "war" in politics usually invokes the mobilization of all means available and produces fear and uncertainty. If policy makers choose to avoid the term "war" for describing the large-scale use of force, or if they decide to label a terrorist act (such as the attacks of September 11, 2001) as an "act of war," then this will enable and restrain certain state practices. It will also influence the dominant framing of an act of violence and shape the political narratives (Devetak 2009).

This chapter analyzes political discourses about military missions of unified Germany since the 1990s, with the main focus on the later phase of the International Security Assistance Force (ISAF) mission in Afghanistan. The concept of "war" had been avoided in these debates by most parts of the German political elite until a gradual change in discourse emerged in 2008–9. The ISAF mission, mandated by the United Nations (UN), had been framed as a "stabilization operation" for a long time but gradually turned into a counterinsurgency mission in large parts of Afghanistan. It was the so-called Kunduz airstrike on two fuel tankers, ordered by a German colonel and resulting in many civilian deaths, that further intensified the German public debate on the "character" of the Afghanistan mission.

Basic concepts "are deeply political" and provide "sources and/or sites of contestation between political actors" (Hobson 2015, 37–38). William Connolly (1993, 6) has forcefully argued that conceptual contests are central to politics. Hence, analyzing political concepts "at work" turns our scholarly attention to (de)politicization processes. Avoiding naming the Afghanistan (ISAF) mission a "war" has many reasons, but I will interpret this as a *depoliticization* move in the hegemonic political culture of the "civilian power" Germany that eventually spurred a huge conceptual contest. Quite some actors, among them soldiers and journalists, increasingly challenged the government's depiction of the ISAF mission as a "stabilization operation." The consequence of the resulting conceptual contest about "(no) war" in Afghanistan was a *repoliticization* of the issue.

The extent to which the German discourse is "special" in this regard can only be established by comparative research. However, related empirical research indicates that Germany *is* rather special among Western democracies (Malici 2006; Geis, Müller, and Schörnig 2013). The heavy burdens of the past are still interpreted by many as resulting in specific responsibilities, in "learning lessons" from history, and in avoiding "normalization." While the term "normalization" is in itself very problematic—what is "normal" in the contemporary social order of states or regions?—it often implies having fewer reservations about using military means and being willing to adopt greater responsibility in the joint military interventions of the North Atlantic Treaty Organization (NATO) allies.

This chapter will also include—in an illustrative manner—visual representations of "(no) war" in Afghanistan produced in German popular culture.[2] Wilhelm Janssen (1982) has briefly remarked at the end of his conceptual history analysis of the concept "war" that writing a conceptual history of "war" faces challenges that other basic concepts do not entail in the same way: It cannot grasp the intense *emotional* reactions of human beings who experience war—the very concept remains rather abstract, but the concrete individual and collective experiences of the horrors of war, of heinous acts, and the dramatic emotions implied cannot be captured by intellectual accounts of conceptual histories (Janssen 1982, 614–15). Images can express emotions often in a more immediate sense than words can. Images can "symbolize and communicate emotions" (Hutchison 2014, 5). Visual representations of war work "within specific semantic fields where emotions and dispositions to action vis-à-vis the suffering of 'others' are evoked for the spectator" (Chouliaraki 2006, 262).

Conceptual analyses are usually based on verbal statements only, excluding visual material from the investigation. I will tentatively take up an idea put forward by Jan-Werner Müller, who advocated the inclusion of images into conceptual history (2014, 88–89):

> Especially if it ought to focus more on everyday lived experience . . . , it might include metaphors and images. . . . Of course one can object that this is no longer conceptual history at all—images might indeed make arguments, but they are not unavoidable or contested in the way basic concepts are. Yet both images and metaphors . . . might be as important in structuring a social imaginary.

Films, videos, photographs, or cartoons might contribute to conceptual contests in a rather indirect, diffuse way. In political realms where most citizens lack personal experience and imaginaries, such as the contemporary Western military actions in "alien" territories far away (e.g., Afghanistan, Iraq, Libya, and Mali), media of popular culture convey specific imaginations of such missions in the "homeland discourse" (Daxner 2012, 29–56). Films, for example, can shape imaginations of contemporary "wars" or "war-like" operations in cases where "official" imagery is lacking. Their narratives can foster support for a military mission or contestation of its legitimacy (cf. Engelkamp and Offermann 2012; Heck 2017).

This chapter is structured as follows: In the first section, the term "(de)politicization" and the academic debate on the transformation of "war(fare)" will be briefly introduced. In the second section, the German political culture and the role concept of the "civilian power" will be outlined, followed by an analysis of the changing political discourse about the Afghanistan mission of the German army. It is beyond the scope of this chapter to give a detailed account of all the diverse actors involved in the discourse,[3] so only some aspects can be highlighted. The third section will deal more specifically with the reasons for the *avoidance* discourse and point out numerous ambivalences. An outlook in the fourth section will deal with the rather unexpected return of the "Afghanistan question" in the context of the "refugee crisis" in Germany: Is "it" "war" or not?

The Changing Concept of "War": Conceptual Contests as (De) legitimating Discourses and Practices in Politics

All political concepts are fuzzy and vague. The German historian Reinhart Koselleck (2004, 85)—who has established, among others, the subdiscipline of conceptual history (*Begriffsgeschichte*)—described this as a central feature of concepts: "A word presents potentialities for meaning; a concept unites within itself a plenitude of meaning. Hence, a concept can possess clarity, but must be ambiguous." This ambiguity and fuzziness opens up the possibility for "politics," as William Connolly (1993) has argued in his reflections on the terms of political discourse.

> Central to politics . . . is the ambiguous and relatively open-ended interaction of persons and groups who share a range of concepts, but share them imperfectly and incompletely. Politics involves a form of interaction in which agents adjust, extend, resolve, accommodate, and transcend initial differences within a context of partly shared assumptions, concepts, and commitments. On this reading, conceptual contests are central to politics; they provide the space for political interaction. (6)

Koselleck stressed this point in his reflections on the importance of doing conceptual history. He conceived of concepts as both indicators and factors of politico-social change and suggested analyzing the semantic struggles between political or social actors to understand historical transformations. "The struggle over the 'correct' concepts becomes socially and politically explosive" (Koselleck 2004, 79).

Unpacking concepts thus requires analyzing the temporal, ideational, material, and sociopolitical context of a certain concept: how it has been used and is used in a certain society by certain speakers for what purposes and with what kind of connotations and invocations (Berenskoetter 2016, 9–16; Ish-Shalom 2011). The notion of *struggles* over concepts, of concepts as sites of *contestation,* implies adopting an analytical perspective of permanent (de)politicization processes in societies. There are different meanings of (de)politicization in political science and in politics, partly also used in derogatory terms (Jenkins 2011). Politicization in a simplified manner means "making collectively binding decisions a matter or an object of public discussion. This definition can be operationalized via three indicators: rising awareness, mobilization, and contestation" (Zürn 2014, 50). Politicization is understood in this chapter as a strategy entailing "exposing and questioning what is taken for granted, or perceived to be necessary, permanent, invariable, morally or politically obligatory and essential. Simultaneously, this process helps to reveal and contribute towards contingency, openness and autonomy" (Jenkins 2011, 159–60). Conversely, a strategy of depoliticization—which in itself is a political act—"entails forming necessities, permanence, immobility, closure and fatalism and concealing/negating or *removing* contingency" (Jenkins 2011, 160; emphasis in original).

The language, terms, and interpretations of social phenomena in politics and political science are, of course, not strictly separable from each other. Since most social scientific concepts are vague, academics need to engage in conceptual controversies as well. Terms, concepts, and ideas that are intensely debated in social science might be used in politics to legitimate or delegitimate certain practices or policy options.[4] The more recent conceptual debates on the transformation of war provide an important example in this regard. For a long time, war has been attached to state entities in international politics and law (Freedman 2014, 19). Since the 1990s, the transformation of war and warfare has become a major theme in international relations: the debate on so-called humanitarian interventions, new wars, asymmetric warfare, the war on terrorism (a term from the political realm), and the future of "cyber wars" and other types of war have been the most prominent topics in international relations security studies since the later 1990s.[5] These academic debates involve conceptual controversies about the "nature" of war, about definitions of war, about stretching the concept, and about potential consequences of an (in)appropriate understanding of "war" for political and military strategic planning, mostly in Western countries.

Such concepts serve to (de)legitimate certain types of violence and certain types of political reactions. They structure societal threat conceptions and imaginaries, they seem to bring (putative) "order" into the disorder of

global politics and diverse phenomena of violence, and they offer orientation for policy makers and military strategists to design intervention and
prevention strategies. However sophisticated the intensive academic expert
debates on the transformation of war(fare) have been since the 1990s, the
German political discourse around the Afghanistan mission suggests that
not many of these reflections have reached out to a broader audience.
Attempts of political leaders to open up the concept of "war" and explain,
for example, "asymmetric warfare" to the public had rather little resonance
(cf. Robotham and Röder 2012, 209–13).

The "Civilian Power" Germany Does Not Engage in "Wars"

Germany as a "Civilian Power": A Slow Farewell to Illusions?

Following the end of World War II, (West) Germany's foreign policy
was strongly influenced by the burdens of its Nazi past and by being the
(divided) front state in the Cold War. German leaders had to learn how
to strike a balance between very heterogeneous interests in the West and
the East and to avoid any political move that might be interpreted as the
resurgence of a new, inappropriate power politics (Haftendorn 2001). In
the precarious constellation of the Cold War, a defeated, occupied, and
outlawed West Germany gradually developed a distinctive form of exercising "soft" power that enabled its rehabilitation and integration into the
Western community. The reliance on soft power and a highly internation-
alized state identity has characterized Germany's foreign policy profile ever
since (Katzenstein 1997, 19–29).

These traits of German foreign policy have led some scholars to call
Germany a "civilian power" (e.g., Harnisch and Maull 2001b).[6] This foreign policy role conception is based on the assumption that international
relations changed fundamentally with the end of the Cold War. Problems
in international politics were now considered to arise predominantly in
economic, social, and cultural spheres. Such problems could best be tack-
led by the establishment of multilateral, participatory arrangements, the
strengthening of the UN system, the juridification of international relations, and the promotion of democracy, human rights, and sustainable
development. Although civilian powers have strong reservations about the
use of force, they are not *pacifist* powers. Since they are actors that are willing and able to shape international relations actively, they might also use

force, if need be, to implement their principles on the basis of collective decision-making (Harnisch and Maull 2001a).

The role ideal type "civilian power" is often used to highlight characteristics of (West) German foreign policy since 1949: West Germany had completely renounced all the negative traits of its past policy and culture. It acted multilaterally, it abandoned sovereignty, it featured a "culture of restraint," and its population had "anti-militarist" attitudes (Baumann and Hellmann 2001). The (benign) self-conception of German foreign policy can be summarized by the two phrases "never again war" and "never alone" (Harnisch and Maull 2001a). The former refers to the break with the past, that is, gives the highest priority to the maintenance and promotion of peace; the latter refers to Germany's integration into the Western multilateral frameworks, which alleviated the fears of its neighbors and facilitated confidence building (Haftendorn 2001). The regimes of Imperial Germany and National Socialist Germany defined their state identity as aggressive, expansive, and bellicose great powers, with the National Socialist regime explicitly based on racist ideology. The Federal Republic of Germany and unified Germany struggled to establish a "never again"–based identity of a restrained and peaceful partner (Baumann and Hellmann 2001; Schwab-Trapp 2002).

The increasing participation of German troops in NATO, the UN, and the European Union military missions since the 1990s has challenged this self-image of Germany as a "civilian power" and as an actor hesitant to engage in military affairs (Buras and Longhurst 2004). Following unification and the end of the Cold War, Germany's allies and partners have increasingly emphasized new expectations concerning Germany's role in international politics: The bottom line of this new narrative was that Germany should transform from a passive "consumer" of security, provided by its NATO allies during the Cold War, into an active "producer" of security. This included fair burden sharing within NATO and participation in military missions (Geis 2013, 261–65). This transformation of German security policy is well reflected in the public discourse on "war" in unified Germany: The cases of Bosnia, Kosovo, the so-called war on terrorism, Afghanistan, and the highly controversial Iraq War in 2003 have enhanced public and academic debates on the use of force and how Germany should relate to these crises.

In particular, the changing ruling parties from left-wing to conservative in the 1990s and 2000s carefully avoided speaking of "war" in public discourse for many years when the German army's missions were to be described. Many others, scholars from political science included, do not hesitate to use the terms "Kosovo war" or "Afghanistan war"—but many politicians refrain from this usage. There are, among others, juridical reasons why German politicians avoid the term "war" but also political reasons (see the third section). During the Kosovo war in 1999, domestic advocates of Germany's participation in the military intervention avoided calling this "air campaign" or "humanitarian intervention" a "war." The German Armed Forces (Bundeswehr) not only participated in their first combat mission after World War II but did so without a UN mandate and in a country that had been occupied by the Wehrmacht of Nazi Germany. The very concept of "war" would promote public rejection of a German participation while the (not uncontested) framing of a "humanitarian intervention," remarkably pushed forward by a new left-wing government with strong anti-militarist roots, had a stronger appeal to larger parts of the public (Geis 2013, 246–53).

Two cases in point are the justifications employed by then foreign minister Joschka Fischer (Green Party) and Chancellor Gerhard Schröder (Social Democratic Party) at the beginning of the NATO intervention: "We are not fighting a war; we are resisting, we are defending human rights, freedom and democracy" (Fischer); and "We are not fighting a war, but we are called to enforce a peaceful solution in Kosovo also by military means" (Schröder; both cited in Schwab-Trapp 2002, 379).[7]

Post–World War II Germany's creed "Never again war!" seemed to lose credibility in light of diverse types of violent conflicts and grave human rights violations. This led to various contradictions within the public discourse. A public that had largely preferred not to think (about) "war" anymore and leave the past behind was prompted to think (about) "war" and the changing character of war again—and whether it will engage in the use of military force abroad again. However, it was the Afghanistan mission of the German Armed Forces that induced a slow change of the political discourse.

"Stabilization Operation," "War-like Circumstances," "War"? The Political Discourse on the Afghanistan Mission of the Bundeswehr

The German Bundeswehr is a so-called parliamentary army: the German parliament (Bundestag) possesses comparatively far-reaching control and oversight mechanisms. Military missions other than for humanitarian assistance require the prior approval of the parliament (Bake and Meyer 2012). During the time of the Afghanistan deployment of the Bundeswehr (2001–14), four different coalition governments ruled in Germany, starting with a left-wing government of the Social Democratic Party (SPD) and Green Party (until 2005), followed by a Grand Coalition of the Christian Democratic Union/Christian Social Union (CDU/CSU) and Social Democratic Party (2005–9) and a liberal-conservative coalition of CDU/ CSU and the Free Democratic Party (FDP) (2009–13), again followed by a Grand Coalition (2013–17). The ministers of defense, who also act as commanders in chief, played an important role in shaping the political discourse on the Afghanistan mission (Schroeder and Zapfe 2015, 178). The only parliamentary party that has never been part of the ruling coalitions is the far left party PDS/Die Linke. It has consistently presented itself as "the only" true "anti-war" and "anti-militarist" party in the Bundestag, often using the concept of "war" to criticize the other parties' decisions.

Following the terrorist attacks of September 11, 2001, in the United States and the invocation of NATO's collective defense commitment clause (for the first time in history), the German parliament approved in November 2001 of German participation in the US-led military mission Operation Enduring Freedom (OEF). The operation was conceptualized as a counterterrorist mission operating in several deployment theaters in Afghanistan and beyond, including maritime areas such as the Red Sea, the Gulf of Aden, and the Somalia coast. In December 2001, the German parliament also approved of participation in ISAF in Afghanistan. ISAF had been authorized by UN Security Council Resolution 1386 to support the Afghan Interim Authority in the maintenance of security in Kabul and its surrounding areas so that the Interim Authority and the UN staff could operate in a secure environment. In the years to come, the ISAF mission would change significantly in territorial scope and military character, resulting in counterinsurgency operations and increasing casualties among civilians and soldiers, also among the German troops (Noetzel 2010, 2011; Hilpert 2014, 137–69). German participation with up to 5,350 soldiers would develop into the biggest Bundeswehr mission to date.

A large majority in the German parliament maintained a fairly optimistic view on the first years of the German "engagement" in Afghanistan and emphasized the normative commitment to bringing democracy and human rights to the war-torn country. A few years later, the vague concept of "stabilization" became ever more prominent in the parliamentary discourse and replaced the idealistic goals of the first years (Müller and Wolff 2011, 215). However, the extent and scope of the German deployment and geographical responsibility broadened, as the changing mandates by the Bundestag showed over the years. The changed rules of engagement notwithstanding, the political discourse of the "stabilization operation" kept "lagging behind" the (counterinsurgency) military realities on the ground (Noetzel 2011, 416–17).

The slow change in the political discourse on the Afghanistan mission in Germany came about in 2008–9, with the further deterioration of the security situation in Afghanistan and with the so-called Kunduz affair in September 2009. It was relevant for the German political discourse that the military operations in Afghanistan were based on different mandates that the parliament was requested to extend on a regular basis. These mandates were met with differing degrees of critique and opposition over the years (Meiers 2011). The formal separation of the OEF and the ISAF mandates resulted in some artificial rhetoric operations in the parliamentary debates since speakers carefully tried to avoid creating the impression of being (perhaps) involved in a "war" (Robotham and Röder 2012, 205–7).

> With the beginning of the ISAF mission, which was strongly promoted by Germany, a central political narrative began to emerge in Berlin that constructed a normative dichotomy between ISAF and OEF. While ISAF was presented as the "good" defensive peacekeeping operation, OEF was portrayed as the "bad" offensive counterterrorism operation. . . . The obvious intention of this dissociation was to have a military presence in Afghanistan without waging war, thereby keeping the German public in its comfort zone. (Schroeder and Zapfe 2015, 179)

The reference to the UN mandate for the ISAF mission was important for many members of parliament since this seemed to imply for them that a reconstruction mission based on a UN mandate simply *cannot* be(come) a "war." A prominent leftist member of the Green Party, Jürgen Trittin, for example, stated in a parliamentary debate on June 25, 2008—at a time when the security situation had worsened in Afghanistan—"It is a basic error to think that there is a war in Afghanistan" (cited in Chauvistré 2009, 47). As late as in October 2010, Trittin declared regarding the northern provinces that the Bundeswehr there does "an excellent job. . . . They do not fight a war there, dear colleagues from the Left Party, but they safeguard the (re)construction there" (cited in von Krause 2011, 222).

Many opinion polls, conducted among the German population since the 1990s, have shown that the approval of a Bundeswehr deployment is fairly high as long as a mission is framed as "humanitarian." Approval rates drop massively when a mission is framed in terms that suggest combat operations (Jacobi, Hellmann, and Nieke 2011, 177–79; Fiebig 2012). This enduring feature of the German strategic culture might tempt elected politicians, who have to meet the expectations of both their domestic constituencies and their international partners, to establish strategic narratives that deemphasize or even conceal the "military" character of deployments—mainly for domestic use (cf. Hilpert 2014, 109; Nonhoff and Stengel 2014, 55).

Deemphasizing terms such as "stabilization operation" or "reconstruction operation" for the Bundeswehr mission in Afghanistan match an image of the soldiers that has been promoted for years in the political culture of the "civilian power" Germany: If there are pictures presented to the German public, then these often portray German soldiers as "armed social workers," not killing and not being killed in their missions abroad. While the role differentiation of the "postmodern" soldier in "postmodern wars"—being a fighter, a social worker, and a diplomat with intercultural skills all in one person—is a phenomenon that affects all Western interventionist armies, the notion of Bundeswehr soldiers actually fighting in combat operations "out-of-area" remains troubling to large parts of the German public today (Mannitz 2011; Dörfler-Dierken 2012, 228–29). This ambivalence is also reflected in the visual realm of popular culture. Several German films, produced for public TV channels or cinema, dealt with the combat experiences and traumas of German soldiers returning from Afghanistan, providing the spectators with (fictionalized) representations of the Afghan theater of war and rather stereotyped Orientalist images of Afghan civilians. These films sought to frame the difficult Afghanistan mission of the Bundeswehr as "good and necessary" (Engelkamp and Offermann, 2012, 250).

It is interesting to note that representatives of the military prepared the changes within the political discourse in 2008–9. They pointed out that the Bundeswehr was involved in combat operations and that the soldiers' experiences on the ground differed quite from the political rhetoric far away in Berlin. The soldiers also claimed that their "war-like" experiences in Afghanistan were not understood at home, complaining about a lack of recognition for their difficult mission by the political leadership and population in Germany.[8] Against this background, the first subtle but still significant change in discourse appeared in using the war-acknowledging term "fallen soldier" for German soldiers killed in Afghanistan. When reporting or speaking about Bundeswehr casualties in the German public, it would usually be said or written in rather neutral terms that they had been "killed" or that they had "died." The term "fallen soldier" (*Gefallene*) is associated with combat, connotes large-scale war, and, as a legacy of the German past, also reminds some of a problematic and obsolete rhetoric of glorifying war experiences.[9]

Whereas the US, British, and Canadian armies had far higher numbers of casualties in Afghanistan, the Germans who stayed in the comparatively "calm" northern provinces lost fifty-five soldiers, thirty-five of them killed in action (Nieke 2016, 85). The death of larger numbers of soldiers killed in combat was a new experience for the Federal Republic of Germany. It was Defense Minister Jung (CDU) who first referred to "fallen soldiers" at a funeral ceremony for two killed soldiers on October 20, 2008. This change of rhetoric was quite well received in the German media and by the soldiers (Dörfler-Dierken 2010, 140). A detailed analysis of twelve such funeral ceremonies for soldiers killed in the ISAF mission between 2007 and 2011 shows how the "official" rhetoric of the political leadership began changing around 2009–10 (Nieke 2016). The respective ministers of defense and in three cases also Chancellor Angela Merkel took part in the ceremonies and delivered a speech.

It was the young minister Karl-Theodor zu Guttenberg (CSU) who began to change the framing of the whole Afghanistan mission most significantly, speaking now of "war-like circumstances" and also of "war." Chancellor Merkel (CDU) also began using this wording in her speeches and declarations in 2010 (Schroeder and Zapfe 2015, 186–87). Importantly, the minister and chancellor either adopted the subjective perspective of the German soldiers who *experienced* combat situations that *might* be *perceived* as "war" or distinguished between an international legal terminology and a colloquial use of the concept "war." For example, Guttenberg said in his speech at the funeral ceremony for three German soldiers who had been killed in the so-called Good Friday combat on April 2, 2010: "What we had to live through on Good Friday near Kunduz, most people call it war, understandably. Me too." Chancellor Merkel stated in her speech at the same funeral ceremony: "In international law, one calls this, what exists in large areas of Afghanistan, a non-international armed conflict. Most soldiers call it civil war or simply war. And I understand this well" (both quotes cited in Nieke 2016, 91). By using the terms "understand" or "understandably," both speakers tried to show their sympathy and empathy with the soldiers, expressing acknowledgment and gratitude by the state that had sent them into harm's way and also their very personal compassion.

The change in the ministers' and chancellor's rhetoric in the funeral speeches reflects the change in the larger public discourse in which members of civil society, members of parliament, the military, the media, and other actors had been involved in discussing intensely around 2009–10 whether Germany was now in a "war in Afghanistan." In particular, one incident played a key role in the whole debate: It was the so-called Kunduz airstrike of September 4, 2009, in Afghanistan and the subsequent so-called Kunduz affair in the German public that received a lot of media attention. The German colonel Georg Klein ordered an airstrike on two fuel tankers near Kunduz City since the tankers were considered (intelligence was given by one informant) to be captured by Taliban insurgents. Two US fighter jets bombed the tankers. Estimations of the casualties range from 90 to 140 people, many of them civilians. As a consequence, the questions of what the Bundeswehr was actually *doing* in Afghanistan and what the political goals of this mission were sparked debated in the public more intensely than ever before.[10] The leading weekly political news magazine *Der Spiegel* (2010) reconstructed the "bloodiest military operation of the German military since the end of the Second World War" in a detailed account as a "war crime."

It remains unclear whether the insurgents had indeed intended to attack the German camp with "rolling fuel bombs," as claimed by the informant, and it became a matter of strong controversy whether Colonel Klein's order was to be assessed as an act of "self-defense" or as a "war crime." The Bundestag conducted a parliamentary inquiry; its final report (October 2011) revealed both quite divergent perspectives of the political parties *and* many highly problematic aspects of the colonel's decision and the political reactions in Germany. In sum, the ruling parties came to the conclusion that the colonel had acted in a "comprehensible" way, given the conditions under which he had to decide, and should not be personally denounced for this.[11] In contrast, a secret NATO report revealed heavy criticism of the US general Stanley McChrystal, then the commander of the ISAF and the US troops in Afghanistan, since the high number of civilian casualties violated the key counterinsurgency principle of protecting the civilians (Noetzel 2011, 411). All juridical inquiries in Germany regarding Colonel Klein's decision either collapsed or ended in an acquittal; he remained in the army and was later promoted to the rank of brigadier general. However, three other persons lost their office in the aftermath of the incident: Defense Minister Jung initially denied that there were any civilian casualties and incurred strong criticism but stayed in office until after the federal election had passed three weeks later. He was replaced by Guttenberg, who forced the highest-ranking general, Wolfgang Schneiderhan, and the undersecretary of state, Peter Wichert, to resign.

The "Kunduz airstrike" not only engaged expert circles in the defense ministry, the parliament, and the military but also became a "game changer" for a wider public (Noetzel 2011, 308; Heck 2017, 376). Remarkably, it also inspired the production of a docudrama called *A Murderous Decision*, starring quite some prominent German actors, shown in September 2013 at prime time on a major public TV channel in Germany (Heck 2017). The award-winning docudrama offers narratives about the personality of Colonel Klein as a military commander, the circumstances under which the German soldiers in Afghanistan were acting at that time, and representations of the Taliban as fanatic enemies. In addition, the film shows the suffering of families who lost relatives in the bombing and portrays the family of a German soldier who was killed by insurgents some weeks before the airstrike. "The specific audiovisual and narrative construction of this film promotes the interpretation that Colonel Klein was driven into the decision by his advisers to take revenge for the increasing violence and the rising number of victims among German armed forces" (Heck 2017, 366). In this sense, the film might rather promote a depoliticization of the "Kunduz affair."

In conclusion to this section, the military incidents and combat experiences in Afghanistan, the changed rules of engagement, and the weak prospects of "success" in the mission resulted in a political contestation of the concept "war" in which many diverse actors were involved. The political leadership hesitated to use the concept of "war" but conceded the compromise wording of "war-like circumstances" or "experiences like war" and thus pointed to the subjective perspective of the soldiers on the ground. Other actors, *both* advocates and critics of the Afghanistan mission, were less shy to refer to the concept of "war" and complained about an insincere, evading, and hypocritical German discourse in this regard. Journalists of different political leanings were especially outspoken about this perception of an "avoidance" discourse (Chauvistré 2009, 16, 53; Kornelius 2009). The biggest German tabloid newspaper, *BILD-Zeitung*, ran the following title in huge letters after the death of three German soldiers in June 2009: "Three German Soldiers Have Fallen in Combat—*Bundeswehr in War!*—Injured Persons, Heavy Combat—How Much Bloodier Will Afghanistan Get?" (cited in von Krause 2011, 232). The perception of a rising gap between inadequate political statements in Berlin and unsettling news from Afghanistan increased the pressure on politicians to rethink their public assessments of the situation in Afghanistan.

The Ambivalence of (Not) Being in a "War"

Why did ministers, the chancellor, and many members of parliament—the core of the political elite—avoid the term "war" for so long?[12] They rather reacted to a discursive pressure from other actors, including media reports and soldiers' depictions of their experiences on the ground, when they finally used terms such as "war-like circumstances" or "experiences of war." No other group of actors had these reservations. Interestingly, *both* advocates and critics of the Afghanistan "engagement" demanded to use the concept of "war" and reproached the government with dishonesty, hypocrisy, and evasive behavior. In this section, several reasons for this avoidance will be discussed. These reasons are grounded in legal considerations, in collective imaginaries shaped by memory politics, and in attempts to maintain a widely favored self-image of a "civilian power." They are usually invoked in a manner that fosters depoliticization and a closure of public discourse, that is, an attempt to avoid contestation and potential rejection of a military mission that has been framed as "good and necessary" for so long.

There are several juridical reasons why high-ranking politicians usually avoid the term "war" in this context (von Krause 2011, 235–38), but only one will be considered here: The Bundeswehr was not involved in an interstate armed conflict with the Afghan government. The ISAF troops were legitimated by a UN mandate and later developed into conflict parties in an asymmetric violent conflict with nonstate actors. The term "war" has been replaced in contemporary international law by terms such as "armed conflict" and "non-international armed conflict" for civil war–like situations. However, the argument that the usage of the concept "war" in Afghanistan would imply the recognition of the Taliban as a legitimate conflict party—put forward, among others, by Defense Minister Jung—is incorrect (Schörnig 2009, 3).

Legal terminology and controversies notwithstanding, many academic disciplines and many "ordinary" people keep on using the concept "war" and seem to have certain intuitions of what this entails. In the specific context of the German debate, the imaginary of "war" is still largely shaped by World War II. Some journalists and politicians in the "war/no war" discourse on Afghanistan have pointed out that many elderly Germans would still invoke their own (or their parents') experiences of World War II when they hear the concept of "war." "War" in this sense is associated with a maximum of destruction and annihilation of civilians and arouses strong emotions whenever the term is invoked (Robotham and Röder 2012, 208–9). Defense Minister Jung referred exactly to this aspect of vivid memories of World War II when he expressed his strong reservation about calling the "war on terrorism" in Afghanistan a "war" (von Krause, 2011, 234–35). While images of both world wars are still very present in the contemporary social imaginaries of the "Western" world, a differentiated imagery about new forms of war(fare) or the hybrid roles of soldiers in peace-building and peace-enforcement missions has not developed yet (Daxner 2012, 38–51).

The most compelling explanation for the concept avoidance is that all German governments since 1990 have feared to alienate their voters and the public at large since the "out-of-area" use of force by German troops has been a "taboo."[13] A controversial ruling by the Federal Constitutional Court in 1994 clarified the legal circumstances under which such missions can be legitimated. By gradually expanding the scope of Germany's participation in military missions, the governments only gradually confronted the public with changing realities (Chauvistré 2009; Naumann 2010; Geis 2013). Given Germany's cherished self-perception as a "civilian power," the deliberate avoidance of the term "war" by many politicians *can* be intended to lower the domestic political inhibitions to engage in international military interventions. Parts of the political leadership see a critical gap between rising international expectations of Germany to adopt more "responsibility" in international affairs, implying military burden sharing, and a majority of the population that is rather unwilling to do so.

Less benign interpretations of the political discourse on military missions accuse the political leadership of a blatant lack of strategic thinking and the population of a problematic indifference toward their own army and their missions, increased by the suspension of the conscription in 2011 (Naumann 2010). Not speaking of "wars" appears in this interpretation more like a manifestation of self-deceptions, illusions, and incapability of policy makers (cf. Chauvistré 2009). Another interpretation argues that Germany lacks pluralist deliberative forms of security communication that would enhance public disputes and controversial engagements about the contingencies and complexities of modern security politics (Jacobi, Hellmann, and Nieke 2011).

In sum, avoiding naming the Afghanistan ISAF mission a "war" has certainly many reasons. In the given context of this volume on "political concepts at work," I interpret this avoidance as a *depoliticization* move that eventually instigated an enormous conceptual contest. This contest, in turn, resulted in a *repoliticization* of the issue: the legitimation and "good" purpose of the mission *were* contested; its "necessity" and "success" *were* disputed. However, with hindsight, one can see that the consequences for the governments were not critical: Neither did the "Kunduz affair," which occurred three weeks before the federal election in September 2009, noticeably affect the results of the election, nor were the German troops withdrawn from Afghanistan. The German governments, who are often depicted as especially sensitive to voters' attitudes about military deployments (Naumann 2010, 19), continued the mission in Afghanistan although the approval rates by the population had been dropping since 2008. Since 2010, a majority has been rejecting the deployment (Fiebig 2012, 188, 197–98).

The repoliticization is an ambivalent phenomenon: The reintroduction of the semantics of war into the political culture of the "civilian power" Germany is also regarded as problematic by those who question the gradual socialization into a less *"civilian"* power and fear a remilitarization of society (cf. Dörfler-Dierken 2010, 2012). Some actors have argued that the Afghanistan mission has changed both the Bundeswehr and Germany itself. One prominent advocate of this transformative view was the conservative defense minister Thomas de Maizière, who stated in a remarkable interview with *Spiegel Online* on December 23, 2011:

The Afghanistan-mission has not only drastically changed the *Bundeswehr* but the entire Federal Republic. With this mission, as controversial as it was and still is, Germany has proven itself as an adequate and resilient member of NATO. Before the ISAF-mission few of our partners believed that German soldiers are indeed able to fight and that their leadership dares to give the order to do so. We have proven that we are able to do that and that we are also willing to make sacrifices. We have abandoned the image of armed medics and election observers and have become a full-fledged army that is well respected by our partners. The fight in Afghanistan, the broad use of the army in battle, has transformed the *Bundeswehr* and Germany, and so it will remain. (cited in Schroeder and Zapfe 2015, 190)

While the minister's assessment is a positive one, his view is more controversial in the domestic public.

Once again, the inclusion of visual material can further enrich the analysis of verbal statements and point to visually mediated depoliticization moves, in the following instance promoted by military actors who veil the risks and the violence of the ISAF mission. Interestingly, the visual self-representation of the ISAF mission produced by the Bundeswehr does not match the political discourse in 2009–10. David Shim and Frank Stengel (2017) analyzed all thirty-four photo albums focused on the ISAF operation that are included on the Bundeswehr's official Facebook page. The army itself provided the photographs. They reinforce a rational-technocratic image of the ISAF mission. The photographs convey the image of the war in Afghanistan as nonthreatening, as essentially under control. Three aspects are striking in their absence: the enemy, emotions, and destruction. The "enemy" is invisible in the photographs such that almost all the pictures from actual military operations could just as well be photographs from training sessions or maneuvers. Both physical and emotional effects of the armed conflict are absent from the pictures. Furthermore, the photographs show no traces of destruction or of Afghan casualties. "Not only are the Taliban absent but also are fallen Afghan National Army members. . . . This absence makes war even more acceptable . . . , as dead Afghans remain hidden from view and thus present no obstacle to 'our' waging war 'over there'" (Shim and Stengel 2017, 341). In an allusion to the political discourse in Germany, the authors conclude: "What is lacking in these pictures from 'war-like situations' . . . is war" (341). To be sure, all interventionist armies will be aware of the risks involved in disseminating photographs on social media that must not undermine the political legitimacy of the mission and irritate the domestic publics. However, such pictures only add to the confusion back home in Germany about the question of what "it" is in Afghanistan? Are "our" troops really engaged in "wars" nowadays—what is "peace (building)," what is "war"?

The Gray Zone between "War" and "Peace" and the Return of the "Intervened"

The leading German conservative newspaper *Frankfurter Allgemeine Zeitung* titled its report about a short trip of Chancellor Merkel to Afghanistan (December 19, 2010): "Merkel Calls It a War." Michael Daxner argues that the "it" in this headline can be immediately filled with meaning by everyone in what he has called the "homeland discourse" (*Heimatdiskurs*) of the interventionist society. And yet, this "it" remains unconceived to date. "War" ties the social collectives of the interventionist societies and the "intervened" societies together and unites them in a kind of complicity (Daxner 2012, 19). However, the "homeland discourse" in Germany (or in any other of the intervening countries) has not resulted in a deeper understanding of its entangled relationships with the "intervened" society in Afghanistan.

As argued in the previous section, the repoliticization of the ISAF mission in 2009–10 was ambivalent. I would like to add for the purpose of an outlook that it was also a rather moderate repoliticization. If we conceive of politicization as a strategy entailing "exposing and questioning what is taken for granted, or perceived to be necessary, permanent, invariable, morally or politically obligatory and essential" (Jenkins 2011, 159–60), then a politicized debate on a military mission abroad should not remain as self-centered, as the German conceptual contests largely were, often focusing on German casualties, the military experiences of the German or ISAF troops, and the German political leadership. Both Afghan casualties and Afghan political agency were largely absent from the verbal and visual narratives. Differentiated knowledge about the Afghan government, political structures, and society has hardly been enhanced through this debate (cf. Daxner 2012, 31–33). The asymmetric warfare by the insurgent groups and the counterinsurgency measures of the ISAF troops led to an escalation of violence that claimed many civilian casualties. The "Kunduz affair" notwithstanding, the main focus of the German "war/no war" debate was the intervening society, less so the "intervened." Narrative representations of the Afghan population in the German political discourse rather frame parts of the people as potential risks for the intervention "project," and Afghan political actors appear as corrupt and unreliable (Kühn 2014, 206–7).

"Afghanistan" became a minor issue (again) in German politics once the decision to withdraw the ISAF troops by the end of 2014 had been taken (Kühn, 2014, 198). The deployment of up to 980 *Bundeswehr* soldiers to the successor NATO mission "Resolute Support" has not aroused larger interest or attention in the German public. The accumulation of crises and violent conflicts during the last years has shifted priorities. It was the so-called "refugee crisis" that brought Afghanistan back on the German political agenda, now framed as a securitized domestic issue within a larger politicized refugee discourse: Among the 1,667,000 officially registered asylum seekers (which only cover a part of all migrants) in 2015–2019, Afghan nationals were the fourth largest group in 2015, the second largest in 2016, the third largest in 2017, the six largest in 2018 and the fourth largest group in 2019 (BAMF 2020, 17).

During the peak of the "refugee crisis," a renewed controversial debate started on the security situation in Afghanistan: Is there "war" in this country such that asylum seekers in Germany stand a good chance of being recognized as refugees? Or is the country to be assessed as a "safe country of origin" such that tens of thousands of Afghan asylum seekers have a very slight prospect of a legal entitlement and would be deported to Afghanistan? While the German government first claimed that Afghanistan is "safe enough" to deport the asylum seekers, following recent massive violent attacks in spring 2017 the government suspended this decision and engaged in a "reassessment" of the security situation in Afghanistan. To date, asylum seekers support organizations that criticize the inappropriate response of German state organizations to asylum proposals from Afghan citizens.[14]

These unexpected consequences of conceptual contests underline the ambiguities of concepts such as "war" and "peace" in contemporary settings of violent conflict. The confusion about the legal recognition of asylum seekers from Afghanistan highlights that the "it" in the question

"Is it war in Afghanistan?" is still contested. Again there is one striking absence from this securitized debate: whether the past interventionist practices of the "Western" troops have anything to do with the current situation in Afghanistan and the forced migration of hundreds of thousands of "locals." In the ambiguities of contemporary peace-building practices (Kühn 2016), in the blurring of "war" and "peace," the issue of political responsibility should be one of the major questions to address.

This chapter dealt only with the concept of "war," not with its positive counter-concept of "peace." As scholars of conceptual analysis have argued, all concepts are enmeshed in a larger net of related concepts (see Ish-Shalom, this volume) such that analyses of only one concept have clear limitations. Koselleck (2004, 155–91) introduced the notion of "asymmetrical counter-concepts"—such as Hellene and barbarian, Christian and heathen, superhuman and subhuman—that structure political discourse and practice. While Koselleck discussed actor-related concepts and the implications for the (non)recognition of social actors in his historical examples, "war" and "peace" denote more abstract conditions of human existence. Clear-cut notions of such conceptual opposites veil the gray zones in between them and the inherent ambiguities in all of them. It is a truly *political* endeavor to reveal the gray zones and the ambiguities.

Notes

1. I thank Lennard Eccarius for his research assistance and Piki Ish-Shalom, Hanna Pfeifer, and Gabi Schlag for their instructive comments on a former draft of this chapter.

2. It is beyond the scope of the chapter to address methodological and conceptual issues of using visual material of popular culture in international relations studies; see, e.g., Heck (2017); Michalski and Gow (2007); Schlag and Geis (2017); and Weber (2006).

3. See the detailed accounts of the Afghanistan discourse in Chauvistré (2009); Daxner (2012); Dörfler-Dierken (2010); Hilpert (2014, 106–37); Jacobi, Hellmann, and Nieke (2011); Nieke (2016); Robotham and Röder (2012); Schroeder and Zapfe (2015); and von Krause (2011, 217–46).

4. The "democratic peace" literature is a case in point where academic debates have traveled into politics and been used by policy makers for legitimating questionable foreign policy options (Ish-Shalom 2015).

5. These debates produced a huge body of literature on the transformation of war/ warfare; see overviews, to name but a few, in Bousquet (2016); Geis (2006); Gray (2012); Kaldor (2006); Münkler (2002); Lindley-French and Boyer (2014); Strachan and Scheipers (2013); and Van Creveld (1991).

6. The concept of a "civilian power" emerged in the early 1970s and was introduced by François Duchêne to describe the distinct modes and type of power of the European Community; for a critical engagement with this morally charged concept, see Diez (2005).

7. Translations from German are by the author.

8. See Noetzel (2010, 489, 496) and Dörfler-Dierken (2010, 145–47; 2012, 225). However, the experiences of German soldiers in Afghanistan differ considerably, depending on where they have been deployed and which military assignments they have to fulfill. Only a part of them experienced direct or indirect violence themselves (Seiffert, 2012, 81–89).

9. In a similar vein, the (heavily contested) term "veteran"—hitherto associated with the many millions of German soldiers returning from World War I and II— was (re)introduced into the political discourse via injured and traumatized soldiers "returning" from the Afghanistan mission (Engelkamp and Offermann 2012; Weber 2017).

10. It is beyond the scope of the chapter to reconstruct the incident in detail; see *Der Spiegel* (2010).

11. See http://www.bundestag.de/dokumente/textarchiv/2011/36783945_kw48_sp_kundus/207070 (accessed 17 February 2020).

12. For a completely different conflict setting, Israel and the Lebanon "War" in 2006, see Ish-Shalom's (2011) analysis, which shows the broad variety of aspects that are addressed, explicitly or implicitly, when an armed conflict is (not) called a "war."

13. This also applies to the Japanese society.

14. See, e.g., https://www.proasyl.de/thema/fakten-zahlen-argumente/ (accessed 20 February 2020).

References

Bake, Julia, and Berthold Meyer. 2012. "The German Bundeswehr Soldier between Constitutional Settings and Current Tasks." In *Democratic Civil-Military Relations: Soldiering in the 21ˢᵗ Century Europe*, ed. Sabine Mannitz, 67–84. Abingdon: Routledge.

BAMF (Bundesamt für Migration und Flüchtlinge). 2020. *Das Bundesamt in Zahlen, 2019—Asyl.* Nürnberg: Bundesamt für Migration und Flüchtlinge.

Baumann, Rainer. 2006. *Der Wandel des deutschen Multilateralismus.* Baden-Baden: Nomos.

Baumann, Rainer, and Gunther Hellmann. 2001. "Germany and the Use of Military Force: 'Total War,' the 'Culture of Restraint' and the Quest for Normality." In *New Europe, New Germany, Old Foreign Policy? German Foreign Policy since Unification*, ed. Douglas Webber, 61–82. London: Cass.

Berenskoetter, Felix. 2016. "Unpacking Concepts." In *Concepts in World Politics*, ed. Felix Berenskoetter, 1–19. London: Sage.

Bousquet, Antoine. 2016. "War." In *Concepts in World Politics*, ed. Felix Berenskoetter, 91–106. London: Sage.

Buras, Piotr, and Kerry Longhurst. 2004. "The Berlin Republic, Iraq, and the Use of Force." *European Security* 13 (3): 215–45.

Chauvistré, Erik. 2009. *Wir Gutkrieger: Warum die Bundeswehr im Ausland scheitern wird*. Frankfurt: Campus.

Chouliaraki, Lilie. 2006. "The Aestheticization of Suffering on Television." *Visual Communication* 5 (3): 261–85.

Connolly, William E. 1993. *The Terms of Political Discourse*, 3rd ed. Oxford: Blackwell.

Creveld, Martin Van. 1991. *The Transformation of War*. New York: Free Press.

Daxner, Michael. 2012. "Heimatdiskurs—ein deutsches Problem?" In *Heimatdiskurs: Wie die Auslandseinsätze der Bundeswehr Deutschland verändern*, ed. Michael Daxner and Hannah Neumann, 15–67. Bielefeld: Transcript-Verlag.

Der Spiegel. 2010. "Ein deutsches Verbrechen." 5:35–57. http://magazin.spiegel.de/EpubDelivery/spiegel/pdf/68885074 (accessed 15 March 2017).

Devetak, Richard. 2009. "After the Event: Don DeLillo's White Noise and September 11 Narratives." *Review of International Studies* 35 (4): 795–815.

Diez, Thomas. 2005. "Constructing the Self and Changing Others: Reconsidering 'Normative Power Europe.'" *Millennium* 33 (3): 613–36.

Dörfler-Dierken Angelika. 2010. "Identitätspolitik der Bundeswehr." In *Identität, Selbstverständnis, Berufsbild*, ed. Angelika Dörfler-Dierken and Gerhard Kümmel, 137–60. Wiesbaden: Springer VS.

Dörfler-Dierken, Angelika. 2012. "Von 'Krieg' und 'Frieden': Zur Wahrnehmung des Afghanistaneinsatzes bei Soldatinnen und Soldaten, Politik und Kirchen." In *Der Einsatz der Bundeswehr in Afghanistan: Sozial- und politikwissenschaftliche Perspektiven*, ed. Anja Seiffert, Phil C. Langer, and Carsten Pietsch, 223–38. Wiesbaden: Springer VS.

Engelkamp, Stephan, and Philipp Offermann. 2012. "It's a Family Affair: Germany as a Responsible Actor in Popular Culture Discourse." *International Studies Perspectives* 13 (3): 235–53.

Fiebig, Rüdiger. 2012. "Die Deutschen und ihr Einsatz: Einstellungen der Bevölkerung zum ISAF-Einsatz." In *Der Einsatz der Bundeswehr in Afghanistan*, ed. Anja Seiffert, Phil C. Langer, and Carsten Pietsch, 187–204. Wiesbaden: Springer VS.

Freedman, Lawrence. 2014. "Defining War." In *The Oxford Handbook of War*, ed. Julian Lindley-French and Yves Boyer, 17–29. Oxford: Oxford University Press.

Geis, Anna, ed. 2006. *Den Krieg überdenken. Kriegsbegriffe und Kriegstheorien in der Kontroverse*. Baden-Baden: Nomos.

Geis, Anna. 2013. "Burdens of the Past, Shadows of the Future: The Use of Military Force as Challenge for the German 'Civilian Power.'" In *The Militant Face of Democracy: Liberal Forces for Good*, ed. Anna Geis, Harald Müller, and Niklas Schörnig, 231–69. Cambridge: Cambridge University Press.

Geis, Anna, Harald Müller, and Niklas Schörnig. 2013. "Liberal Democracies as Militant 'Forces for Good': A Comparative Perspective." In *The Militant Face of Democracy: Liberal Forces for Good*, ed. Anna Geis, Harald Müller, and Niklas Schörnig, 307–44. Cambridge: Cambridge University Press.

Gray, Colin. 2012. *War, Peace, and International Relations: An Introduction to Strategic History*. 2nd ed. London: Routledge.

Haftendorn, Helga. 2001. *Deutsche Außenpolitik zwischen Selbstbeschränkung und Selbstbehauptung: 1945–2000*. Stuttgart: DVA.

Harnisch, Sebastian, and Hanns W. Maull. 2001a. "Conclusion: 'Learned Its Lesson Well?' Germany as a Civilian Power Ten Years after Unification." In *Germany as a Civilian Power? The Foreign Policy of the Berlin Republic*, ed. Sebastian Harnisch and Hanns W. Maull, 128–56. Manchester: Manchester University Press.

Harnisch, Sebastian, and Hanns W. Maull, eds. 2001b. *Germany as a Civilian Power? The Foreign Policy of the Berlin Republic*. Manchester: Manchester University Press.

Heck, Axel. 2017. "Analyzing Docudramas in International Relations: Narratives in the Film 'A Murderous Decision.'" *International Studies Perspectives*, 18 (4): 365–90.

Hilpert, Carolin. 2014. *Strategic Cultural Change and the Challenge for Security Policy: Germany and the Bundeswehr's Deployment to Afghanistan*. London: Palgrave Macmillan UK.

Hobson, Christopher. 2015. *The Rise of Democracy*. Edinburgh: Edinburgh University Press.

Hutchison, Emma. 2014. "A Global Politics of Pity? Disaster Imagery and the Emotional Construction of Solidarity after the 2004 Asian Tsunami." *International Political Sociology* 8 (1): 1–19.

Ish-Shalom, Piki. 2011. "Defining by Naming: Israeli Civic Warring over the Second Lebanon War." *Journal of International Relations* 17 (3): 475–93.

Ish-Shalom, Piki. 2015. *Democratic Peace: A Political Biography*. Ann Arbor: University of Michigan Press.

Jacobi, Daniel, Gunther Hellmann, and Sebastian Nieke. 2011. "Deutschlands Verteidigung am Hindukusch: Ein Fall misslingender Sicherheitskommunikation." *Zeitschrift für Außen- und Sicherheitspolitik* 4 (1): 171–96.

Janssen, Wilhelm. 1982. "Krieg." In: *Geschichtliche Grundbegriffe: Historisches Lexikon zur politisch-sozialen Sprache in Deutschland*, ed. Otto Brunner, Werner Conze, and Reinhart Koselleck, 3:567–615. Stuttgart: Klett-Cotta.

Jenkins, Laura. 2011. "The Difference Genealogy Makes: Strategies for Politicisation or How to Extend Capacities for Autonomy." *Political Studies* 59 (1): 156–74.

Kaldor, Mary. 2006. *New and Old Wars*. 2nd ed. Cambridge: Cambridge University Press.

Katzenstein, Peter J. 1997. "United Germany in an Integrating Europe." In *Tamed Power: Germany in Europe*, ed. Peter J. Katzenstein, 1–48. Ithaca, NY: Cornell University Press.

Kornelius, Stefan. 2009. *Der unerklärte Krieg. Deutschlands Selbstbetrug in Afghanistan*. Hamburg: Edition Körber-Stiftung.

Koselleck, Reinhart. 2004. *Futures Past: On the Semantics of Historical Time*. Trans. Keith Tribe. New York: Columbia University Press.

Krause, Ulf von. 2011. *Die Afghanistaneinsätze der Bundeswehr: Politischer Entscheidungsprozess mit Eskalationsdynamik*. Wiesbaden: Springer VS.

Kühn, Florian. 2014. "'We Are All in This Together . . .': Deutschland in der Ambiguität der Afghanistanintervention." In *Deutschland in Afghanistan*, ed. Michael Daxner, 193–212. Oldenburg: BIS Verlag.

Kühn, Florian. 2016. "International Peace Practice: Ambiguities, Contradictions and Perpetual Violence." In *The Politics of International Intervention: The Tyranny of Peace*, ed. Mandy Turner and Florian Kühn, 21–38. Abingdon: Routledge.

Levy, Jack S. 2002. "War and Peace." In *Handbook of International Relations*, ed. Walter Carlsnaes, Thomas Risse, and Beth A. Simmons, 350–68. London: Sage.

Lindley-French, Julian, and Yves Boyer, eds. 2014. *The Oxford Handbook of War*. Oxford: Oxford University Press.

Malici, Akan. 2006. "Germans as Venutians: The Culture of German Foreign Policy Behavior." *Foreign Policy Analysis* 2 (1): 37–62.

Mannitz, Sabine. 2011. "Redefining Soldierly Role Models in Germany." *Armed Forces & Society* 37 (4): 680–700.

Meiers, Franz-Josef. 2011. "Der wehrverfassungsrechtliche Parlamentsvorbehalt und die Verteidigung der Sicherheit Deutschlands am Hindukusch, 2001–2011." In *Zehn Jahre Deutschland in Afghanistan*, ed. Klaus Brummer and Stefan Fröhlich, 87–113. Wiesbaden: Springer VS.

Michalski, Milena, and James Gow. 2007. *War, Image and Legitimacy*. Abingdon: Routledge.

Müller, Harald, and Jonas Wolff. 2011. "Demokratischer Krieg am Hindukusch? Eine kritische Analyse der Bundestagsdebatten zur deutschen Afghanistanpolitik, 2001–2011." In *Zehn Jahre Deutschland in Afghanistan*, ed. Klaus Brummer and Stefan Fröhlich, 197–221. Wiesbaden: Springer VS.

Müller, Jan-Werner. 2014. "On Conceptual History." In *Rethinking Modern European Intellectual History*, ed. Darrin M. McMahon and Samuel Moyn, 74–93. Oxford: Oxford University Press.

Münkler, Herfried. 2002. *Neue Kriege*. Reinbek: Rowohlt.

Naumann, Klaus. 2010. *Einsatz ohne Ziel? Die Politikbedürftigkeit des Militärischen*. Hamburg: Hamburger Edition.

Nieke, Sebastian. 2016. "Gefallene Helfer: Das Soldatengedenken der Bundesrepublik zwischen militärischer Zurückhaltung und professionsethischer Würdigung der Bundeswehr." *Zeitschrift für Außen- und Sicherheitspolitik* 9 (1): 79–100.

Noetzel, Timo. 2010. "Germany's Small War in Afghanistan: Military Learning amid Politico-strategic Inertia." *Contemporary Security Policy* 31 (3): 486–508.

Noetzel, Timo. 2011. "The German Politics of War: Kunduz and the War in Afghanistan." *International Affairs* 87 (2): 397–417.

Nonhoff, Martin, and Frank A. Stengel. 2014. "Poststrukturalistische Diskurstheorie und Außenpolitikanalyse." In *Diskursforschung in den Internationalen Beziehungen*, ed. Eva Herschinger and Judith Renner, 39–74. Baden-Baden: Nomos.

Paul. Gerhard. 2004. *Bilder des Krieges—Krieg der Bilder*. Paderborn: Ferdinand Schöningh.

Robotham, Christopher, and Sascha Röder. 2012. "Die Bundeswehr in Afghanistan: Analysen an den Grenzen des Heimatdiskurses." In *Heimatdiskurs: Wie die Auslandseinsätze der Bundeswehr Deutschland verändern*, ed. Michael Daxner and Hannah Neumann, 201–42. Bielefeld: Transcript Verlag.

Schlag, Gabi, and Anna Geis. 2017. "Visualizing Violence: Aesthetics and Ethics in International P\olitics." *Global Discourse* 7 (2): 193–200.

Schörnig, Niklas. 2009. "In der Opferfalle: Die Bundesregierung und die zunehmenden Gefallenen der Bundeswehr in Afghanistan." *HSFK-Standpunkte* No. 2. Frankfurt.

Schroeder, Robin, and Martin Zapfe. 2015. "War-Like Circumstances." In *Strategic Narratives, Public Opinion and War: Winning Domestic Support for the Afghan War*, ed. Beatrice de Graaf, George Dimitriu, and Jens Ringsmose, 177–98. London: Routledge.

Schwab-Trapp, Michael. 2002. *Kriegsdiskurse: Die politische Kultur des Krieges im Wandel 1991–1999*. Opladen: Leske und Budrich.

Seiffert, Anja. 2012. "'Generation Einsatz': Einsatzrealitäten, Selbstverständnis und Organisation." In *Der Einsatz der Bundeswehr in Afghanistan*, ed. Anja Seiffert, Phil C. Langer, and Carsten Pietsch, 79–99. Wiesbaden: Springer VS.

Shim, David, and Frank Stengel. 2017. "Social Media, Gender and the Mediatisation of War: Exploring the German Armed Forces' Visual Representation of the Afghanistan Operation on Facebook." *Global Discourse* 7 (2): 330–47.

Strachan, Hew, and Sibylle Scheipers, eds. 2013. *The Changing Character of War*. Oxford: Oxford University Press.

Weber, Christian. 2017. *Veteranenpolitik in Deutschland—die neuen Bande in den zivil-militärischen Beziehungen?* Baden-Baden: Nomos.

Weber, Cynthia. 2006. *Imagining America at War: Morality, Politics and Film*. Abingdon: Routledge.

Zürn, Michael. 2014. "The Politicization of World Politics and Its Effects: Eight Propositions." *European Political Science Review* 6 (1): 47–71.

CHAPTER 5

Encountering Nomads in Israel Defense Forces and Beyond

Philippe Beaulieu-Brossard[1]

> YOTAM FELDMAN, JOURNALIST, 2007: What do you think Deleuze would think about your use of his ideas?
>
> BRIGADIER GENERAL (RET.) SHIMON NAVEH, LEADING SYSTEMIC OPERA-TIONAL DESIGN THEORIST AND INSTRUCTOR, 2007: He would be enthusiastic, go wild over it.
>
> BEN ZWEIBELSON, JOINT SPECIAL OPERATIONS UNIVERSITY (JSOU) · SOF DESIGN AND INNOVATION PROGRAM DIRECTOR, 2016: D&G likely would be most pleased with it, and find it ironic that current postmodernist defenders of their work would try to deny the application by the military. D&G might call those defenders of their concept as the new establishment—the guardians of an assemblage that they cannot begin to guard or protect. It is all an illusion. . . . When radical concepts work, they radicalize in all directions.[2]

In October 2016, I organized a workshop gathering sixteen current and retired military commanders, planners, defense scientists, and instructors.[3] They had one point in common. They had all used critical theory and reflexive informed concepts in the classroom, in headquarters, and/ or on the battlefield in the last decade. While some had worked together in the past or knew each other's publications, this was the first time these defense professionals had met as a group. Perhaps because this was a prime opportunity, these defense professionals sought to find a concept consolidating their collective identity, implicitly. Gilles Deleuze and Félix Guattari's (1980) nomad became, surprisingly or not, one of the most reiterated concepts to represent group members. Yet, "nomad" was not specific enough for some defense professionals. Ben Zweibelson, the SOF design and innovation program director at the Joint Special Operations University (JSOU), was the first to suggest pandas, a wildlife metaphor, to gain in specificity. For Zweibelson, this metaphor captured the solitary intellectual life of group members, and an "embarrassment of pandas," rare and unexpected gatherings such as this workshop. Later, Dr. Alex Ryan, a praised military and public policy systemic design consultant, suggested a metaphor he deemed more precise.[4] He compared the group's history to a journey of giraffes: "Contrary to a flock or a herd, giraffes will come together and travel together for a while and depart on another path. So, there is a sense of community, but no obligations to remain part of the herd." Beyond a great sense of humor, these defense professionals had another point in common. In the last two decades, most had crossed the path of retired Israeli brigadier general Shimon Naveh. Against all odds, this general contributed in diffusing the least expected concepts in the least expected organizations, some in operational language, some in doctrinal form, and some as a farce. In echo of the introduction of this volume, this chapter will nonetheless take these concepts seriously.

Two decades earlier, Naveh and his colleagues founded the Operational Theory Research Institute (OTRI) in Israel. For a growing number of senior officers, conventional concepts used by the Israel Defense Forces (IDF) proved more and more obsolete from 1973 onward.[5] These concepts were not adapted for asymmetric conflicts becoming the norm rather than the exception for the IDF, leading to an impression of failure. As Luke Campbell, Brent J. Steele, and Anna Geis offer in this volume, the concept of success/failure in war is contingent and deeply political. In this case, it provided organizational political legitimacy for an alternative. And OTRI was tasked with providing such an alternative. To do so, Naveh and his colleagues sought to develop a methodology and a course for senior officers called the Advanced Operational Command and Staff Course (AOCSC). Both aimed at unleashing the critical and creative capacities of officers.[6] As the traditional rationalist military literature was partly to blame for IDF failures to adapt, Naveh and his colleagues departed from it. They found inspiration in various subfields sharing a more or less reflexive and neo-pragmatic epistemology such as complex systems thinking, architecture, and postmodern social theory. The IDF was not alone in exploring this radical turn. Again, the impression of failures in Iraq and Afghanistan pushed the US Army to also undertake this turn. Senior officers found in OTRI's products a promising remedy. The US Army School of Advanced Military Studies (SAMS) recruited Naveh in 2005 to develop a variant of his methodology now called the US Army Design Methodology (ADM). US Special Operations Forces (SOF) also hired Naveh in 2007 to translate this methodology at the strategic level, that is, to practice the art of anticipating, adapting, and preparing a military organization to face future contingencies. Both the US Army (2015) and SOF (2016) made their preferred version of design mandatory in 2015—the former for planning officers and the latter for general staffers.

Of all the hundred concepts inspiring design-informed defense professionals (hereafter defense professionals), Deleuze and Guattari's concepts seem to withstand the test of time for a small number of enthusiasts. Once central to Naveh's methodology, these concepts turned into footnotes, and footnotes into analogies. While some in military and business circles still perceive Deleuze and Guattari's concepts and postmodern social theory more broadly as the cutting edge to be further developed, the content and functions of these concepts are still unclear to both users and observers. As these concepts are used to manage violence, bringing their multiple functions to consciousness is more important than ever.

As caveats, defense professionals building on Deleuze and Guattari, and design and system thinking more broadly, do not linearly apply theory to practice as some may assume in academia. As I explore elsewhere, they rely on a craft or tinkering attitude toward knowledge using what they find useful to build their way of thinking and acting without necessarily being consistent with the philosophy (Beaulieu-Brossard 2019). Sometimes, what is seen as useful is only the mental representation, the "sound-image" according to Ferdinand de Sausurre (1916). This is the case for most defense professionals explicitly or implicitly referring to the concept of nomad. For instance, Ofra Graicer and Ben Zweibelson are among the few exceptions who are explicitly and substantially using the concept in this chapter. Second, and contra Eyal Weizman (2007), only a minority of a minority of a minority is finding inspiration in Deleuze and Guattari in comparison to the growing military design movement's preference for more accessible seminal sources, especially in professional military journals & blogs, doctrine or in management.

In this chapter, I seek to expose three of the numerous functions Deleuze and Guattari's concepts can take in the military, mostly in the IDF but also in US SOF. Building on the sociological perspective presented in the introduction of this volume, I argue that these concepts offer mental representations to conceptualize the "world around us . . . *and* ways to act in the world to achieve one's goals" (see Ish Shalom, this volume). These concepts do so in the IDF and beyond inside at least three functions: narrative framing, political, and instrumental. Narrative framing means that these concepts allow so-called military designers to generate a plot giving intent to actors, giving meaning to artifacts, and weaving sequences of events, constituting stories that enable them to make sense of their community in time and space. In other words, the concept of the nomad contributes in consolidating the identity of the community of military designers and gives it a purpose (Bruner 1991; Roberts 2006). As advanced in the introduction of this volume, concepts are not only socially but also politically meaningful in three senses: concepts "offer normative stands and commitments" dovetailing in political measures, concepts enable the inclusion and exclusion of individuals in communities, and concepts can be a vehicle of persuasion. I would add to this that conceptual language may amplify or undermine the authority of defense professionals in military or civilian decision-making processes. This political function is especially observed in organizational politics, and exceptionally, in domestic politics. Last but not least, the instrumental function means that defense professionals directly apply these concepts to improve military practices related to planning in most instances and to tactics in rare instances (Eriksson and Norman 2011, 418). The instrumental function remains the explicit rationale for adapting Deleuze and Guattari's concepts. For defense professionals and observers, the narrative framing and political functions are most often implicit, unconscious, and therefore nonintentional. As a caveat, the simple move of assigning a function to a concept is a political gesture in itself. Neither this chapter nor defense professionals can escape it, as expressed in the introduction of this volume. For instance, skeptics often accuse supporters of seeking political or economic gains over instrumental ones in contrast to supporters stressing the instrumental potentials of a concept. The narrative, political, and instrumental functions are the few central ones among several functions possible to understand how concepts work in military practices.

In this chapter, I first offer a brief introduction to Deleuze and Guattari's nomad in relationship to the concepts of war machine and smooth space. This introduction reveals how these opaque concepts provided clues to the IDF to make sense of their environment, on the one hand, and to an idealized self, on the other. In so doing, I seek to clarify these concepts and nuance the impression of incommensurability between the military profession and post-1968 postmodern philosophy. I then move on to expose what Deleuze and Guattari's concepts can do once translated from philosophy to military contexts. I develop examples for each of the three functions summarized above. For the narrative function, I show how several defense professionals found inspiration in Deleuze and Guattari's nomad to make sense of organizational suppression despite bringing the very same organization closer to professional excellence, from their perspective. For the political function, I focus mainly on how these concepts may enhance or reduce authority in civil-military relations. For the instrumental function, I present the examples of walking through walls in the IDF and of goal setting in the US Special Operations Forces Command (SOCOM) white paper on design thinking of 2016.

Deleuze and Guattari's Nomad(s)

> In order to achieve desired Degrees of Freedom one must first identify his/her biases, prejudices and axioms carved in institutional "stone." These are the borders they must transgress *in order to be liberated. And this is why I coined that phase the nomadic one. For nomad people have no baggage, no shackles that tie them to their place, no doctrines or dogmas to adhere to, no fortresses to defend but their own individual freedoms: of movement, of thought, of identity. Nomad people have no ego.*
>
> —Dr. Ofra Graicer (2017), IDF Generals' Course co-instructor

In the midst of the occupation of Southern Lebanon (1982–2000) and the first intifada (1987–93), a puzzle became of pressing importance for the IDF. While the IDF could easily win battles, these seemed pointless in changing the political status quo over time. For Naveh and his colleagues, discovering Deleuze and Guattari's (1980) radical proposition about war provided clues to resolve this enigma from the late 1990s onward.[7] This proposition lies on a counterintuitive understanding of the relationship between organizations, conventions, and war. Naveh and his colleagues found inspiration in this proposition, especially for making sense of asymmetric conflicts and for developing a military professional ideal based on an essence of movement.

Deleuze and Guattari lay their proposition on a close reading of Carl von Clausewitz's (1976) aphorism "War is the continuation of politics by other means." In contrast to the numerous interpreters of Clausewitz, Deleuze and Guattari found their proposition on the very semantic of this aphorism. In this reading, organizations such as states seek to use war to continue politics by other means (Reid 2003). For Deleuze and Guattari, this means that war is an external phenomenon to politics. In turn, politics seek desperately to use war despite never fully controlling it. History abounds with examples not only of states that failed to appropriate war but also of states transformed deeply in attempts to use war (Tilly and Ardant 1975). Some states even collapsed in the process, such as Russia in the midst of World War I. For Deleuze and Guattari, this shows that states are powerless in comparison to the power of war. For this reason, they understand war as the most powerful phenomenon in transforming the human condition as a whole, including political realities.[8] In other words, war makes more the state than the state makes war.

Deleuze and Guattari rely on a heuristic move to better take this proposition seriously. This move locates war as an extrinsic phenomenon to the state.[9] This results in the concept of war machine in the sense that war is its own machine escaping appropriation from any organization, including the state. This is especially the case as war may demand disrupting all conventions in the struggle for survival. The state is the opposite in this regard as it lies on a set of more or less rigid conventions to continuously actualize its existence. These conventions may include a fixed territory, a national identity, and a set of rules in the form of a constitution, to name a few. As states depend on these conventions, using war involves translating these conventions to the battlefield. States develop formal military institutions for this purpose. For Deleuze and Guattari, the objective of military institutions is to mediate between conventions sustaining the state, on the one hand, and the absence of conventions in war, on the other hand. Military institutions do so by disciplining soldiers with rigorous procedures, training, and education. These efforts, however, can only be in vain when faced with the contingencies of war. Sooner or later, war will disrupt conventions and, by extension, military institutions and the very states they seek to serve.

Yet, not all organizations require the same respect for conventions. Deleuze and Guattari found inspiration in the anthropology of nomadic tribes to better appreciate nuances in relationships between organizations, conventions, and war.[10] If the essence of the state depends on sustaining conventions at all costs, the essence of nomadic tribes lies on the opposite. Movement in all respects—from one space to the next, from one identity to the next, or from one rule to the next—is both literally and figuratively the essence of nomadic tribes for Deleuze and Guattari. Being a nomad depends on perpetually refusing conventions as they formalize. The essence of nomads and the essence of war are therefore the same. They are both based on an absence of conventions. Nomads are in harmony with war for this reason. War disrupts the emergence of conventions that may lay the groundwork for state formation within or outside nomadic groups. In other words, as the conventions of nonstate actors such as nomads are more flexible than state conventions in general, the conventions of the former tend to be more moldable to the contingencies of war. This proposition provided an understanding as to why Israel could not leverage war to change political realities especially when fighting against nonstate actors. Sooner or later, war would become too disruptive for state conventions in contrast to nonstate actors. War, in itself, would end up tearing down all conventions of the Israeli state before politically defeating nonstate adversaries once and for all. Naveh (2002) and his colleagues feared asymmetric conflicts more in the long run than conventional conflicts in part for this reason.

No matter the efforts states invest in appropriating war with military institutions, these efforts will always be in vain in comparison to nomad-like groups escaping the burden of sustaining rigid conventions. These groups will always be in a better position to innovate faster than state armies since their essence is in harmony with war. Deleuze and Guattari (1988, 368) compare state science with nomadic sciences to support this point. State science tends to forbid intuitions in order to develop so-called universal conventions to understand an independent reality. In turn, these conventions provide the required legitimacy for ordering the human condition over a territory in the form of state governance. Nomadic sciences have neither this pretension nor this desire. They are intuitive and holistic as they relate to all aspects of everyday life rather than acting as conventions for supporting an order. While states outmatched nomads by consolidating wealth, production, and technology from the late fifteenth century onward, they always lacked the critical and creative potentials made possible by more flexible scientific practices (De Landa 1991, 12). States ensured survival by co-opting nomadic innovations for their own interests in time of struggle. This co-optation is nonetheless a risky, if not a Faustian, bargain. The radical freedom that nomads demand for innovating is just not compatible with the exercise of governance. This radical freedom may end up disrupting the very conventions that states require to govern. For this reason, state-nomadic partnerships can only turn into tragic cycles. Despite saving the state in critical moments, the state usually ends up suppressing all forms of nomadic essence until it has no choice but to enlist it again. In short, the critical and creative potentials of nomads spoke to defense professionals for making sense of insurgencies that proved more resilient, adaptive, and innovative than state armies in contemporary conflicts. For the same reasons, nomadic ways of thinking would become a professional model to emulate despite inherent risks of suppression from military institutions.

Movement as essence, the cornerstone of nomadic ways of thinking, became a core principle of Naveh's methodology from the late 1990s to this day (Graicer 2017).[11] As seen above, this means to continuously refuse military conventions as they formalize. Among those, movement as essence implies a radical understanding of space. Nomads never let the idea of a bounded territory formalize. Instead, they continuously reframe their understanding of territory as they travel. They continuously deterritorialize and reterritorialize in Deleuze and Guattari's terminology. Accordingly, they do not seek to respect predetermined routes but continuously adapt direction to evolving circumstances as they travel in between necessary stopping points for survival, such as oases, wells, or shelters. These points are always temporary in comparison to the movement in between. This is why Deleuze and Guattari (1980, 472) understand nomadic space as smooth: it is only defined by continuous movement in vast empty and unbounded space such as oceans, deserts, or steppes. States, in contrast, structure a territory—or striate space, in Deleuze and Guattari's terminology—in an attempt to hold and control it against evolving circumstances. They do so by imposing both material and ideational structures. For instance, the former can take the form of gridding space (urbanism) and the latter the form of fixed binary identities such as governors/governed, legal/illegal, and so on. States develop desperately against space, while nomads continuously adapt to spatial circumstances. This understanding inspired some defense professionals not only to think more in nonlinear ways about space for military operations but also to think about time as they set goals to accomplish in the future, as I will develop in instrumental functions below.

Although Deleuze (1978) repeatedly voiced opposition to the Zionist ideal, that is, the formation of an Israeli state in claimed historical lands, his professional ideal was not far from defense professionals' building on his writings (Dosse 2009).[12] Deleuze embraced movement as essence as a life-work ideal, if not as an objective. He found in war the perfect metaphor for this. As Julian Reid (2003, 59) observed: "The possibility of a form of thought so radical that it wages the violence of war on existing orders of knowledge conditions Deleuze's politico-philosophical project in its entirety." Deleuze developed concepts with the aim of disrupting all conventions by building on war as a metaphor. In his own terminology, he sought to turn his work into a nomadic war machine against the state and its conventions, on the one hand, and against the order of thoughts in academia, on the other hand. This would, Deleuze hoped, bring to consciousness what was not thinkable before and, therefore, lead to continuous intellectual emancipation. In a nod to this ideal of philosophical excellence, Deleuze (1990, 103) called his colleague Michel Foucault a "warrior." He saw in Foucault a formidable philosopher based on his capability to develop concepts "waging war" and disrupting taken-for-granted orders. This specific intellectual emancipatory project is in harmony with the intellectual emancipatory project of Naveh and his colleagues, albeit in different fields, as seen in Ofra Graicer's (2017) quote that opens this section. While Deleuze's vocation responds to his ideal of philosophical excellence, the vocation of defense professionals responds to an ideal of military excellence. Translating Deleuze and Guattari's concepts to respond to this latter vocation nonetheless involves greater stakes even if these concepts are poorly understood or used superficially at first sight. Indeed, violence is not only metaphorical but actual in this vocation. Deleuze and Guattari's concepts may fill multiple functions beyond intellectual emancipation in the military and society more broadly. The following sections provide examples of implicit (narrative and political) and explicit (instrumental) functions.

Narrative Framing Functions

> If Doctrine stands for the State Apparatus (or institutional
> interiority), Systemic Operational Design (SOD) could be its War
> Machine (or explorer of institutional exteriority).
>
> —Ofra Graicer (2017)

Deleuze and Guattari made available a rich pool of mental representations inspiring alternative narratives for making sense of selves and others in several sectors. For instance, several scholars rely on the nomadic war machine to make sense of phenomena escaping state control such as viruses, self-organized armed groups such as ISIS, or globalized capitalism (Du Plessis 2017). Defense professionals rely on the nomadic war machine as a concept to make sense of the same elements as well. Naveh, for instance, portrays Israel and the West's elusive "other" as a Wahhabi war machine manifested in "nomadic terrorists" in several PowerPoint presentations. This mental representation stresses the lack of Saudi Arabian state control over violent extremists. Another narrative, however, seems more unique to the military. The nomad against the state provides a powerful mental representation for developing stories that provide meaning to a group at the fringe of military institutions risking suppression for a professional ideal. This professional ideal lies on becoming an "institutional war machine" (Graicer 2017). The institutional war machine is a mental representation of an idealized self across time saving the state from itself thanks to intellectual emancipation. Sooner or later, however, tragedy awaits those getting closer to this ideal in this narrative. The more this ideal appears within reach, the more the state will come to fear for its foundational conventions. As a response, the state will resist, co-opt, or purge the institutional war machine until a next crisis requires it. This narrative takes the form of a tragic cycle as it involves a rise in nomadic ways of thinking, then a resistance to them, and, finally, forgetting them in military institutions.

While Naveh (2007a) developed this narrative to make sense of three Israeli experiences across time, some US, Australian, and Canadian defense professionals expressed a similar narrative to make sense of their experiences with design (Beaulieu-Brossard and Dufort 2017). Naveh's study of the evolution of operational art in the IDF is, perhaps, most explicit in using this narrative by weaving past, present, and future stories.[13] Naveh develops this narrative into three episodes: the Palmach (1941–48),[14] Moshe Dayan's paratroopers (1953–67), and Naveh's OTRI (1995–2005). The Palmach episode is most faithful to both the potential and the fate of the nomadic war machine in Naveh's narrative. This is more than a coincidence since this episode takes place during the early state formation of Israel. The Palmach found a mentor in the unorthodox British general Orde Wingate and inspiration in Russian military tradition. From Wingate, the Palmach borrowed the capability to transform its identity to adapt to changing circumstances, and from also the Russian a smooth understanding of space according to Naveh.

Rather than obeying to a "sedentary" approach "imposing a pre-designed grid of universal forms," the Palmach would generate thinking and practices unique to each operation, making the survival and establishment of the Israeli state possible (Naveh 2007a, 41). Yet, tragedy — in the form of a "purge" — awaited this success as expected in this narrative. As part of the consolidation of the Jewish state, Prime Minister Ben Gurion rapidly disbanded the Palmach for a more cohesive IDF (Naveh 2007a, 51).[15] Furthermore, Naveh (2007a, 52) claims that this "coup" turned into suppression as the state prohibited any discussion about Palmach's operational excellence. Likewise, the British Army suppressed Wingate's legacy despite enthusiastic praises for turning a likely defeat into a decisive victory in the Burma campaign in World War II, according to Graicer (2015, 5). Considering Wingate's legacy as too "divisive," army council members vowed to "write him down" to avoid any more "Wingates" in the British Army, based on Michael Calvert's account (Graicer 2015, 239). For both the Palmach and Wingate episodes, mythical legacies to build on turned into legacies to be suppressed and suppression turned into amnesia in this narrative.[16]

Naveh's journey toward developing an "institutional war machine" inside the IDF gains in significance when inserted as the third and last episode of this series between 1995 and 2005. While Naveh does not refer explicitly to the nomad in this episode, his narrative bears resemblance with the same tragic cycle. Toward the end of this episode, Naveh (2007a, 33) assesses that with OTRI, the IDF had the same ingredients that brought the Palmach to excellence. AOCSC-educated colonels and generals would prove worthy of this inheritance in Operation Defensive Shield in the West Bank in 2002 and in the disengagement of Gaza in 2005. Naveh reports an absence of civilian casualties during both and a near absence of Israeli casualties in the former (Matthews 2008). Naveh (2007a, 34) even praises the latter as "one of the most unique and successful operations in [IDF] history." As Graicer (2017) observes, Naveh's "private armies could run loose" as long as the institution did not feel threatened or feared an upcoming war. These two conditions did not last long. Some generals soon perceived AOCSC graduates as a threat to their authority, especially in light of operational successes in this narrative. As for war, the second intifada between 2000 and 2005 followed by the Second Lebanon War in 2006 sustained an emergency atmosphere that proved unfertile for theoretical nuances. Major General (Ret.) Itzak Ben Israel offered that "sometimes we fight, and things become clear" to explain this lack of appetite for nuances when I met him.[17] What became clear for Ben Israel and his colleagues against OTRI's program was that the IDF could not operate properly with conceptual and terminological confusion in contrast to policy makers thriving on vagueness, as Neta Kramer observes in this volume. In the end, war is the only tribunal of military knowledge from Ben Israel's perspective and as Barkawi and Brighton (2011) compellingly developed elsewhere.

Beyond confusion, Naveh's (2007a, 6) narrative understands this episode explicitly as a purge awaiting the right event to be put into motion. He recalls the comments of Major General Moshe Kaplinski, the vice chief of the general staff, that the IDF must "get rid of Shimon Naveh and Dov Tamari because they could not be controlled." As a result, the general staff gradually suppressed Naveh and OTRI's supporters through financial irregularity charges, forced retirement, or organizational disbandment in this narrative.[18] "Purging" the key agents did not completely suppress their concepts from the IDF but sent them back at the fringe, under censorship or in "exile." Again, promises to build on would turn into promises to be suppressed and suppression into amnesia or what Naveh (2007a, 24) calls deliberate institutional "anti-learning" in this narrative.

In some instances, this tragic cycle narrative refers explicitly to Deleuze and Guattari's nomadic war machine; in other instances, it bears resemblance with it. The nomad may well save the state from itself, but the more the state regains in confidence and develops, the more nomadic ways of thinking are suppressed as they run contrary to the possibility of governance. This cyclical narrative generates a symmetry between Naveh's experiences and those of great military legacies, thus consolidating the nomadic war machine as an ideal and appropriating these legacies as part of the very same historical movement. This narrative ran in direct opposition to the official institutional narrative by turning what some perceived as "mumbo jumbo" into institutional conservatism, "charlatans" into avantgarde underdogs, and heretics into the very definition of military excellence. This narrative also provided group solidarity, a road map for renewing motivation and pursuing attempts at transforming the military despite likely rejection.[19] This narrative was political at least at the institutional level, as the next section develops further.

Organizational Political Functions

> When you come with this knowledge, with reasoned insights, to
> someone who feels helpless, . . . the political echelon is happy to buy
> what you offer it. Then you look for partners that will do it together
> with you, that will challenge you intellectually, and you don't find
> them.
>
> —Moshe Ya'alon (Michael 2007, 441)

Naveh and his colleagues prefer contemplating how the nomadic war machine and other critical concepts could serve instrumental functions or provide mental representations for better understanding new phenomena. Despite this intent, these concepts could not remain isolated in a planning room. They would trickle down in transforming the everyday life of defense professionals inspired by them. Surprisingly or not, I was unable to find a correlation between defense professionals learning these concepts and their political views. Perhaps defense professionals refrained from disrupting deep ontological commitments in their private vocation despite the potential of nomadic ways of thinking to do so. Defense professionals seemed to be still able to compartmentalize in concordance with a military professional ideal separating military from civilian lives. This was less the case in terms of organizational politics. Nomadic ways of thinking turned into a perpetual reform agenda against military conventions, as already observed above. In other words, the nomad would serve a counterhegemonic project in the military realm. In political and public realms, conceptual capacities made possible by the nomad and other concepts contributed in amplifying the authority of the IDF above civilian institutions. This was especially the case during the tenure of Moshe Ya'alon, general staff member (1995–2005), from regional commander to chief of general staff. In this section, I present the often implicit political functions of sophisticated concepts, including those from Deleuze and Guattari in civil-military relations.

Ya'alon, a key instigator, sponsor, and supporter, was aware of the multiple functions of these concepts, including the political ones. He understood these concepts as a tool for an "organizational revolution" in the IDF (Adamsky 2010, 103). These concepts would expand at the organizational levels following Ya'alon's progression in the IDF. In each new position from Central Command covering the West Bank (1995–98) up to chief of the general staff, Ya'alon would integrate these concepts and seek to diffuse them to all general headquarters (Michael 2007, 434). Once these concepts trickled down (following Ya'alon's command) or trickled up from AOCSC graduates, the organization would be likely disrupted and would change. Adapting Deleuze and Guattari's nomadic war machine made this institutional political function possible. Naveh, like Graicer, was explicit about this function as a by-product. In an interview with Weizman (2007), Naveh claims that the primary purpose of using critical theory was "to critique the military institution itself—its fixed and heavy conceptual foundations" and that OTRI has "become a subversive node within it." In other words, the narrative function shared above provided purpose by informing a political function of perpetual reform.

Skeptics, however, understood this political function very well. For some like IDF colonel Yehuda Vagman, "The more those ideas were blurred, incomprehensible and non-implementable, the more creative they were considered, and accordingly, the more they enhanced their producer's status in the organization" (Michael 2007, 435). Most skeptics in the IDF and US armed forces followed Vagman in trading the instrumental function for this political function to make sense of these defense professionals, finding inspiration in Deleuze & Guatarri. As Neta Kramer suggests in this volume, vagueness, whether intended or not, does something. In this case, vagueness both hindered the effectiveness of the opposition to these concepts between 1995 and 2004 and bolstered the same opposition after the Second Lebanon War in 2005. Also in echo to Kramer and observed by several members of the military design community, the meaning of design has been enlarged to the point of making the concept meaningless and simply used as a cliché or slogan to dissolve its initial disruptive nature. The story of the translation of design in the US army is an expression of this phenomenon.

Using sophisticated concepts enabled performing an implicit demarcation that provided a higher status to those using them and a lower status to those not using them, skeptics observed. As a result, several officers attempted to follow these defense professionals to fulfill this political function without paying attention to the instrumental function. In so doing, sophisticated concepts turned into fashionable buzzwords uttered to be accepted as an equal, if not the avant-garde, in a well-respected group. Vagueness associated with these concepts could also consolidate authority by giving the impression to fellow officers that they did not understand their profession despite years of experience, according to an interviewee requiring anonymity. In other words, speaking the language of sophisticated concepts made the difference between inclusion and exclusion from an elite group of military intellectuals, as presented in the introduction of this volume.

Some even claimed that these concepts served mostly political economic functions. Suspicious, they accused enthusiasts of making themselves indispensable in understanding and teaching incomprehensible concepts for economic gains. Others, like US Army Special Forces Lieutenant Colonel Grant Martin (2017), developed a similar argument with regard to the proliferation of sophisticated concepts as a means to legitimate more resources and promotions in military organizations.

For Naveh and his colleagues, these by-product political functions were a double-edged sword in retrospect. On the one hand, using sophisticated concepts including those from Deleuze and Guattari raised their status as unique experts able to develop cutting edge alternative methodologies. On the other hand, democratizing sophisticated concepts including Deleuze and Guattari to as many officers as possible turned it into ridicule in some cases. Ridicule damaged prospects for individual learning and changing the military institution in the end. When I met him in 2015, Naveh regretted distributing copies of a *Thousand Plateaus* in the IDF and listing it as a mandatory reading at SAMS for this reason.[20] Canadian Major general Jennie Carignan, once an international SAMS student, remembered the disdain of her colleagues for this opaque book.[21] The production of SAMS student monographs provides evidence of this. Since 2007, an average of only a single officer student per year quoted Deleuze and Guattari, the peak being four students right after Naveh's tenure in 2009.[22] This phenomenon not only occurred at SAMS but also cursed Naveh and some of his colleagues along their path, including during a contract with US SOCOM. An interviewee taking part in Naveh's SOCOM design- course relied on an infection metaphor to make sense of this phenomenon. For him, the opacity of these sophisticated concepts combined with Naveh's arrogance generated "antibodies" to the point that he abandoned the course after two classes. In short, the political function in the form of amplifying authority was limited to those curious enough to pay attention. Otherwise, these concepts were more counterproductive in this respect.

Consistent with Deleuze and Guattari's holistic assumptions, the political function of concepts applies beyond the military. Accordingly, integrating sophisticated concepts can only bring operational successes with organizational change in the long run, defense professionals believe. Likewise, organizational change can only be sustainable with society-wide changes in the long run since organizations are not isolated. Therefore, defense professionals mobilize Deleuze and Guattari for holistic critiques and holistic transformation beyond the military. As Naveh put it: "Theories do not only strive for a utopian socio-political ideal with which we may or may not agree, but are also based on methodological principles that seek to disrupt and subvert the existing political, social, cultural, or military order" (Weizman 2007, 215). As these concepts are intrinsically holistic, they also incite defense professionals to include as many sectors deemed relevant as possible for a better understanding. This may or may not include political, economic, social, infrastructure, or cultural sectors, to name a few, although the military does not have jurisdiction over them. Indeed, defense professionals must think beyond the military sector since contemporary issues rarely, if ever, fall into a single sector in the twenty-first century. However, the temptation to move from understanding to influencing the political decision-making process into these sectors is often difficult to resist. This is especially the case in states without robust civilian institutions, as Yoram Peri (2006) observes in Israel. Concerned by this phenomenon, Ya'alon explains that this tends to naturally occur, especially when the gap of knowledge, in both qualitative and quantitative terms, is unbridgeable with civilian institutions (Michael 2007, 444). For instance, Ya'alon observes that political directives would become clearer once it could relate to a military plan rather than the other way around, from civilian planning to military planning. While the IDF already had the upper hand in civil-military relations in Israel for reasons beyond the scope of this chapter, developing a sophisticated methodology amplified its authority over civilian institutions.

This political function was therefore a by-product, as it was unintentional in this specific Israeli case. In other cases, the contrary can be easily imaginable depending on the intents of defense professionals. For instance, some skeptics trade the instrumental for the political function to explain the development of the US Army counterinsurgency manual of 2006 also relying on social scientific concepts (Price 2011). Skeptics claim that the objective of the manual was intended more to sell the "surge" to the US Congress than to develop counterinsurgency operations. In short, the political functions of Deleuze and Guattari's nomad and other sophisticated concepts must be nuanced. While using or promoting these concepts may amplify authority in some instances, it may also contribute to the contrary, especially when the audience is skeptical. Further research needs to be conducted to investigate the extent to which nomadic ways of thinking contributed to IDF political support for the disengagement of Gaza in 2005. While these concepts clearly reinforced Naveh's conviction that Israel should not actualize a fixed territorially bounded space based on past historical narratives, rare are those who took a Deleuzian detour to take this controversial position (Rynhold and Waxman 2008).

Instrumental Functions

> Our movement through the buildings will push them into the streets and alleys, where we will hunt them down. By doing that we will smoothen the intrinsic striation of the enclave.
>
> —Colonel Aviv Kochavi,
> IDF 35th Paratrooper Brigade, 2002 (Naveh 2005)

For defense professionals, the primary function of Deleuze and Guattari's nomadic war machine is instrumental. They seek to apply these concepts directly to inform better military practices, especially for developing operational and strategic approaches. This function aims at provoking a reimagination of military practices away from military conventions perceived as a source of failures in contemporary conflicts. For some, applying these concepts enables increasing efficacy manifested in minimal casualties, destruction, and use of force. For others, applying these concepts contributes to radical humanist ideals in the form of emancipation from structural constraints to reach individual and professional potentials more fully. In this section, I develop two examples of instrumental functions. The first example illustrates how the IDF 35th Paratrooper Brigade built on smooth space during the Second Intifada in 2002. The second shows how specific individuals relied implicitly on nomad-like analogies for goal-setting purposes when explaining the US SOCOM white paper on design thinking of 2016.

Deleuze and Guattari's nomadic war machine in a collision course with striated space became operational concepts in the development of Operation Defensive Shield in the West Bank in 2002. Before this episode, the

IDF refrained from conducting operations in dense urban environment. The urban environment posed heavy casualty risks either in IDF soldiers or in civilians, as fighters would easily set ambushes and hide among civilians. Colonel Gal Hirsch (2016, 166), the chief of operations (J-3) and an AOCSC graduate, was convinced of the opposite. He saw operating in Palestinian urban environments as the proper response to heightening violence in the form of suicide bombings and as a stepping stone to controlling the West Bank as a whole. Hirsch was alone in sharing this perspective. Against all odds, he disrupted the general staff's assumptions to the point that his operational concept was accepted. This decision set a precedent by disrupting the taboo of operating in a dense urban environment. By operating in an urban environment, the IDF sought to signal that there would be no safe haven anymore for fighters seeking to use violence. This, they hoped, would provide incentives for a peaceful settlement. The more time passed, the more what is now called urban warfare would become the "new normal" for the IDF.

Understanding the urban environment as striated space and the IDF as a nomadic war machine transcending it contributed in setting this precedent. Aviv Kochavi, the 35th Paratrooper Brigade commander (now deputy chief of general staff) and also an AOCSC graduate, commanded the operation in Balatta camp in the Nablus area. Naveh's (2005) dramatization of a brainstorm session between Kochavi and his officers suggests how they implemented nomadic ways of thinking. The script begins with Amir, an IDF officer, reminding the group that the IDF had never seized an urban area since 1982, that this instance was not successful, and that this contradicted training. Kochavi replies by finding reinforcement in the concepts of smooth and striated space. He portrays Palestinian fighters as respecting a striated understanding of space in the very act of fortifying an urban environment. The brigade would surely be unsuccessful by respecting the same logic. Rather, IDF soldiers would be more effective by transforming the striated space into a smooth one. To concretely turn striated space into smooth space, IDF officers generated the military tactic of "walking through walls" on an unprecedented large scale to bypass ambushes set by Palestinian fighters (Weizman 2006). Officers reinterpreted the battle space by reversing training habits. Opening doors and moving along roads and sidewalks were now forbidden. Instead, soldiers would ignore the urban structure by piercing holes in apartment walls and ceilings and move from block to block until they gained military control of an area. Israel recorded a single casualty. The United Nations recorded 497 Palestinian casualties and large-scale destruction of nongovernmental properties (Annan 2002). Deleuze and Guattari's concepts proved useful to make sense of and operate in unfamiliar contexts such as asymmetric conflicts. In this specific case, these concepts contributed in enabling the IDF to reengage urban space instead of abandoning it. In other words, and in a nod to Anna Geis in this volume, these concepts "serve[d] to (de) legitimate certain types of violence," bringing an impression of potential control, superiority, and orientation in a complex urban space.

After departing Israel for the United States in 2005, Naveh joined Booz Allen Hamilton's Centre for the Application of Design (CAD). This military contracting firm acted as a medium enabling Naveh, Ryan, and other internationals to work for American defense organizations. In return, CAD became the highest concentrated pool of intellectual capital on the application of sophisticated concepts for military purposes in the United States at the time.[23] Naveh would first teach and conduct research at SAMS under this organization between 2005 and 2007. In late 2007, William "Joe" Miller, the director of strategy, plans, and policy (J5) at US SOCOM and Naveh's personal friend, requested assistance as his office lacked a methodology for strategic projection.[24] SOCOM contracted CAD to assist in the form of research, development, and courses taught by Naveh, James Schneider, and Timothy Challans. A few years later, SOCOM departed from this team to develop their own design teaching and research capacities at JSOU. When I met Miller, his team, and JSOU faculty in 2016, none referred to Deleuze and Guattari's nomad explicitly, to the exception of Ben Zweibelson, quoted at the beginning of this chapter.

For others working for JSOU in 2016, this concept turned into footnotes and footnotes into analogies, where its sound image seemed sufficient to achieve a specific function. This was the case for defense professionals taking part in developing the US SOCOM white paper on design thinking (2016) or teaching from it. They relied on nomad-like analogies to explain an alternative to the traditional practice of goal setting (i.e., the end state) in the US military. In conventional planning, officers usually reverse engineer the commander's end state to develop a linear path toward achieving it, according to Colonel (Ret.) Richard Newton, the lead author of the SOCOM white paper on design thinking.[25] Then, officers seek to respect this path at all costs as if the context would be as fixed as the preestablished "end state." To show progress, officers rely on as many quantifiable elements as available from body counts to square miles under control for instance. Newton saw this practice as counterproductive. Several officers also confessed that this practice leads them to tweak reports to give the impression of consistency with the linear path and preestablished goal. The linear path as the fixed end state would end up being irrelevant to the emerging context, thus leading to fight in a world that no longer exists on the ground.

Newton suggested alternatives following the literature on foresight. Instead of the end state, he suggested imagining a range of acceptable and unacceptable futures. Instead of the linear path, he suggested becoming familiar with unexpected detours. Newton relied on a seventeenth-century navigation analogy. Reaching a destination was possible only by muddling through rather than by following a linear path. While nonlinearity navigation may seem ineffective, ships reached their destination more effectively by continuously adapting to external circumstances, thus leading to a more flexible goal-setting process, according to Newton. For Zweibelson, who became the design and innovation program director at JSOU in 2017, Newton's vision was at odds with poststructuralism, including Deleuze and Guattari, despite relying on nomad-like analogies to explain the US SOCOM white paper on design thinking of 2016. From Zweibelson's perspective, Newton as well as several contractors for JSOU taught and applied design in a more linear way and closer to mainstream design thinking developed in the US Army before 2017. In a struggle over defining the future of design education at JSOU in 2016, some individuals may have used nomad-like analogies not only for instrumental functions but also for organizational political ones as developed in the section above.

In contrast, Zweibelson attempted to develop JSOU's design and innovation program as consistently as possible with design philosophy and also by explicitly building on poststructuralism, including Deleuze and Guattari's concepts of rhizome, assemblage, and the nomad, as he developed elsewhere (Zweibelson 2017). For instance, Zweibelson found in Kenneth Stanley and Joel Lehman's (2015) studies on artificial intelligence a more persuasive analogy of the unconventional practice of goal setting presented above. According to Stanley, artificial intelligence proceeds more effectively toward a desired end state when they are not programmed to reach it. Stanley found that simply assigning a fixed goal incites both artificial and human intelligence to filter out elements that may not directly lead to the goal at first sight. Yet Stanley showed how these very dismissed aspects may provide stepping stones leading to a satisfactory goal. Both this goal and the means to reach it were more or less thinkable before. This analogy provided an intelligible way to translate Deleuze and Guattari's nomad introduced in US SOCOM a few years earlier by Naveh and reintroduced by Zweibelson in 2016. Only time will tell whether this new understanding of time and space will prevent, minimize, or enable more violence in the years to come.

Deleuze and Guattari's nomad is among several sophisticated concepts that may serve instrumental functions in the military and other professions. In most cases, implementing deliverables resulting from these concepts remains the greatest challenge for defense professionals. Cultural, institutional, and idiosyncratic logics often lead to filing and forgetting these deliverables despite their promises. For products surviving these logics, they may make the human condition worse or better depending on one's viewpoint. On the one hand, the military instrumentalization of these concepts may contribute to further violence by enabling operations that were unthinkable before such, as in the Ballata camp case. On the other hand, these concepts may provide less violent alternatives than conventional military concepts, especially by familiarizing officers with more flexible ways of thinking such as in goal setting in US SOCOM. The greatest danger may lie in literally taking war as an extrinsic phenomenon to the state, thus dispelling state responsibility in contemporary conflicts or romanticizing the unique disruptive capacities of war found in Deleuze and Guattari.

Conclusion

Deleuze and Guattari contributed to the military design- movement by making visible alternative ways of thinking about the relationship between organizations, conventions, and war. This perspective is far from consensual in the literature. Several contributors are quick to denounce the militarization of social sciences and humanities, and especially post-1968 postmodern social theory (Weizman 2006, 2007; Feldman 2007; Price 2011; Levine 2012). They find defense professionals and postmodern social theorists to be at extreme odds in terms of vocation. The former aims at executing the state monopoly over the legitimated use of physical force, to borrow Max Weber's (2004) terms. The military institution is responsible for making sovereign power possible over a territory and beyond. On the contrary, postmodern social theorists seek to disrupt the state apparatus and especially the oppressive means making it possible. Despite these differences of vocation, I sought to demonstrate that both groups share the will to disrupt any convention potentially hindering respective ideals of professional excellence. In other words, both communities share an essence of movement. Translating this essence in military contexts nonetheless enables different functions than academic ones. As the military profession involves managing violence, these concepts fulfill functions that may profoundly transform the human condition for better or worse.

Once translated into narratives, Deleuze and Guattari's nomad provided alternatives to make sense of selves and others. The nomad collapsed into an idealized self, contributing to group formation that provided a purpose and to a political program of continuous reform. Translated into the logic of politics, the holistic nature of these concepts incited defense professionals to take into account all spheres of human existence and to contribute to decision-making processes in some instances, such as in Israel. While these concepts could provide authority and a higher status in some cases, their opacity also led to the contrary and even to ridicule, depending on the audience. The act of associating functions to these concepts, such as political economic ones, was also an integral part of political struggles within and beyond the military institution. Moreover, the nomad provided inspiration for reimagining movement in time and space. On the one hand, unthinkable military operations became thinkable, and even normal. On the other hand, the nomad contributed to opening less violent possibilities by legitimating flexibility over prized ontological commitments such as holding a fixed territory at all costs, as in the case of the disengagement of Gaza in 2005, for example. Last but not least and from the perspective of Gramscian theory presented in the introduction of this volume, military design is both counter-hegemonic and hegemonic. Military design is counter-hegemonic as it compels people to "critically reflect on the social, economic, and political structure into which [human beings] are locked" and find ways to disrupt these structures to change the status quo. Yet, design could be understood as attempting to manipulate human beings in following specific frames without involving their agency in the process, thus strengthening the agency of military designers over subalterns, again from a Gramscian perspective.

Further research needs to be conducted on the potentials, limits, and dangers involved in the military use of concepts. Developing further this research program from the perspective of the sociology of knowledge offers promising ways to do so. This research program can focus on how the military produces and uses knowledge and, in return, on what this knowledge makes defense professionals think and do. This research is needed for a better understanding of how the military works, on the one hand, and of how some unexpected concepts may inspire more the military than others in various directions, on the other hand. Without this richer understanding, defense professionals as well as academics advising or criticizing the military may well contribute to aims contrary to their intents without being aware of it. While we will never know whether Deleuze and Guattari would "go wild over" the military use of their ideas, as Naveh put it, contemporary commentators criticizing this military movement, such as Eyal Weizman (2007), became seminal in contributing to it. In other words, more research needs to be conducted not only on extrinsic militarization but mostly on intrinsic militarization. While the former debates to what extent defense professionals made "children in the back" of social theorists, in Deleuze's (2003, 15) own terms, the latter debates to what extent the logic of war is already embedded in social theories and, perhaps, in the human condition.

Notes

1. This chapter would not have been possible without the initiative, leadership, and patience of Piki Ish-Shalom. I also thank all interviewees who generously gave their time and stories, without which this chapter would have been impossible. Many thanks to all participants of the workshop on concepts at work held in Jerusalem in 2015 for their comments. Special thanks to Ofra Graicer and Ben Zweibelson for their comments on previous versions.

2. The first two lines are from Feldman (2007). The third line comes from the author's personal interview with Ben Zweibelson, recalling his answer to the same question asked by a PhD student in Tampa, Florida, 6 March 2016.

3. Assistant Professor Philippe Dufort (Saint Paul University) and I organized this workshop, called Hybrid Warfare: New Epistemologies and Ontologies in Armed Forces, which was held at Canadian Forces College in Toronto, Canada, on 16–17 October 2016. The Canadian National Department of Defence's Defence Engagement Program provided funding.

4. After several years adapting concepts in US Armed Forces, Alex Ryan became vice-president of the MaRS Solutions Lab, a prestigious innovation driven startups hub in Toronto in June 2017.

5. While some senior officers started to doubt IDF conceptual capacities after the Yom Kippur War of 1973, difficulties during the occupation of Southern Lebanon (1982–2000) and the first intifada (1987–93) accelerated this trend.

6. General Amnon Schachak, the chief of staff, and his deputy, Major General Matan Vil'nai, passed a resolution to launch both OTRI and the first AOCSC in 1995 (Naveh 2007b, 97). Four themes composed the curriculum: early Soviet operational art (e.g., Tukhachevsky, Isserson, Varfolomeev), epistemology (e.g., Kuhn, Cohen, Wilkins), systems theory (e.g., Capra, Maturana), and space perception (Virilio, Deleuze and Guattari, Tschumi) (Adamsky 2010, 101). Naveh and his colleagues named this methodology Systemic Operational Design.

7. Beaulieu-Brossard's personal interview with Brigadier General (Ret.) Shimon Naveh in Herzlya, 12 May 2015.

8. For Tarak Barkawi and Shane Brighton (2011), this phenomenon is so important that it deserves its own field of inquiry.

9. Deleuze and Guattari found in early mythology the ground to support this claim. In this mythology, the gods of war are in a deeply rooted opposition to the gods of sovereignty (Reid 2003, 63).

10. Deleuze and Guattari uses sedentary groups instead. This category includes states. I directly use states for clarity purposes.

11. Indeed, turning movement into essence into a core principle is a paradox, as this would imply moving away from this notion before it becomes a principle.

12. For instance, in an op-ed published by *Le Monde* in 1978, Deleuze (1978) condemned Israel not only for developing a repressive colonial regime but also for trying to sell this model around the world.

13. Andrew Marshall's Office of Net Assessment of the US Department of Defense, a key US military figure for launching the Revolution in Military Affairs in 1990s, ordered this study (Rosen 2012). In the study, Naveh reveals a thorough research of the nomad as a concept building on Bruce Chatwin's anthropological, Henri Lefebvre's geographical, and Deleuze, Guattari, and De Landa's philosophical perspectives, to name a few.

14. The Palmach was a group akin to a Jewish special force established during the British Mandate of Palestine between 1941 and 1948.

15. Naveh's (2007a, 51) narrative finds support in Eliot Cohen's study, according to which "Ben Gurion's decision to disband the PALMACH provided the most crucial condition for the institutionalization of the governmental apparatus and the professionalization of its military component."

16. Of all the great "nomadic-like" colonels and generals feeding this narrative, T. E. Lawrence seems to be the exception to the rule.

17. Beaulieu-Brossard's interview with Major General (Ret.) Itzak Ben Israel at Tel Aviv on 28 May 2015.

18. These charges were abandoned afterward.

19. In a design-tutorial at Canadian Forces College in May 2018, Brigadier General (Ret.) Gal Hirsch, an AOCSC graduate and leading military design practitioner, also relied on the nomad to reward disrupting rules and conventions for military effectiveness.

20. Beaulieu-Brossard's interview with Brigadier General (Ret.) Shimon Naveh at the IDF National Defense College in Herzlya on 12 May 2015.

21. Beaulieu-Brossard's interview with Brigadier General (now Major General) Jennie Carignan at Canadian Forces College in Toronto on 29 March 2016.

22. See SAMS monographs collection at the Ike Skelton Combined Arms Research Digital Library at Fort Leavenworth, http://cgsc.contentdm.oclc.org/cdm/landing-page/collection/p4013coll3 (accessed 2 March 2017).

23. Interview with Rolly Dessert, Booz Allen Hamilton CAD's former senior associate, Fort Leavenworth, Kansas, 22 February 2016.

24. Beaulieu-Brossard's interview with William "Joe" Miller in Tampa, Florida, on 14 March 2016.

25. Beaulieu-Brossard's interview with Colonel (Ret.) Richard Newton in Tampa, Florida, on 7 March 2016.

References

Adamsky, Dima. 2010. *The Culture of Military Innovation: The Impact of Cultural Factors on the Revolution in Military Affairs in Russia, the US, and Israel.* Stanford, CA: Stanford University Press.

Annan, Kofi. 2002. *Report of the Secretary-General on Recent Events in Jenin, Other Palestinians Cities.* New York: United Nations.

Barkawi, Tarak, and Shane Brighton. 2011. "Powers of War: Fighting, Knowledge, and Critique." *International Political Sociology* 5 (2): 126–43.

Beaulieu-Brossard, Philippe. 2019. "Critique for Action: Outline of a Craft Turn in Security Practices." Unpublished paper.

Beaulieu-Brossard, Philippe, and Philippe Dufort. 2017. "Conclusion: Researching the Reflexive Turn in Military Affairs and Strategic Studies." *Journal of Military and Strategic Studies* 17 (4).

Bruner, Jerome. 1991. "The Narrative Construction of Reality." *Critical Inquiry* 18 (1): 1–21.

Clausewitz, Carl von. 1976. *On War.* Princeton, NJ: Princeton University Press.

De Landa, Manuel. 1991. *War in the Age of Intelligent Machines.* Swerve edition. New York: Zone Books.

Deleuze, Gilles. 1978. "Les gêneurs." *Le Monde,* 7 April.

Deleuze, Gilles. 1990. *Negotiations: 1972–1990.* New York: Colombia University Press.

Deleuze, Gilles. 2003. "Lettre à un critique sévère." In *Pourparlers,* ed. Gilles Deleuze, 11–23. Paris: Editions de minuit.

Deleuze, Gilles, and Félix Guattari. 1980. *Mille plateaux, Capitalisme et schizophrénie / Gilles Deleuze, Félix Guattari.* Paris: Éditions de minuit.

Deleuze, Gilles, and Félix Guattari. 1988. *A Thousand Plateaus: Capitalism and Schizophrenia.* London: Athlone Press.

Dosse, François. 2009. "Les engagements politiques de Gilles Deleuze." *Cités* 40 (4): 21–37.

Du Plessis, Gitte. 2017. "War Machines Par Excellence: The Discrepancy between Threat and Control in the Weaponization of Infectious Agents." Critical Security Studies 5 (1): 45-61.

Eriksson, Johan, and Ludwig Norman. 2011. "Political Utilisation of Scholarly Ideas: The 'Clash of Civilisations' vs. 'Soft Power' in US Foreign Policy." Review of International Studies 37 (1): 417–36.

Feldman, Yotam. 2007. "Dr. Naveh, or, How I Learned to Stop Worrying and Walk through Walls." Haaretz, October 25. Accessed 4 October 2013. http://www.haaretz.com/

Graicer, Ofra. 2015. Two Steps Ahead: From Deep Ops to Special Ops—Wingate the General. Dayan Base: IDF.

Graicer, Ofra. 2017. "Self Disruption: Seizing the High Ground of Systemic Operational Design (SOD)." In Special Issue: Reflexive Military Practitioners: Design Thinking and Beyond, ed. Philippe Beaulieu-Brossard and Philippe Dufort. Journal of Military and Strategic Studies 17 (4): 21–37.

Hirsch, Gal, and Reuven Ben-Shalom. 2016. Defensive Shield: An Israeli Special Forces Commander on the Front Line of Counterterrorism: The Inspirational Story of Brigadier General Gal Hirsch. Jerusalem, Israel: Gefen.

Levine, Daniel J. 2012. Recovering International Relations: The Promise of Sustainable Critique. New York: Oxford University Press.

Martin, Grant. 2017. "Of Garbage Cans and Paradox: Reflexively Reviewing Design, Mission Command, and the Gray Zone." In Special Issue: Reflexive Military Practitioners: Design Thinking and Beyond, ed. by Philippe Beaulieu-Brossard and Philippe Dufort. Journal of Military and Strategic Studies 17 (4): 194–208.

Matthews, Matt. 2008. We Were Caught Unprepared: The 2006 Hezbollah-Israeli War, Long War Occasional Paper. Fort Leavenworth, KS: Combat Studies Institute Press, US Army Combined Arms Center.

Michael, Kobi. 2007. "The Israel Defense Rorces as an Epistemic Authority: An Intellectual Challenge in the Reality of the Israeli–Palestinian Conflict." Journal of Strategic Studies 30 (3): 421–46.

Naveh, Shimon. 2002. "Asymmetric Conflict: An Operational Reflection on Hegemonic Strategies." Unpublished paper.

Naveh, Shimon. 2005. "Between the Striated and the Smooth: Urban Enclaves and Fractal Manoeuvres." Paper delivered at the conference An Archipelago of Exception, Barcelona, 11 November.

Naveh, Shimon. 2007a. "Operational Art and the IDF: A Critical Study of a Command Culture." Center for Strategic & Budgetary Assessment (CSBa)(September 30, 2007), written for the Director of Net assessment, Office of the Secretary of Defense, Contract: DaSw01–02-D-0014–0084.

Naveh, Shimon. 2007b. Operational Art and the IDF: A Critical Study of a Command Culture. Washington, DC: Department of Defense, Office of Net Assessment.

Peri, Yoram. 2006. Generals in the Cabinet Room: How the Military Shapes Israeli Policy. Washington, DC: US Institute of Peace Press.

Price, David H. 2011. Weaponizing Anthropology: Social Science in the Service of the Militarized State. 1st ed. Oakland, CA: AK Press.

Reid, Julian. 2003. "Deleuze's War Machine: Nomadism Against the State." *Millenium* 32 (1): 57–85.

Roberts, Geoffrey. 2006. "History, Theory and the Narrative Turn in IR." *Review of International Studies* 32 (4): 703–14.

Rosen, Stephen P. 2012. "The Impact of the Office of Net Assessment on the American Military in the Matter of the Revolution in Military Affairs." In *Contemporary Military Innovation: Between Anticipation and Adaptation*, ed. Dima Adamsky and Kjell Inge Bjerga, 39–50. New York: Routledge.

Rynhold, Jonathan, and Dov Waxman. 2008. "Ideological Change and Israel's Disengagement from Gaza." *Political Science Quarterly* 123 (1): 11–37.

Saussure, Ferdinand. 1916. Cours de linguistique générale. Paris : Payot.

Stanley, Kenneth O., and Joel Lehman. 2015. *Why Greatness Cannot Be Planned: The Myth of the Objective*. Heidelberg: Springer.

Tilly, Charles, and Gabriel Ardant. 1975. *The Formation of National States in Western Europe: Studies in Political Development*. Princeton, NJ: Princeton University Press.

US Army. 2005. *Army Planning and Orders Production (FM 5–0)*. Washington, DC: Department of the Army Headquarters.

US Army. 2015. *Army Design Methodology (ATP 5–0.1)*. Washington, DC: Department of the Army Headquarters.

US SOCOM. 2016. *Design Thinking for the SOF Enterprise*. Tampa, FL: US Special Operations Command Headquarters.

Weber, Max. 2004. *The Vocation Lectures: "Science as a Vocation"; "Politics as a Vocation."* Indianapolis: Hackett.

Weizman, Eyal. 2006. "Walking Through Walls: Soldiers as Architects in the Israeli-Palestinian Conflict." *Radical Philosophy* 136 (March–April): 8–22.

Weizman, Eyal. 2007. *Hollow Land: Israel's Architecture of Occupation*. London: Verso.

Zweibelson, Ben. 2017. "Blending Postmodernism with Military Design Methodologies: Heresy, Subversion, and Other Myths of Organizational Change." *Journal of Military and Strategic Studies* 17 (4): 139–64.

CHAPTER 6

Political Concepts and Vagueness

Cyberattacks in the Israeli Political Discourse

Neta Strunin-Kremer

Language is an integral part of social life (Bourdieu 1991, 1). It allows humans to communicate and to create shared knowledge and social norms, which in turn shape and dictate their life as a society. Concepts are a mental representation of an element or phenomenon of the physical, social, or psychological world (see Ish-Shalom, this volume). While a word refers to a specific object, a concept combines different elements and experiences. As a result, it is difficult to find a single, clear, and consensual definition of concepts, as every definition contains normative perceptions and emphasizes certain elements over others (Berenskoetter 2016).

Conceptual politics is an interdisciplinary research area that combines different research methods and can be based on different paradigms (see Ish-Shalom, this volume). Some scholars claim that the conceptualization of political concepts should be examined as a process occurring within an epistemic community of scholars and decision makers. Others examine the interaction between the academic and political arenas as a main mechanism behind the conceptualization process of political concepts (Bueger and Bethke 2014, 33–34).

This chapter is based on the sociological approach, which relies on the assumption that discourse is a type of practice (see Bueger, this volume). Therefore, by examining and understanding how a certain concept was conceptualized, we can understand its exemplars and predict how different actors will use and react to the concept. According to this approach, the conceptualization of a new concept is shaped through the bidirectional interaction between the political arena and academy. It is influenced by the normative and ideological perceptions of the involved actors (Kurki 2010, 363, 371). Since discourse is a type of practice, actors, in conceptualizing a political concept, shape reality according to their perceptions and interests knowingly or not.

Political actors, therefore, may use the conceptualization of a certain concept to shape the public perception of reality according to their own interests and to promote certain policies while avoiding criticism (Ish-Shalom 2011, 41–43; see also Ish-Shalom, Berenskoetter, this volume). In this chapter, I combine the literature of conceptual politics and securitization to examine how Israeli decision makers conceptualize cyberattacks, in particular how they use vagueness to securitize the discourse regarding this phenomenon (see Ish-Shalom, Steele and Campbell, Geis, Beaulieu-Brossard, this volume). By doing so, they can justify many decisions and actions that Israel takes in the cyber domain without damaging its image as a liberal democracy.

Over the last few years, decision makers and scholars have presented cyberattacks as one of the most significant threats in the international arena. Given the hidden and undetectable nature of this threat, most countries see cyber defense as a major national interest. Such perceptions have led to allocating national resources to establish national organizations such as the Israeli National Cyber Bureau[1] and the US Cyber Command,[2] as well as to create regional cyber defense strategies (European Commission 2020).

Currently, scholars, practitioners, and decision makers identify the cyber domain as a combat zone per se. However, attacks performed in the cyber domain are different from attacks performed in the physical world. In contrast to other domains, the entry barriers in the cyber domain are relatively low. The attacks conducted in this domain are not limited by tangible borders. They are almost impossible to identify while being launched, less costly than launching a missile or a bomb, and yet may cause severe physical damage. Such properties create an incentive for different actors to use this type of weapon in the international arena.

The fact that cyberattacks are perceived as a major international threat, as well as that such attacks have a tremendous impact on relations between international actors, makes it clear that the concept of cyberattack indeed has political significance. Therefore, to understand how different actors respond to cyberattacks, we need to examine first how they define this threat. An examination of how principal Israeli decision makers present the concept of cyberattack, however, reveals a certain vagueness surrounding this phenomenon.

Vagueness is a well-known phenomenon within political discourse analysis literature, which identifies several motivations for its use within political discourse. In this chapter, I will examine Israel's use of vagueness to securitize its cyber discourse. To do so, I will analyze speeches and statements made by the Israeli prime minister Benjamin Netanyahu between the years 2011–15 that refer to cyber threats or cyberattacks. Since one of the assumptions of this research is that concepts are created within discourse, which is a type of practice, I will perform discourse analysis based on a critical approach (also known as critical discourse analysis, or CDA). According to this approach, any textual unit contains ideas and perceptions that construct, justify, and perpetuate social power relations, while the speaker represents the dominant group (van Dijk 1993, 249–54). Therefore, CDA serves well my aim of identifying the social power relations and understanding how the conceptualization of cyber preserves and constructs them.

The Concept of Cyber

"Cyber" is a common short form for "cybernetics." The concept of cybernetics is based on a Greek verb that means "to direct" or "to navigate." In 1948, Norbert Wiener used the concept of cybernetics to describe the dynamics between different biological systems that are able to transfer information to form actions (Afek 2013, 18–19). The cyber domain contains different networks, devices, and infrastructures, and its development and structure are inherently woven with the history of the Internet.

The Internet was an American military development, designed as a decentralized network that guaranteed transmission of information even if some of its components were damaged. This system breaks information into bytes to enable it to run easily and to challenge the ability of potential hackers to understand it (Melzer 2011, 257–58). Today, the Internet is used by different actors who can access it from different devices, some less protected than others. As a result, the cyber domain has become vulnerable. The dependence of different systems and devices on the same networks and infrastructures means that a single attack can cause severe damage to both military and civil targets (Kerschischnig 2012, 7).

Cyberattacks involve an invasion into a system of computers or networks with the purpose to destroy information, steal it, or damage a certain target within the cyber domain (Melzer 2011, 1–4). An examination of the academic literature reveals that most scholars differentiate between different types of attacks (e.g., cybercrimes or cyberterrorism) based on the identity of the attacker or the target (Carr 2015, 643; Deibert 2003, 158–59; Rid 2012, 10–15). However, the same means (such as worms, viruses, or Trojan horses)[3] can be used to launch any of these attacks.

Certain features of the cyber domain may make the attacks conducted within it a significant national and international threat. One of the most important and unique of these is the dependence that exists among this domain's various components, making it almost impossible to conduct a discriminate attack. An attack conducted within the cyber domain has the potential to cause severe damage to different targets simultaneously. The main concern of politicians and scholars is the ease within this domain of damaging critical infrastructures.[4] Since these infrastructures depend on one another, one cyberattack may destroy many of them and potentially prevent nation-states from being able to provide essential services to its civilians (Kerschischnig 2012, 7–8, 47–48).

The cyber domain's intangibility challenges the effectiveness of national borders and the sovereignty of nation-states. It also enables actors to maintain secrecy, making it almost impossible to identify an attack while it is being launched. Because the ability to launch such an attack is not limited to nation-states, the use of cyberattacks is very appealing to nonstate actors (Kerschischnig 2012, 9–10).

However, history indicates that although the cyber domain creates incentives for different actors to use it in order to damage different targets, the actual damage caused through this domain is not as catastrophic as feared. Many scholars agree that cyberattack alone is not likely to cause irreversible damage and does not pose a threat to the very existence of a nation-state (Gartzke 2013, 41–59).

Such claims contradict the threat portrayed in speeches and statements of different decision makers regarding the cyber domain. Some scholars explain this gap by claiming that decision makers have an interest in exaggerating the cyber threat. They argue that the cyber discourse was successfully securitized, as evidenced by the establishment of the American Commission on Critical Infrastructure developments, the attribution of cyber security issues to the American Department of Homeland Security, and by the creation of the NATO-backed cyber defense center in Estonia (Hansen and Nissenbaum 2009, 1156–67). In this chapter, I will turn to the case of Israel and examine whether and how Israeli decision makers securitize the country's cyber discourse by creating vagueness with regard to the concept and phenomenon of cyberattack.

Securitization and Political Vagueness

The main idea behind securitization theories is that it is not the objective aspects of a phenomenon that make it a security issue but rather the way in which it is presented by political actors (Balzacq and Guzzini 2015, 98–99). Securitization is a discursive act of constructing a certain issue as an existential threat. Through this act, the securitizing actor is able to control the relevant discourse and define the appropriate strategies and means to cope with the phenomenon in question (Stritzel 2007, 357–60). To securitize a certain phenomenon, securitizing actors need to know their audience in order to draw upon images, metaphors, and stereotypes that suit the audience's identity, culture, and history (Balzaq 2010, 9–10). Indeed, in securitizing the Israeli cyber discourse, Israel's decision makers demonstrate a keen awareness of the role of security threats in Israeli society's identity.

A significant part of Israel's identity is the constant struggle against different existential threats. Even before the foundation of the state of Israel, the leaders of the Zionist movement justified its establishment based on the various threats Jews have faced throughout history. A similar justification exists in Israel's independent declaration, which reflects the identity of the state of Israel ("Declaration of Establishment of State of Israel" n.d.).

This background is crucial to understanding the sensitivity of the Israel public to security threats, as this sensitivity affects the efficiency of the securitization process. Since political actors use existential threats as a principle legitimation for the existence of Israel, one can anticipate that the Israeli public will tend to support any policy framed as part of a campaign against national threats. This situation promotes the domination of political actors with security background over other actors.

Examination of Netanyahu's electoral campaign reveals the use of different slogans constructing his reputation as a security expert. Examples of such a strategy can be seen, for example, from the 2013 campaign: "Strong prime Minister—Strong Israel"; or from 2006: "Strong against the Hamas—Netanyahu, Likud" ("Slogans in Israeli Politics" 2019). Both slogans successfully constructed Netanyahu's image as a security expert, a perception that became quite popular among Israelis. For example, a Google search of the phrase "Mr. Security" in Hebrew results in a majority of hits focusing on Netanyahu. This image of Netanyahu enables him to securitize different issues, which in a reciprocal process strengthens further his image as Mr. Security.

To securitize a certain issue, political actors use different rhetorical means. Vagueness refers to uncertainty about the boundaries of a certain concept: when a concept is vague, we will struggle to decide whether certain borderline cases are included within it. Scholars differentiate between *essentially* vague concepts and *epistemic* vagueness. Essentially vague concepts have no clear boundaries (Tye 2012, 535–36), whereas epistemic vagueness exists when a certain concept has clear boundaries but those using it do not know them (Merricks 2001, 146). When a concept is epistemically vague, different actors will be in conflict over certain borderline cases, arguing whether they represent empirical implementation of that concept.

To securitize a phenomenon, the securitizing actor must create a clear and unquestioned perception of threat in the public domain. By using epistemic vagueness, the securitizing actor is able to prevent the public from accessing information that would enable them to question the definition of the phenomenon as an existential threat. Therefore, if Israeli decision makers wish to construct cyberattacks as an existential threat, they need to shield the Israeli public from information that would enable them to criticize this perception. By creating vagueness about the limits of cyberattacks, they can include other phenomenon within the concept of cyberattacks, creating an illusion that this threat is more extensive and severe than it really is.

As mentioned above, by securitizing a certain phenomenon, decision makers can justify in advance the use of extreme measures against it and control the relevant discourse. Similarly, by securitizing phenomena occurring in the cyber domain, Israeli decision makers can control the cyber discourse and legitimize decisions that otherwise would have been questioned and criticized.

Why Use Vagueness?

Several motivations exist for using vagueness in political discourse. Political actors may use vagueness when they are addressing different audiences that have different interests and perceptions with regard to a certain issue. By being vague, these actors guarantee that every group understands the statement according to their perception and at the same time avoids making a statement that costs them public support. Using vagueness also serves political actors addressing a sensitive issue or social taboo; when they cannot avoid such issues but know that making any clear and firm statement would anger certain groups, they can resort to vagueness (Garver 1990, 1–6). Actors may also use vagueness when they aspire to achieve contested interests. We see some vagueness in resolutions of the UN, for example, where there is a need to create a clear instruction, on the one hand, and to maintain flexibility and openness to interpretation, on the other (di Carlo 2013, 1–10; see Mitrani, this volume). Martha Finnemore and Henry Farrell claim that the United States actively hides the gap existing between its reputation as a leader of the free and liberal world and its secret aim to promote its own interests (Farrell and Finnemore 2013).

Deborah Housen-Couriel made similar claims with regard to Israel, pointing to the vagueness in Israeli cyber discourse that allows Israeli decision makers to ignore the contesting aspects of the phenomenon of cyberattacks and to act within the cyber domain, while condemning other actors that are acting in the exact same way (Housen- Curiel 2012). In fact, the use of vagueness in Israeli political discourse is not a new phenomenon. One of the most well-known examples is Israel's vague nuclear policy: this policy is the outcome of Israel's aspiration to develop nuclear power, free from any limitation or international supervision, while maintaining its relation and status within the international community. Israel also wished to gain a strategic advantage over its neighbors while preventing the creation of a regional nuclear arms race. These conflicting interests led to the creation of a vague policy that, over time, has been recognized as such by Israeli decision makers (Buchner 2010, 37–38).

The main criticism directed against Israel's vague nuclear policy focuses on the fact that despite Israel's repeated claims that it is a liberal democracy (Ravid 2011), its nuclear policy contradicts one of the main principles of liberal democracy: that is, transparency (Kohen 2005, 11). It is not unusual for liberal democracies to push aside liberal and democratic principles temporarily (Meijer 2013, 431); but when this situation becomes permanent, the identity of the state as a liberal democracy is endangered (Yaniv 1993, 1–2).

A use of vagueness can be detected if the audience becomes aware that the speaker, instead of using wording that would maximize the amount of information, had chosen to use wording that prevented relevant knowledge (Blume and Board 2014, 856). Actors can do this by using professional terminology that is unfamiliar to the audience or by using complicated and ungainly sentences. In other cases, they create vagueness by using a wide and general concept to address very different phenomena or by employing metaphors and comparisons without explaining them. In the next section, I will analyze Netanyahu's use of these tools to create vagueness and disguise it at the same time.

Analysis and Findings: Vagueness in Israeli Cyber Discourse: Speeches of Israeli Prime Minister Benjamin Netanyahu

Since 2011, the concept "cyber" has appeared in many of Netanyahu's speeches and statements. In fact, he presents cyber defense and cyber development as key national interests. These claims have been backed by the establishment of the Israeli National Cyber Bureau under the prime minister's office. As the Israeli prime minister and as a political actor who focuses on security policy and cyber-related phenomena, Netanyahu plays a crucial role in the construction of the concept of cyber in the Israeli discourse.

A corpus of twenty-two relevant text units by Netanyahu reveals the use of several means that create an epistemic vagueness regarding the phenomenon of cyberattack and that disguise it. Analyzing the texts by methodologies of the CDA reveals different linguistic and conceptual means, the first of which are related to the speaker's choice of words, images, and metaphors (Foss 2009, 66–68).

In his speeches, Netanyahu explicitly argues that the phenomena that occur within the cyber domain pose a national and existential threat. As mentioned above, such an argument is quite controversial. The use of vagueness enables Netanyahu to make such an argument without addressing this controversy and exposing himself to criticism or damaging his perception as an expert who has the knowledge and capability to face this threat. Such vagueness is manifested as Netanyahu obscures the relations and limits between different cyber-related concepts such as cyberterrorism, cybercrime, and cyber espionage and defines them all as one main national threat.

For example, at the Annual Cyber Security International Conference of the Yuval Ne'eman Workshop for Science, Technology, and Security in 2013,[5] Netanyahu defined cyber as a "national problem" and argued that actors such as Iran, Hizballah, and Hamas were launching cyberattacks against critical national systems but also against economical and civil targets ("Prime Minister Netanyahu's Speech" 2013). In this speech Netanyahu does not differentiate exemplars of cyberterrorism and cybercrimes but addresses them all as cyberattacks, which he defines as a main national problem. This conflation of concepts is in stark opposition to the well-grounded and familiar conceptual distinctions we find in international and domestic law and also in cyber-oriented literature, as mentioned above (Ballard 2010). In light of the efforts of both scholars and legislators to conceptually differentiate these phenomena, it seems that Netanyahu's decision to ignore that differences exist between these phenomena is in fact a strategy used to construct these phenomena as a wide national threat. By choosing to use a wider concept that represents various differentiated phenomena, Netanyahu can define it as a wide threat without explicitly contradicting the arguments and information delivered by scholars regarding these phenomena.

In that sense, the use of vagueness enables Netanyahu to construct the phenomena occurring within the cyber domain as a national and existential threat, while avoiding potential criticism. These conflicting interests could be caused by the context of this speech. The International Cyber Conference of the national Cyber Forum and Yuval Ne'eman Workshop is an annual event, organized by the Blavatnik Interdisciplinary Cyber Research Center and the National Cyber Bureau, where political actors, scholars, and practitioners discuss cybersecurity-related issues. The event is open for anyone who registers in advance and is covered by the press media. In that sense, this event presents an opportunity for the speakers to shape the Israeli public's perception regarding the phenomena occurring within the cyber domain, while taking under consideration the fact that their arguments might be publicly contradicted by the other speakers. Vagueness can be useful under these conditions as it enables them to construct a certain perception, while it avoids making contested statements and undermining their image as experts.

When using strategies of vagueness, the speaker must disguise these strategies, or he may confront opposition from citizenry who can feel deceived by him. Indeed, an examination of Netanyahu's speeches thus reveals various strategies to disguise the existence of vagueness. For instance, when presenting the government decision to establish a National Cyber Authority under his own office, Netanyahu describes the cyber threat as a "dynamic and strategic threat" ("Government Approved" 2015). This statement was made in a governmental meeting. However, it was published by different press media organizations and even by the prime minister's office itself. Therefore, one can assume that Netanyahu in fact wanted to address a wider audience than the one attended in that meeting.

At first sight it seems that by using the phrase "dynamic and strategic threat" Netanyahu is explaining how cyber activities are threatening Israel; but this description does not really help to explain the extent of the threat posed by the cyber domain or how creating the National Cyber Authority under the prime minister's office will protect Israel from that threat. In fact, this description could be used to describe any other threat and therefore does not contribute to the audience's knowledge about this specific phenomenon. Instead, it creates an illusion of clarification and by doing so helps to disguise the vagueness surrounding the threat in question and the manner in which the establishment of the National Cyber Authority can protect Israel from this threat. Such an illusion is crucial for decision makers of liberal democracies, who are expected to maintain transparency although it might damage their ability to efficiently make decisions and execute them. In this case, Netanyahu creates this illusion to justify the establishment of the National Cyber Authority under his office, a decision that maintains his domination over the relevant discourse and the decision-making process while excluding every rival actor.

Based on the arguments mentioned earlier suggesting that the creation of cybersecurity authorities by the United States and NATO indicates the success of a securitization process, it is possible to argue that the establishment of a designated national cybersecurity authority under Netanyahu's office is evidence of the success of a securitization process. The justifications made by Netanyahu at the speech mentioned above support this argument.

Netanyahu's attempt to create and disguise an epistemic vagueness is also exemplified in his tendency to use complicated phrasing and ungainly sentences, which characterizes the following quotation: "The threat within the cyber domain has the ability to paralyze states. This is a strategic threat, which has the ability to paralyze and damage, no less than other threats, in some fields even more, and we have to take all precautions, at a national and an international level" ("Government Approved" 2015).

At first sight, it seems that the second sentence is meant to clarify the first; however, closer examination reveals that it does not add any clear information explaining how cyberattacks can paralyze states. In fact, this sentence not only fails to clarify the claim presented in the first sentence but also disguises this fact. It is a complicated and ungainly structure and thus challenges the audience's ability to identify the information buried within it or to notice that, in fact, the amount of knowledge shared is very small.

The same can be seen in Netanyahu's speech from the Annual Cyber Security International Conference of the Yuval Ne'eman Workshop for Science, Technology, and Security in 2013: "Everything we do, everything that our friends are doing as well, countries friendly to us; in some manner we are all in the dark, sensing our way through or in the dark, sensing and making decisions in a reality that changes rapidly" ("Prime Minister Netanyahu's Speech" 2013). In this sentence, Netanyahu is referring to Israel's actions within the cyber domain. The complex, fragmented structure of this sentence not only challenges the audience's ability to understand what Israel is doing within the cyber domain but also confuses the listeners to such an extent that by the end of the sentence they will forget its main issue. The use of this convoluted kind of phrasing disguises the limited amount of information transmitted to the audience, as well as the fact that the audience is not able to determine, based on this scarce information, whether different margin cases qualify as cyberattacks. Such phrasing thus arguably contributes to the creation of epistemic vagueness regarding this phenomenon.

To identify the main motivation that led Netanyahu to use such phrasing, one should examine the contextual aspect of each speech. The speeches addressed above were delivered in quite different contexts. One was delivered in a governmental meeting, which is a closed event for only certain political actors, while the other was delivered at the annual cyber conference featuring different Israeli and foreign speakers (political actors, scholars, and practitioners) in front of a wide audience. In that sense, the context of the second speech posed a challenge for Netanyahu as a speaker. When a speaker addresses a wide and varied audience, he must balance between multiple interests and therefore is more likely to use different strategies and tools, such as vagueness. Furthermore, as the prime minister, Netanyahu dominates the discourse created in governmental meetings, especially when he addresses cyber-related issues, which were defined as part of his office's authority when the National Cyber Bureau was established. However, at the annual cyber conference, Netanyahu is one of many speakers from different fields who were chosen due to their expertise and knowledge regarding the cyber domain and the phenomena that occur in it. As such, they might challenge Netanyahu's arguments and compete over dominating the cyber discourse. Based on these differences, one might be puzzled that in both contexts Netanyahu uses complicated phrasing.

This finding can be explained by the fact that both speeches were documented and quoted not just by the press media but also by the prime minister's office. Therefore, it is safe to assume that each speech was written and phrased to address a wide audience composed of different groups and individuals with different levels of knowledge regarding the cyber domain, different interests, and different views. In other words, when Netanyahu speaks at a closed governmental meeting, he is aware that his audience contains not only those who are present at this meeting. The use of complicated phrasing and ungainly sentences enables Netanyahu to construct certain perceptions regarding the cyber domain and the manner in which it poses a national threat, instead of arguing the issue literally and being criticized by some in the audience. Therefore, this language pattern is used in different speeches and statements to address a wide and diverse audience.

Netanyahu's attempt to create vagueness and securitize the cyber discourse manifested in his use of various security images and metaphors. For example, in his speech from the Annual Cyber Security International Conference in 2013, he uses the metaphor of a digital Iron Dome: "We aim to establish what I call a digital iron dome to face these attacks, which will only increase in quality and quantity. This obliges us to always be one step ahead of our adversaries in this never ending contest. That is why the previous government established the National Cyber Bureau" ("Prime Minister Netanyahu's Speech" 2013).

The Iron Dome is presented as one of the most popular and familiar inventions in current Israeli security discourse, by military speakers, politic actors, and media reporters. It is perceived as a successful defense system (Zitun 2014). Therefore, when Netanyahu presents the aspiration to create a digital Iron Dome to protect Israeli national and civil systems from cyberattacks, he constructs cyberattacks as an existential national threat, similar to the missile threat that led to the development of the Israeli Iron Dome. The use of this metaphor also constructs a perception according to which, by establishing the National Cyber Bureau, the Israeli government can efficiently protect national and civil targets from cyberattacks, similar to the missile protection provided by the Iron Dome.

By using this metaphor, Netanyahu can construct and assimilate these perceptions in the public consciousness without arguing it literally. As mentioned above, there are several motivations that led actors to use vagueness in political discourse. One of these motivations is the necessity to address a sensitive or controversial issue. In this case, the perceptions mentioned earlier contradict the properties and structure of the cyber domain as it is presented by different scholars. Based on its properties and structure, it is impossible to create a "digital Iron Dome" that will fully shield all national and civil targets linked to the cyber domain. Also as mentioned above, different scholars have doubted the ability of a cyberattack to pose a national and existential threat.

Therefore, instead of making controversial arguments and taking the chance that the other speakers might contradict them publicly, Netanyahu uses a metaphor to construct these perceptions. By using such a well-known and popular defense system as a metaphor, he also disguises the fact that he neither substantiates nor explains whether and how the National Cyber Bureau can protect Israeli national and civil targets from the threat posed by cyberattacks.

Another interesting example of how Netanyahu uses the Iron Dome can be seen in the following quotation, taken from his speech at the inauguration of Israel's cyber park: "At the end of the day, our life depends on the Iron Wall. We are building the Iron Wall, the Iron Dome, and we have an iron will—that is what gives us the power to defend ourselves and also to say to those who aim to hurt us: 'You should not.' These are the foundations of Israel's defense. Everything else happened now" ("Prime Minister Netanyahu Inaugurated" 2013).

This was yet another public event covered by media and attended by other political actors, academic actors such as the president of the Ben Gurion University of the Negev, and practitioners such as KUD International president and CEO Marvin J. Suomi. In that sense this speech, like the one given by Netanyahu at the annual cyber conference, addressed a wide audience composed by different groups. This kind of context forces Netanyahu to carefully phrase his arguments and avoid making statements that might jeopardize this image and the different interests he aspires to maintain. Therefore, in this quotation Netanyahu uses different metaphors that construct cyberattacks as national and existential threats and a perception according to which the Israeli government can provide effective and complete protection from this threat.

The metaphor of the Iron Wall is quite common in Israeli discourse, symbolizing tenacity. It originated in an article by Ze'ev Jabotinsky—an article that qualifies as a constitutive text within Israeli cultural history.[6] Jabotinsky explained that, since the implementation of Zionism in the land of Israel is unlikely to be acknowledged by the Arabs living in this area, it is necessary to create an "Iron wall" that represents a strong military defense force (Lustick 1996, 199). Jabotinsky's article thus constructs the perception, mentioned above, of Israel as a state that deals with constant existential threats. Netanyahu's decision to use the metaphor of the Iron Wall at the initiation ceremony of the cyber park constructs a perception according to which the cyberattacks pose a national and existential threat, similar to Arab armies or Hamas's missiles. At the same time, it creates a perception according to which the decision to establish this park will enable the Israeli government to protect its citizens from this threat.

As mentioned above, some scholars and practitioners have questioned whether cyberattacks can pose a national and existential threat and whether it is possible to create a protection means that will resemble a protection wall or a dome. Therefore, by using a metaphor, Netanyahu is able to construct this perception without a literal argument that such an idea is achievable. Furthermore, by choosing such familiar metaphors he is able to create an illusion among the public that they understand how the establishment of the cyber park can provide this kind of protection. In doing so, Netanyahu not only securitizes the cyber discourse but also constructs and maintains Israel's image as a constantly threatened state, as well as the domination of security-oriented decision makers. Therefore, this quotation exemplifies how the creation of an epistemic vagueness contributes to constructing a certain phenomenon as an existential threat.

Conclusions

This chapter examined the creation of epistemic vagueness surrounding the phenomenon of cyberattacks within speeches and statements by Israeli prime minister Benjamin Netanyahu. It presented the different means used to create and disguise the creation of epistemic vagueness and how using these means contributed to the securitization of Israeli cyber discourse. In light of the size of the corpus and its focus on single-actor texts, the conclusions of this study should be cautiously applied to the conceptualization of cyberattacks in particular and certainly to the conceptualization of political concepts in general.

However, these findings emphasize and exemplify several theoretical arguments. They support the arguments presented by several scholars, according to which the cyber discourse is securitized by different political actors to justify decisions that otherwise would have been criticized or questioned (such as the decision to establish a national cyber authority under the prime minister's office) and to dominate the relevant discourse.

This chapter also revealed how the creation of vagueness enables actors to control the perception of certain phenomena and to securitize. This fact may lead some to claim that the use of vagueness contradicts the very essence of the securitization process. However, as this research indicates, when actors use vagueness regarding some aspects of the securitized phenomenon, they can increase the sense of threat among the public. The lack of knowledge challenges the public's ability to question the extent of the threat, or even its construction as an existential threat, as it is presented by the securitizing actor.

In the age of mass media, it is very difficult to shield the public from information or to exclude rival actors from the public discourse. Therefore, when constructing a certain phenomenon as a national and existential threat, political actors are exposed to criticism that can damage their image and interests. As exemplified in this chapter, the creation of epistemic vagueness enables them to construct this phenomenon as a national and existential threat without making explicit arguments that contradict the existing knowledge regarding the phenomenon in question and therefore to shield them from potential criticism.

These findings also correspond with some main arguments regarding the motives and interests that shape and affect the way actors conceptualize political concepts. As mentioned above, the analysis conducted in this research exemplifies how the conceptualization of cyberattacks as it is manifested by Netanyahu's speeches represents his interest to dominate the relevant discourse and decision-making process. In that sense, it supports the argument presented by scholars that political actors may use the conceptualization of a certain concept to shape reality according to their own interests and to promote certain policies while avoiding criticism. Thus, it emphasizes the importance of the involvement of different actors from different arenas in the conceptualization of political concept.

Notes

1. This is an advising body to the Israeli government and the Israeli prime minister, established in 2011.

2. The US Army Cyber Command was established in October 2010 to lead cyber missions while reporting directly to the Headquarters of the Department of the Army ("U.S. Cyber Command" n.d.).

3. These are different malwares, programs or codes designed to steal, pollute, damage, or destroy data, servers, or networks.

4. Critical infrastructures are the infrastructures necessary to provide the most basic needs of a state's civilians, such as energy supply, water supply, and communication infrastructures (Kerschischnig 2012, 7–8, 47–48).

5. This workshop was launched in 2002 by Professor Issac Ben Israel (see Beaulieu-Brossard, this volume).

6. Ze'ev Jabotinsky was a Zionist leader and the founding father of the Revisionist movement ("Ze'ev Jabotinsky—Biography" n.d.).

References

Afek, Sharon. 2013. "The Cybernetic Attack: Legal Character Lines: Implementation of International Law on Warfare in Cyber Space." *Eshtonot* 5:1–149.

Ballard, Mark. 2010. "UN Rejects International Cybercrime Treaty." *Computerweekly.*

Balzaq, Thierry. 2010. "A Theory of Securitization: Origin, Core Assumptions, and Variants." In *Understanding Securitisation Theory: How Security Problems Emerge and Dissolve*, ed. Thierry Balzaq, 1–30. New York: Routledge.

Balzacq, Thierry, and Stefano Guzzini. 2015. "Introduction: 'What Kind of Theory—If Any—Is Securitization?'" *International Relations* 29 (1): 97–102.

Berenskoetter, Felix. 2016. "Unpacking Concepts." In *Concepts of World Politics*, ed. Felix Berenskoetter, 1–19. London: Sage.

Blume, Andreas, and Oliver Board. 2014. "Intentional Vagueness." *Erkenntnis* 79 (S4): 855–99.

Bourdieu, Pierre. 1991. *Language and Symbolic Power*. Ed. John B. Thompson, Gino Raymond, and Matthew Adamson. Cambridge: Polity Press.

Buchner, Oded. 2010. *Deterrence and Nuclear Ambiguity: Mordechai Vanunu as a Soldier of Ambiguity*. M&P Publishing.

Bueger, Christian, and Felix Bethke. 2014. "Actor-Networking the 'Failed State'—An Enquiry into the Life of Concepts." *Journal of International Relations and Development* 17 (1): 30–60.

Carlo, Giuseppina Scotto di. 2013. *Vagueness as a Political Strategy: Weasel Words in Security Council Resolutions Relating to the Second Gulf War*. Newcastle upon Tyne: Cambridge Scholars.

Carr, M. 2015. "Power Plays in Global Internet Governance." *Millennium: Journal of International Studies* 43 (2): 640–59.

"Declaration of Establishment of State of Israel." n.d. Israel Ministry of Foreign Affairs. Accessed 11 December 2016. http://www.mfa.gov.il/mfa/foreignpolicy/ peace/guide/pages/declaration of establishment of state of israel.aspx

Deibert, R. J. 2003. "Black Code: Censorship, Surveillance, and the Militarisation of Cyberspace." *Millennium: Journal of International Studies* 32 (3): 501–30.

European Commission. 2020. "Shaping Europe's Digital Future: Cybersecurity." European Commission, May 28. https://ec.europa.eu/digital-single-market/en/ cybersecurity

European Commission. n.d. "Cybercrime." European Commission Migration and Home Affairs. Accessed 3 October 2015. http://ec.europa.eu/dgs/home-affairs/what-we-do/ policies/organized-crime-and-human-trafficking/cybercrime/index_en.htm

Farrell, Henry, and Martha Finnemore. 2013. "The End of Hypocrisy: American Foreign Policy in the Age of Leaks." *Foreign Affairs*, November–December.

Foss, Sonja K. 2009. *Rhetorical Criticism: Exploration and Practice*. 4th ed. Long Grove, Illinois: Waveland Press.

Gartzke, Erik. 2013. "The Myth of Cyberwar: Bringing War in Cyberspace Back Down to Earth." *International Security* 38 (2): 41–73.

Garver, Eugene. 1990. "Essentially Contested Concepts: The Ethics and Tactics of Argument." *Philosophy and Rhetoric* 23 (4): 251.

"The Government Approved the Establishment of a National Cyber Authority." 2015. Prime Minister's Office. Accessed 12 May 2015. http://www.pmo.gov.il/media center/spokesman/pages/spokecyber150215.aspx

Hansen, Lene, and Helen Nissenbaum. 2009. "Digital Disaster, Cyber Security, and the Copenhagen School." *International Studies Quarterly* 53 (4): 1155–75.

Housen-Curiel, Deborah. 2012. "Constructive Ambiguity in Cyber Space: The Legal and Policy Challenges." In *The Annual Cyber Security International Conference Proceeding 2012*, ed. Lior Tabansky, 83–86. Tel Aviv: Tel-Aviv University Press.

Ish-Shalom, Piki. 2011. "Conceptualizing Democratization and Democratizing Conceptualization: A Virtuous Circle." In *The Conceptual Politics of Democracy Promotion*, ed. Christopher Hobson and Milja Kurki, 38–52. New York: Routledge.

Kerschischnig, Georg. 2012. *Cyberthreats and International Law*. The Hague, Netherlands: Eleven International Publishing.

Kohen, Avner. 2005. *The Last Taboo: The Secret of Israel's Nuclear Situation and What to Do with It*. Or-Yehuda: Kinneret Zmora-Bitan Dvir.

Kurki, Milja. 2010. "Democracy and Conceptual Contestability: Reconsidering Conceptions of Democracy in Democracy Promotion." *International Studies Review* 12 (3): 362–86.

Lustick, Ian. 1996. "To Build and to Be Built By: Israel and the Hidden Logic of the Iron Wall." *Israel Studies* 1 (1): 196–223.

Meijer, Albert. 2013. "Understanding the Complex Dynamics of Transparency." *Public Administration Review* 73 (3): 429–39.

Melzer, Nils. 2011. *Cyberwarfare and International Law*. Geneva, Switzerland: United Nations Institute for Disarmament Research. https://www.unidir.org/files/publi cations/pdfs/cyberwarfare-and-international-law-382.pdf

Merricks, Trenton. 2001. "Varieties of Vagueness." *Philosophy and Phenomenological Research* 62 (1): 145–57.

"Prime Minister Netanyahu Inaugurated the High Tech Park in Be'er Sheva, Which Will Also Serve as the National Cyber Center." 2013. Prime Minister's Office. Accessed 18 August 2015. http://www.pmo.gov.il/mediacenter/events/pages/ eventbeersheva030913.aspx

"Prime Minister Netanyahu's Speech at the International Cyber Conference of the National Cyber Forum and Yuval Ne'eman Workshop." 2013. Prime Minister's Office. Accessed 20 May 2015. http://www.pmo.gov.il/mediacenter/speeches/ pages/speechcyber090613.aspx.

Ravid, Barak. 2011. "Netanyahu: Israel Is a Democracy and Won't Tolerate Discrimination." Haaretz.com. http://www.haaretz.com/israel-news/netanyahu-israel-is-a-democracy-and-won-t-tolerate-discrimination-1.403473

Rid, Thomas. 2012. "Cyber War Will Not Take Place." *Journal of Strategic Studies* 35 (1): 5–32.

"Slogans in Israeli Politics." 2019. Wikiquote. https://he.wikiquote.org/wiki/ סיסמאות_בפוליטיקה_הישראלית

Stritzel, H. 2007. "Towards a Theory of Securitization: Copenhagen and Beyond." *European Journal of International Relations* 13 (3): 357–83.

Tye, Michael. 2012. "Vague Objects." *Mind* 71 (282): 241–43.

van Dijk, T. A. 1993. "Principles of Critical Discourse Analysis." *Discourse & Society* 4(2): 249–83.

"U.S. Cyber Command." n.d. U.S. Army Cyper Command. Accessed 17 December 2016. http://www.arcyber.army.mil/Pages/USCyberCommand.aspx

Yaniv, Avner. 1993. *National Security and Democracy in Israel.* Boulder, CO: Lynne Rienner.

"Ze'ev Jabotinsky—Biography." n.d. Knesset. Accessed 4 January 2017. https://knes set.gov.il/vip/jabotinsky/eng/Bio_frame_eng.html.

Zitun, Yoav. 2014. "90% Success for Iron Dome, 10 Missiles Were Intercepted in the Gaza Strip." Ynet. http://www.ynet.co.il/articles/0,7340,L-4558376,00.html

CHAPTER 7

Shifting Tides

The Blue Economy and Concepts in Practice

Christian Bueger

Blue economy is a recent concept that stands for a major reevaluation of the potential of the oceans. The concept has made a remarkable career journey across the world. Starting its travel in the sustainable development discourse, it has become one of the main ways for how the oceans and seas are discussed in public policy and world political debates. This chapter analyzes the trajectory of the concept of blue economy to sketch out a practice-driven form of concept analysis.

Concepts are one of the basic linguistic materials of international politics. The study of concepts, however, is too often seen as a concern for historians of international thought only. That concepts are also a productive entry point for understanding contemporary international politics and its transformations has been only gradually recognized. This new recognition is linked in many ways to the appreciation of linguistic structures conducted in the frame of discourse-theoretical and post-structuralist analyses in the discipline of international relations (IR). Such "textualist" perspectives have well advanced our understanding of why and how language matters in international politics (see Beaulieu-Brossard, this volume). They, however, tend to focus on larger systems of meaning and hardly ever scrutinize single concepts, their evolution, and their career. In this chapter, I argue for basing the study of concepts on a practice theoretical perspective (see Strunin-

Kremer, this volume).[1] I use the case of the concept of blue economy to develop three interrelated claims on how to do conceptual analysis.

First, following the work of Ludwig Wittgenstein and John Dewey, I suggest that the meaning of a concept lies in its use. Concepts have no inherent meaning outside of their use. For Wittgenstein, concepts are part of what he called "language games." Dewey employed the notion of "conjunct activities" of a community of functional language use, of which concepts are part. Drawing on those basic insights, I suggest the more established term "practice" to refer to the sets of activities within which concepts are used (see Ish-Shalom, this volume). In consequence, the study of concepts implies studying the practices of which concepts are part and the collectives that carry and enact those practices (practical configurations).

Second, such a perspective implies that concepts do not have a definite origin or a birthday. New concepts draw on, and organize, the relations between existing concepts in novel ways. It is no surprise that the majority of recent conceptual innovations are composed of two terms that have been in prior use. Think about recent concepts such as "peace building," "human security," "failed state," or "humanitarian intervention." These are examples of concepts that integrate existing concerns and fill words with new meaning. In a quite similar fashion, the concept of blue economy advances preexisting terms. The concept was originally developed to shift emphasis from a "green economy" to a "blue" one. Yet over the course of its trajectory, it gained several related meanings.

Third, the functional perspective of language implies that concepts are used for distinct purposes. Concepts are responses to particular problematic situations and aim at addressing these. To study the evolution of concepts, hence, implies to follow them across the situation to which they are a response. If concepts are used to respond to different problematic situations, their meaning can shift considerably. I make this argument by showing how the concept of blue economy gradually shifted its meaning by being transferred across situations. Starting out as an environmentalist concept of innovation, it became employed as a primarily economic term and later was used as a security concept and a diplomatic tool. I describe these shifts by studying a selected range of situations in which the concept of blue economy is in use.

I organize my discussion in the following way. I start with a brief tour d'horizon on how concepts are studied in the discipline of IR. This is mainly to make my first argument that we should study concepts in action and to introduce my core theoretical presumptions. The second section introduces the empirical case. I discuss the formulation of the concept of blue economy and then proceed to investigate some stations of its travel history. I seek to show how the meaning of the concept has shifted and turned in response to particular needs. In the conclusion, I point to some of the consequences of my outline of a practice-based conceptual analysis. Stressing the importance of giving up the quest for universal definitions of the meaning of concepts, or even measuring their content, I point to the practical value of conceptual analysis for identifying political projects, for understanding sociopolitical change, but also for intervening into public policy debates.

Conceptual Analysis and International Relations: A Very Short Tour D'Horizon

When the linguistic turn reached the discipline of IR (see Berenskötter, this volume), it became clear that much of the discipline had relied on an understanding of language, which philosophers have referred to as a "picture theory of language." The core premise of this position is that language and, in consequence, concepts are neutral and mirror nature. The task that follows from picture theory was to refine concepts so they bring one closer and closer to the reality they describe.[2] It required quite some energy to convince at least some parts of the discipline that there was something wrong with this understanding.[3] Ludwig Wittgenstein's *Philosophical Investigations* and John Dewey's work on language were vital in making this argument, not the least because both philosophers also provided the basic groundwork for the French structuralists and post-structuralists. Since my objective is not to rehearse the ideas of the linguistic turn,[4] let me concentrate on two points vital for my following discussion.

Both Dewey and Wittgenstein rejected the idea that language can have a universal, context-independent meaning.[5] As they argued, the rule of how to use a concept is not inscribed in the concept itself. In consequence, concepts (and language in general) are always dependent on a context and a social configuration that ascribes what the appropriate forms of using a concept are (see Ish-Shalom, this volume). Dewey described these social configurations as "conjoint activities," while Wittgenstein developed the notion of "language games." Here I prefer the term "practical configuration." By practical configuration, I refer to the activities of a collective of language users in which meaning is inscribed. Dewey's work on language goes far beyond the achievements of Wittgenstein and is vital for showing the instrumentality of language. For Dewey, language and concepts are developed for instrumental purposes, to achieve a goal or to address a problem, for instance, a problem of intersubjective coordination. In Dewey's understanding, concepts are technology: they are tools developed and used in response to a particular problematic situation.[6] In consequence, for understanding a concept, we have to study not only the collective of language users but also the situation to which the collective responds.

The instrumentalist perspective on concepts has influenced discussions in IR in various ways, yet the attention has been seldom on practical situations. A wide range of historians of international thought have argued for the importance of concepts in structuring social order and have explored concepts such as anarchy, territory, sovereignty, or global society.[7] Historians do so mainly in large tempo-spatial scales. Their curiosity is with epochs and centuries and how conceptual transformations stand for representations of shifts in structures of meaning and subsequent political practice. Such studies, however, provide little insight about the practitioners and the practical situations in which they develop new concepts, an aspect that becomes more central in studies of contemporary concepts.

Discussions of contemporary concepts and short-term conceptual shifts can be identified primarily in two corners of the IR field, that is, first, critical security studies and their search for the meaning of the concept of security (see Strunin-Kremer, this volume), and, second, policy-oriented studies that are driven by the puzzle that policy practitioners continuously invent new concepts. One of the foundational problems of critical security studies was how to grasp the meaning of the concept of security. Arguing against equating security with realist understandings of national security, it was shown how the concept is broader and wider. A major starting point in the debate was the introduction of Walter Bryce Gallie's notion of essentially contested concepts.[8] Gallie contrasted conceptual confusion with conceptual contestation and argued that some concepts are normatively loaded to a degree that users strongly prefer a particular meaning (Collier, Hidalgo, and Maciuceanu 2006). In security studies, Gallie's work was translated into the argument that the concept of security could not have a determinate meaning and that striving for universal definition would hence be a rather unproductive quest. This in turn led to various perspectives and frameworks that set out to study how the concept of security is made, how it is used, and how it is filled with meaning.[9] The rich set of studies available in the meantime documents how political actors purposefully use the concept of security to pursue political objectives but also show that the concept is often filled with meaning through the routine work of experts and analysts.

In policy-oriented work, the starting point is usually different. Scholars are puzzled about the fact that many of the concepts thriving in policy discourse are ambiguous, indeterminate, or simply fuzzy.[10] These concepts moreover resisted the attempts to define and universalize them. While many scholars proceed to offer definitions of these concepts, or search their luck in quantification, another alternative is to engage in the mapping of meanings and the controversies and political interests that go along with it. Barnett et al. (2007), for instance, provide such a mapping for the concept of "peace building." They argue that "the concept's talents are to camouflage divisions over how to handle the postconflict challenge" and that it "can facilitate collective action because different constituencies can support the symbol without necessarily achieving consensus on the substance" (43). Des Gasper (2005) makes a similar case for the concept of human security: Its strength lies less in its explanatory or guiding power and more in its ability to connect people and discourses. Andrea Cornwall (Cornwall 2007; Cornwall and Brock 2005) makes similar arguments in development studies, analyzing concepts such as "participation" and "empowerment." She argues that these are "buzzwords" that have the capacity to mobilize resources. Following up on these works, Bueger and Bethke (2014) study the concept of the "failed state." Drawing on a practice theoretical framework, they demonstrate empirically how this concept led to the assembling of a large network of diverse actors that through their participation changed their identity. The study demonstrates how concepts become points of convergence for different collectives and enable cooperation and coordination among disparate actors.

Together these studies give us a rich understanding of the multiplicity of conceptual meaning that clearly shows that one of the functions of concepts lies in bringing heterogeneous actors together. Some of these studies risk producing a static picture. They provide a mapping of possible meanings rather than investigating processes of change and the actual use of concepts. Yet, we have to peer at the practical activities by which concepts are used and filled with meaning. If more and more attention has been paid to concept use, the full implications of the instrumentalist perspective are often not recognized. Concepts are tools used to respond to a problematic situation. Without grasping such situations, without studying how these vary and change over time and space, a study of concepts is incomplete.

In the following discussion, I intend to correct this omission. I offer a brief analysis of the rise of a recent concept. The concept of blue economy rose to prominence in the past decade. Its introduction substantially changes the understanding of the importance of the oceans in international politics. Yet, as my discussion shows, there is considerable variety in how the concept is used as a tool across different collectives and situations.

The Concept of Blue Economy

The case of the blue economy is remarkable. Within a very short time span, the concept has been adopted across the globe to revaluate the oceans as a source for economic development. As the World Wildlife Foundation (WWF 2015, 1) stated in a report from 2015: "During the past few years, the term 'Blue Economy' or 'Blue Growth' has surged into common policy usage, all over the world. . . . Despite increasing high-level adoption of the Blue Economy as a concept and as a goal of policy making and investment, there is still no widely accepted definition of the term." In the following discussion, I trace the concept of blue economy and explore the variety of meanings it entails.[11] My guiding question follows from the theoretical discussion: Which practice collectives use the concept of blue economy, how do they use it, and to which situation do they respond?

To answer the question, my research strategy was to follow the concept across different situations. Following the concept across time and space reveals some surprising twists and turns in the concept's life. My story starts with the formulation of blue economy in the so-called Pauli Report, one of the first references one finds. Next, I move to Brussels, where the European Commission further developed the concept to identify an industrial sector. Then I switch continents. I investigate how the blue economy has become a core concept advocated by the government of the Seychelles and shaped the discussion of the African Union's maritime policy.

My discussion draws on the textual analysis of documents published

until 2016 that contain the term "blue economy" or refer to it. I also draw
on a range of conversations with practitioners who have been using the
concept extensively in their work.[12] Such a methodological approach has
severe deficits, since a reconstruction of practices of concept use remains
very limited if it is only based on the interpretation of publicly available
texts.[13] The number of conversations with practitioners I can draw on
hardly offers a corrective. In consequence, my discussion remains on a relatively generic level and an aggregate scale and does not account for zoom-
ing in on concrete (everyday) practical situations, which a full-fledged
practice theoretical investigation would demand. My primary intention
is, however, to open up new ways for practice-based conceptual analysis
and to demonstrate how it allows us to reconstruct the life of concepts
differently. Table 1 provides a summary of the different sites, situations,
and meanings.

The Pauli Report

If one googled the term "blue economy" in 2015, three out of the first five
hits (of 415,000 total hits) would lead to a book titled *The Blue Economy:
10 Years, 100 Innovations, 100 Million Jobs*.[14] What a promise! Who would
not like this concept after reading the title? The book was published in
2010, authored by Gunter Pauli, and written as a report to the Club of
Rome. The two other top Google search results led to the Blue Economy

TABLE 1: The Blue Economy in use

Practical Configuration	Meaning	Use
Pauli Report	Sustainable business strategy	Draw attention for potential of sustainability as a business
Rio+20	Sustainable development of ocean resources	Attention for development concerns of maritime nations
Brussels	Aggregated economic sectors	Integrate economic sectors under EC leadership
Seychelles	Sustainable development strategy	Foreign policy tool to gain authority on world political stages
African Union	New economic sector and source for development	Regional integration, new referent for security policy

Foundation, established in 2015, which follows up on that report. According to Wikipedia (2015), Gunter Pauli "(born 1956 in Antwerp) is a self-styled 'serial entrepreneur,' author and initiator of *The Blue Economy*." *Le Point, The Huffington Post* and *The Tasmanian Times* have called him 'The Steve Jobs of Sustainability.'" According to the Blue Economy Foundation website, work on Pauli's book started in 2004 and was funded by the United Nations Environment Programme (UNEP).

"Blue economy" in the report refers to a business model that builds on a systemic approach and combines seemingly disparate environmental questions with scientific innovations to develop businesses that are beneficial to the environment, create wider social benefits, and promise financial revenues. Drawing attention to Pauli, his team, and the report is not an argument that he "invented" the concept of blue economy. Yet the book and the underlying project mark a moment in which the concept received wide international attention. What can be seen from the text of the report is that the blue economy yokes together elements of earlier concepts that are centrally the concept of a green economy. Attempting to summarize a new way of thinking about the importance of business models and their relation between sustainability, technical innovation, job creation, and international development, Pauli arguably was in search of a new color that could symbolize the switch in perspective. In the report, the color blue has no particular reference to the oceans, sea, or maritime. It was merely meant to be an alternative to green. The intention was to highlight that the planet, which requires protection, is a blue one.

Rio de Janeiro, Brazil

The year 2010 also saw the start of the preparation of the United Nation's Rio+20 conference on sustainable development. The process culminated in a ten-day mega event in June 2012 in Rio de Janeiro. The conference's closing document does not contain the term "blue economy," yet it refers to improving and identifying alternatives to the green economy. Part of the summit and its preparation process included, however, a series of discussions on the blue economy. In contrast to Pauli's concept centered on identifying new business models, the emphasis of the Rio+20 discussions was on the oceans and the sea. This different understanding is visible, for instance, in the title of a preparatory workshop that was organized in 2011:

"Building Ocean and Coastal Sustainability and Greening the Blue Economy."[15] Blue economy hence did not refer to an alternative to the green economy. Instead, it was seen as a distinct segment of the economy that needed to be "greened." At the event, the UN paper "Blueprint for Ocean and Coastal Sustainability" was discussed, which also argued that the blue economy had to be "greened." During the 2012 summit, "blue economy" became largely a term to refer to the ocean aspects of the Rio+20 theme of green economy in the context of sustainable development and poverty eradication. A side event chaired by the governments of Indonesia and Australia, and supported by the Small Island Developing States (SIDS) alliance, discussed blue economy during the summit. As the announcement of the event suggests:

> Around the world, there are a number of innovative efforts underway to achieve a Blue Economy. This event will involve a selection of key Blue Economy leaders showcasing their efforts to conserve and sustainably manage marine resources, and defining key commitments and actions for the future. . . . This event will focus on the issue of "Blue Economy" that is, the conservation and sustainable management of marine and coastal resources in support of sustainable development and poverty eradication. The event will showcase key examples from around the world of leadership towards achieving a Blue Economy.[16]

As an interlocutor observed from the summit discussions, blue economy was primarily used at the summit to refer to the ocean and the sea challenges, yet consistently there was also reference to Pauli's concept. In consequence, confusion abounded over the actual meaning of the concept. However, the concept primarily served the purpose at the summit to highlight the special needs of countries with large coastal zones, such as small island states. The Rio+20 summit soon became considered the birthplace of the concept of blue economy.[17] A 2015 UNEP report, for instance, argues:

> In the lead up to, and during Rio+20, coastal and island developing countries gave a definitive voice to the major role that oceans have to play in all of our futures. It was a discussion which initiated exploration of how concepts and objectives of a Green Economy

could be applied to the unique and irreplaceable role of marine and coastal ecosystems—i.e. the "Blue Economy." (UNEP 2015, 8)

Brussels, Belgium

In September 2012, three months after the Rio de Janeiro summit, the European Commission made a major contribution to defining the blue economy concept. Published and lead-authored by the Directorate-General for Maritime Affairs and Fisheries, the so-called blue growth strategy was meant to reorganize the work of the commission in the maritime domain and integrate the maritime work of the commission and member states under the header of economic growth (European Commission 2012). The strategy complemented the so-called Limassol Declaration, "A Marine and Maritime Agenda for Growth and Jobs," which was adopted on 8 October 2012 by European ministers for maritime policy and the European Commission. The blue growth strategy document contains a lengthy definition of blue economy. The European Commission defined the blue economy by listing different sectors that it sees as interdependent. These sectors include "coastal tourism, offshore oil and gas, deep sea shipping, short-sea shipping, yachting and marinas, passenger ferry services, cruise tourism, ferries, inland waterway transport, coastal protection, offshore wind, monitoring and surveillance, blue biotechnology, desalination, aggregates mining, marine aquatic products, marine mineral mining, [and] ocean renewable energies."

The redefinition that we can see here at work is an attempt to characterize "blue economy" as the descriptor of a reconfigured economic sector. Here the concept does not refer to a type of business model or a sustainability strategy. The intent of the European Commission was quite different. Using the concept of blue economy was first a homogenizing move; it allowed arguing that different types of industries hang together and are interdependent. Second, it allowed the commission to argue that if these industries are seen together, they have significant potential for economic growth of the continent. Developing a strategy for economic growth through emphasizing the connections between different maritime industries was hence the primary purpose of employing the concept. In contrast to the focus on sustainability of the Rio+20 discussion, the blue economy was a tool to identify and establish a new type of economic sector.

Victoria, Seychelles

The government of the Seychelles, a small island state in the Western Indian Ocean with a population of less than one hundred thousand, has become recognized over the years as a leading advocate of what it terms the "blue economy agenda." The government advocates for the concept internationally. According to a governmental document, a series of presentations on the blue economy agenda were given at events such as the 21st African Union Summit (May 2013), the Tokyo International Conference on African Development (June 2013), the 1st Indian Ocean Rim Association for Regional Cooperation Economic and Business Conference (July 2013), and a meeting on the African Integrated Maritime Strategy in the Seychelles (July 2013) (Seychelles 2014). In January 2014, the Seychelles organized a Blue Economy Summit as part of the Abu Dhabi Sustainability Week;[18] the University of the Seychelles launched a Blue Economy Research Institute in March 2014; the government formed a Ministry of Finance, Trade, and the Blue Economy; and presentations included an advocacy event at Chatham House in London (June 2014).[19]

During a conversation with a member of the Seychelles government in 2014, we discussed the concept of blue economy. My interlocutor suggested that parts of the government were not fully convinced about the blue economy agenda spearheaded by the president. As my interlocutor suggested, the concept was too fuzzy and sounded too centered on environmental and sustainability concerns rather than providing a guide to the policies of the island state. As he phrased it, "To make the blue economy useful, we have to define our own version of it." Quite substantial work went into defining the concept and the principles of the agenda. Drawing on an initial concept note drafted for the 2014 UN Conference on Small Island Development States (Seychelles 2014) and the series of speeches and presentations given, the president published a book titled *Rethinking the Oceans: Towards the Blue Economy* (Michel 2016). As the president argues in the book,

> [The blue economy] is clear in its meaning and easy to use, the allusion to colour draws one to the sea, while, in contrast a complicated scientific term would not. I was aware that this term was already in use in a different context, linked with a new business model based on "blue sky" thinking and environmental solutions, but my use

of the same words is quite different. . . . The meaning of the Blue Economy will become clearer the more that it is used, but for me a working definition is that it is about the sustainable use of the sea to meet human needs. To be successful, the concept must embrace environmental as well as economic interests. (Michel 2016, xvi)

The Seychelles version of the blue economy is fairly encompassing. In comparison to its use in the European Union, it is, however, much more centered on environmental concerns, the concept of sustainability, and the centrality of the oceans for development. As Michel's book outlines, blue economy became the central guide for the national policy of the island state. It, however, also became the core concept for its foreign policy. The Seychelles government uses the concept as a tool to access the world political stages. As the president phrased it:

We have taken every opportunity to meet and to make representations to larger countries and international bodies. Just as the Green Economy was previously introduced to the world agenda, we have set ourselves the parallel task of bringing forward the Blue Economy. We are being remarkably successful in doing so. As a result of our advocacy of the Blue Economy, Seychelles is being invited, more and more, to share our thoughts at international conferences and political meetings. The rest of the world wants to know more about the Blue Economy. (Michel 2016, xix)

As the president highlights in this passage, the country is ambitious and uses the concept as a tool to claim expertise in an area and to gain international attention for the micro state. The concept was, moreover, used as a tool to organize the diplomatic coalition of SIDS and place the Seychelles as its leader. According to the president, vast energy was spent "to urge other small island states to adopt the concept too" (Michel 2016, xix). The concept allowed the country to make an international appeal for funding of ocean work but also to act as a regional facilitator. As the minister of foreign affairs outlined at an event at Chatham House:

Most African developing states, and SIDS in particular, lack the technological capacity required to fully realize the benefits of the resources within their exclusive economic zones (EEZs). . . . international cooperation will be important for providing assistance to these states and strengthening their capacity for the effective management and utilization of their EEZs. It is also important for structured international cooperation to be developed, including mechanisms for the governance of sustainable development in waters beyond national jurisdiction. . . . the intention of Seychelles in promoting the blue economy is to engender a change in how oceans are perceived.`. . . there is a need to strengthen the capacity of countries with oceanic territory to better manage those spaces, as well as to promote international cooperation and the sharing of competencies, capacities and resources. (Chatham House 2015 4)

As can be seen in this passage, the blue economy serves the government as a tool to speak on behalf of other states, as well as to make an appeal for development aid and funding for capacity building projects. For the Seychelles, the blue economy is hence much more than a guide for industrial or environmental policy; it is a tool for foreign policy. The concept allows a micro state to be recognized as a lead country, to claim dedicated expertise in an area, and to act on the world political stage.[20] The political functions of the concept also come to the fore in our next situation, where the concept has been used by the African Union (AU) Commission as a tool for regional integration.

Addis Ababa, Ethiopia

As a 2015 report by the United Nations Economic Commission for Africa argues,

The AU plays a crucial role in developing and implementing the Blue Economy policy and strategy in the African region. Over the past decade, the African Union Commission (AUC) has built an enlarged Africa-wide consensus regarding the critical role that the Blue Economy could play in fostering structural transformation in Africa during the next decade. (UNECA 2015, 7)

Indeed, the concept of blue economy has visibly entered and influenced the work of the AUC and is used as a tool for what is termed an

"African renaissance." At the AU, the concept was significant when the commission started its work on an African Integrated Maritime Strategy (known as AIMS 2050). The strategy was developed in a series of events, including a dedicated blue economy event on the Seychelles in 2013. An example of the rationale with which the concept is used here is a keynote address by the chairperson of the AUC, H. E. Dr. Zuma, from 2013. She highlighted the importance of promoting Africa's blue economy and blue growth by stating:

> "To the Green Economy, we must add the Blue Economy, namely maritime resources and the all economy around the maritime industry," a sine qua non condition to Africa's true and meaningful renaissance that guarantees, protects and advances the socioeconomic interests of African populations. (African Union 2013)

The blue economy is in this situation, first of all, used for the distinct purposes of uniting Africa around a distinct theme and as a shared vision for the future. The understanding of blue economy developed within the AU was developed in the process of drafting two documents: AIMS 2050, adopted in 2014, and a follow-up legally binding charter signed at a summit in October 2016. As it is detailed in the AIMS 2050 document, "The overarching vision of the 2050 AIM Strategy is to foster increased wealth creation from Africa's oceans and seas by developing a sustainable thriving blue economy in *a secure* and environmentally sustainable manner" (African Union 2014, 11; emphasis added). Although the concept of blue economy is the core vision of the strategy, the document itself or its "Annex B: Definitions" does not define it. The document only lists and discusses a range of industrial sectors and associated development projects. Notably, in the document the concept gets a distinct twist: it is linked to security concerns. As the vision statement already reveals, the blue economy is an object that needs to be "secured." The link to maritime security marks a core difference to other understandings of the concept. The AIMS 2050 document argues for the importance of recognizing "the backdrop of insecurity" (African Union 2014, 7). The strategy also directly identifies a range of threats. As is argued in the strategy, there is

> a broad array of real and potential threats that could result in mass casualties and inflict catastrophic economic harm to African States.

In addition to loss of revenue, they could fuel violence and insecurity. Some of them, such as drug trafficking, could feed corruption, finance the purchase of illegal weapons, corrupt the youth, pervert democracy/rule of law, distort economies and destabilize communal life. As the actors threatening Africa's maritime domain continue to grow in number and capability, there must be a corresponding African endeavour to address these at the national, regional and continental levels.

If the main emphasis of the AIMS 2050 document remains on economic dimensions, then the fact that the blue economy is understood as a security concern becomes even more forcefully visible in the charter the AU negotiated in 2016. The charter was understood to further advance AIMS 2050 and to add legal force to it. Remarkably, it is titled *African Charter on Maritime Security and Safety and Development in Africa* (African Union 2016). As one of my interlocutors involved in drafting the charter revealed in October 2016, in the negotiation of the charter the concept of blue economy was substantially contested. The debate concerned how blue economy should be defined and whether it should refer to national economies or it projects a shared and integrated African economic space. The latter understanding raised substantial concerns over national sovereignty. This contestation is visible in the document, since it speaks continuously of a "Blue/Ocean Economy." During the negotiations it was decided to solve the issue by negotiating an annex that would define the concept.

In summary, within the AU debate, the blue economy, first, is used as a tool for regional integration. The contestation in negotiating a legally binding charter, however, reveals that by 2016 this attempt had not fully succeeded. Second, and as a major difference to the other understandings of the concept, it is used as a means to speak about maritime security and raise awareness for the economic gains that attention to reducing insecurity at sea promises. The (African) blue economy becomes a reference object of security.

Conclusion

Concepts are important for the creation of social order. As Kratochwil (2006, 25) reminds us, "Concepts are not simple descriptions of observed 'patterns of behaviour' but are a result of agreement on values"; "concepts do their work not via the 'representation' or accurate description of an external reality but are 'productive' of the social world, by always being part of a 'project.'"

My empirical discussion revealed several such projects. The initial project of the Pauli Report was to reinvigorate business models based on sustainability, and blue economy was merely a label that could replace the notion of green economy. On the international stages, we could observe quite different projects. The projects share that they intend to raise awareness for the importance of the sea. While this indicates a shift in how the oceans and its resources are recognized in global politics, by looking closer at the ways the concept of blue economy was employed as a practical tool in concrete situations, we were able to get a better understanding of the variety of political projects actually pursued. For the European Commission, the blue economy was a tool to establish a new type of industrial sector and to argue for the importance of European political integration led by the commission to grow that sector. For the Seychelles, a primary advocate of the concept, blue economy became a tool to act as a global player. It allowed a "micro state" to considerably influence regional and international agendas by claiming expertise but also by rallying the group of SIDS behind their cause. In the context of the AU, the concept was used to strengthen regional integration but also to convince states to recognize the importance of maritime security. The study of blue economy confirms the insight from earlier conceptual analyses that new concepts are invented to bring heterogeneous actors together. Yet, investigating different collectives and situations reveals that this includes very different political projects.

Blue economy is a fascinating case of a contemporary concept, and studying its use leads to some interesting twists and turns in the concept's meaning and appropriation. As I have shown, actors employed the concept for very different purposes in response to problematic situations. Concepts provide temporarily stable fixations of meaning (Ish-Shalom, this volume). Efforts of definition, operationalization, and measurement are political projects. Following concepts across sites shows how the meaning of a concept is dependent on communities of users and their attempts to use them as tools in response to practical situations.

Although concepts are part of the core furniture of international relations, they have not regularly become objects of research, in particular if compared to entities such as "norms" or "ideas." The practice-based understanding of concepts, sketched out in this chapter, as well as the other contributions to this volume document that concept analysis provides a promising gateway to the understanding of contemporary global politics and its shifts. To reconsider concept in such a way implies to give up the quest for universal definitions of the meaning of concepts or even to measure their content and instead treat them as fascinating empirical objects to be studied in their own right. Finally, such forms of concept analysis also have considerable practical value and allow intervention in public policy debates. Policy makers struggle with the meaning of concepts and their ambiguous character. As scholars, we can point out the different meanings of a concept and document how they are part of political projects. We can contribute to a more enlightened use of these concepts and what they foreground and silence.

Acknowledgments

Research for this chapter benefited from a grant by the Economic and Social Research Council (ES/S008810/1) and the Danish Ministry of Foreign Affairs under the AMARIS project administered by the DANIDA fellowship center. For comments and suggestions on earlier drafts, I am grateful to Piki Ish-Shalom, Tim Edmunds, Jan Stockbruegger, the anonymous reviewers, and the participants at the workshop in Jerusalem that gave birth to this volume.

Notes

1. For outlines of the practice theoretical perspective in more general terms, see Adler and Pouliot (2011) and Bueger and Gadinger (2018).

2. The work of Giovanni Sartori is exemplary for such a perspective; see Gerring (2001) for further discussion.

3. See Fierke (2002) for a reconstruction of the career of the linguistic turn in IR. Kratochwil (2007) provides a useful summary from a philosophy of science perspective.

4. See Fierke (2002) and Grimmel and Hellmann (2019) for such a reconstruction.

5. For the interpretations of Dewey and Wittgenstein that I draw on in the following, see Stern (2002); Hickman (1990); and Schatzki 1996.

6. Compare Hickman (1990).

7. See, among others, Bartelson (1995, 2009) and Schmidt (1998), as well as Mitrani, this volume.

8. See Baldwin (1997) and Ish-Shalom, this volume.

9. Of which securitization theory and which security as practice approach are the most developed, see Stritzel (2007); Balzacq et al. (2010); Bueger (2016).

10. See Ish-Shalom; Steele and Campbell; Geis; Beaulieu-Brossard; and Strunin-Kremer, all this volume.

11. For related attempts to reconstruct the history and multiplicity of meaning of the concept of blue economy, see Voyer, Quirk, et al. (2018); Voyer, Schofield, et al. (2018b); Childs and Hicks (2019); Winder and Le Heron (2017).

12. I met interlocutors in Tanzania, Nairobi, Addis Ababa, Brussels, and Victoria between 2013 and 2016 in the frame of several field visits. References to such conversations are based on field notes written by the author.

13. See the methodological discussion in Bueger (2014).

14. Numbers were accurate as of 15 August 2015.

15. See more at http://www.uncsd2012.org/index.php?page=view&nr=423&type=13&menu=27#sthash.V2qsB027.dpuf.

16. See http://www.uncsd2012.org/index.php?page=view&nr=330&type=1000&menu=126#sthash.zoLVeONG.dpuf.

17. However, this is not uncontested, as some actors continue to refer to the Pauli Report as origin. See, for instance, the Indian Ocean Rim Association (2016).

18. See http://www.sids2014.org/index.php?page=view&type=13&nr=59&menu=1515.

19. See Chatham House (2015).

20. For a more extended analysis of how the blue economy is part of the Seychelles foreign policy strategy, see Bueger and Wivel (2018).

References

Adler, Emanuel, and Vincent Pouliot. 2011. "Introduction and Framework." In *International Practices*, ed. Emanuel Adler and Vincent Pouliot, 3–35. Cambridge: Cambridge University Press.

African Union. 2013. *2013 Mo Ibrahim Foundation Forum: The Chairperson of The African Union Commission Highlights the Importance of African Blue Economy.* Accessed 10 September 2016. http://pages.au.int/maritime/events/2013-mo-ibrahim-foundation-forum-chairperson-african-union-commission-highlights-importance-african-blue-economy

African Union. 2014. *2050 African Integrated Maritime Strategy.* Addis Ababa: African Union.

African Union. 2016. *African Charter on Maritime Security and Safety and Development in Africa (Lome Charter).* Addis Ababa: African Union.

Baldwin, David A. 1997. "The Concept of Security." *Review of International Studies* 23 (1): 5–26.

Balzacq, Thierry, et al. 2010. "Security Practices." In *International Studies Encyclopedia Online*, ed. Robert A Denemark. Storrs, CT: International Studies Association.

Barnett, Michael N., et al. 2007. "Peacebuilding: What Is in a Name?" In *Global Governance: A Review of Multilateralism and International Organizations* 13 (1): 35–58.

Bartelson, Jens. 1995. *A Genealogy of Sovereignty.* Cambridge: Cambridge University Press.

Bartelson, Jens. 2009. "Is There a Global Society?" *International Political Sociology* 3 (1): 112–15.

Bueger, Christian. 2014. Pathways to Practice. Praxiography and International Politics, In *European Political Science Review* 6(3): 383–406.

Bueger, Christian. 2016. "Security as Practice." In *Handbook of Security Studies*, 2nd ed., ed. Thierry Balzacq and Myriam Dunn Cavelty, 126–35. London: Routledge.

Bueger, Christian, and Felix Bethke. 2014. "Actor-Networking the 'Failed State'—An Enquiry into the Life of Concepts." *Journal of International Relations and Development* 17 (1): 30–60.

Bueger, Christian, and Frank Gadinger. 2018. *International Practice Theory, 2nd edition*. Houndmills, Basingstoke: Palgrave Macmillan.

Bueger, Christian, and Anders Wivel. 2018. "How Do Small Island States Maximize Influence? Creole Diplomacy and the Smart State Foreign Policy of the Seychelles." *Journal of the Indian Ocean Region* 14 (2): 170–88.

Chatham House. 2015. "The Blue Economy: Seychelles' Vision for Sustainable Development in the Indian Ocean." Accessed 10 September 2016. https://www.chathamhouse.org/sites/files/chathamhouse/field/field_document/20140611BlueEconomy.pdf

Childs, John R., and Christina C. Hicks. 2019. "Securing the Blue: Political Ecologies of the Blue Economy in Africa." *Journal of Political Ecology* 26 (1): 323–40.

Collier, David, Fernando Daniel Hidalgo, and Andra Olivia Maciuceanu. 2006. "Essentially Contested Concepts: Debates and Applications." *Journal of Political Ideologies* 11 (3): 211–46.

Cornwall, Andrea. 2007. "Buzzwords and Fuzzwords: Deconstructing Development Discourse." *Development in Practice* 17 (4): 471–84.

Cornwall, Andrea, and Karen Brock. 2005. "What Do Buzzwords Do for Development Policy? A Critical Look at 'Participation,' 'Empowerment' and 'Poverty Reduction.'" *Third World Quarterly* 26 (7): 1043–60.

European Commission. 2012. "Blue Growth Opportunities for Marine and Maritime Sustainable Growth Brussels." *Communication from the Commission to The European Parliament, The Council, The European Economic and Social Committee and the Committee of the Regions*. 13 September, COM(2012) 494. Brussels: European Commission.

Fierke, Karin M. 2002. "Links across the Abyss: Language and Logic in International Relations." *International Studies Quarterly* 46 (3): 331–54.

Gasper, Des. 2005. "Securing Humanity: Situating 'Human Security' as Concept and Discourse." *Journal of Human Development* 6 (2): 221–45.

Gerring, John. 2001. *Social Science Methodology: A Critical Framework*. Cambridge: Cambridge University Press.

Grimmel, Andreas, and Gunther Hellmann. 2019. "Theory Must Not Go on Holiday. Wittgenstein, the Pragmatists, and the Idea of Social Science." *International Political Sociology* 13 (2): 198–214.

Hickman, Larry A. 1990. *John Dewey's Pragmatic Technology*. Bloomington: Indiana University Press.

Indian Ocean Rim Association 2016. *Blue Economy*. IORA. Accessed 16 September 2016. http://www.iora.net/blue-economy/blue-economy.aspx

Kratochwil, Friedrich. 2006. "History, Action and Identity: Revisiting the 'Second' Great Debate and Assessing Its Importance for Social Theory." *European Journal of International Relations* 12 (1): 5–29.

Kratochwil, Friedrich. 2007. "Evidence, Inference, and Truth as Problems of Theory Building in the Social Sciences." In *Theory and Evidence in Comparative Politics and International Relations*, ed. Richard Ned Lebow and Mark Irving Lichbach, 25–54. Houndmills, Basingstoke: Palgrave Macmillan.

Michel, James Alix. 2016. *Rethinking the Oceans: Towards the Blue Economy.* St. Paul, MN: Paragon House

Schatzki, Theodore R. 1996. *Social Practices: A Wittgensteinian Approach to Human Activity and the Social.* Cambridge: Cambridge University Press.

Schmidt, Brian. 1998. *The Political Discourse of Anarchy: A Disciplinary History of International Relations.* Albany: State University of New York Press.

Seychelles 2014. *Blue Economy Concept Paper.* Accessed 3 April 2015. http://www.sids2014.org/content/documents/275BEconcept.pdf

Stern, David G. 2002. "The Practical Turn." In *The Blackwell Guide to the Philosophy of the Social Sciences*, ed. Stephen P. Turner and Paul A. Roth, 185–206. Malden, MA: Blackwell.

Stritzel, Holger. 2007. "Towards a Theory of Securitization: Copenhagen and Beyond." *European Journal of International Relations* 13 (3): 357–83.

United Nations Economic Commission for Africa (UNECA). 2015. *Africa's Blue Economy: A Policy Handbook.* Addis Ababa: Economic Commission for Africa.

United Nations Environmental Programme (UNEP). 2015. *Blue Economy: Sharing Success Stories to Inspire Change.* UNEP Regional Seas Report and Studies no. 195. Accessed 16 September 2016. http://www.unep.org/ecosystemmanagement/water/regionalseas40/Portals/50221/BlueEconomy_SSSIC_screen_rev.pdf

Voyer, Michelle, Genevieve Quirk, Alistair McIlgorm, and Kamal Azmi. 2018. "Shades of Blue: What Do Competing Interpretations of the Blue Economy Mean for Oceans Governance?" *Journal of Environmental Policy and Planning* 20 (5): 595–616.

Voyer, Michelle, Clive Schofield, Kamal Azmi, Robin, Warner, Alistair McIlgorm, and Genevieve Quirk. 2018. "Maritime Security and the Blue Economy: Intersections and Interdependencies in the Indian Ocean." *Journal of the Indian Ocean Region* 14 (1): 28–48.

Wikipedia. 2015. "Gunter Pauli." Accessed 5 June 2015. https://en.wikipedia.org/wiki/Gunter_Pauli

Winder, Gordon M., and Richard Le Heron. 2017. "Assembling a Blue Economy Moment? Geographic Engagement with Globalizing Biological-Economic Relations in Multi-Use Marine Environments." *Dialogues in Human Geography* 7 (1): 3–26.

World Wildlife Foundation (WWF). 2015. *Principles for a Sustainable Blue Economy.* Report of the WWF Baltic Ecoregion Programme. Accessed 16 September 2016. http://wwf.panda.org/wwf_news/?247477/Principles-for-a-Sustainable-Blue-Economy

CHAPTER 8

Enabling Critique

The Use of "Friendship" in German-Israeli Relations

Felix Berenskötter

This chapter explores how the concept of friendship is used in German-Israeli relations to justify critique. Specifically, it looks at how German intellectuals, members of the government, and media commentators employ the concept to frame and, I suggest, enable critique of Israeli policies and practices. I am not aware of a study exploring this phenomenon, either in the particular case at hand or more generally. Apart from studies on "naming and shaming" (e.g., Hafner-Burton 2008), the scholarly literature has not paid much attention to the practice of critique in foreign policy and international relations. Recent work on friendship has analyzed the causes and consequences of tensions between close allies (Berenskötter and Giegerich 2010; Eznack 2011), and overviews of German-Israeli relations always include descriptions of disagreement (Gardner Feldman 1984; Weingardt 2002; Wittstock 2016), but none of these focus their analysis on the issue of critique.

Relations between Germany and Israel provide an intriguing setting for such an analysis. Both states emerged after World War II and have the memory of the Holocaust burned into their respective national biographies and into the structure of their relationship (see Geis, this volume). Since the establishment of diplomatic relations in May 1965, Germany and Israel have undergone an impressive process of reconciliation, and their close and positive relations were showcased during the "jubilee" in

2015. German government officials, especially, speak emphatically of a close "friendship" between Israel and Germany.[1] At the same time, deep-seated disagreements exist regarding the legitimate borders of Israel, its policies and practices toward Palestinians, and the viability of a "two-state solution." Despite Angela Merkel's strong pro-Israeli stance—she has been described as the most pro-Israeli chancellor in German history (Dempsey 2010)—observers have noted significant tensions in the relationship over these issues (Strenger 2012; Ravid 2014; Economist 2015; *Der Spiegel* 2016). However, the shadow cast by the memory of the Holocaust and associated perpetrator/victim roles make it difficult for German politicians and public intellectuals to openly voice critique of Israeli policies, especially when they concern issues that Israel considers central to its national security. Simply put, how can representatives of the German state and German society criticize Israeli policies and practices without their voices being dismissed as inappropriate and anti-Semitic? The answer put forward in this chapter is that they purposefully employ the concept of friendship to frame their critique of Israeli policies and practices. The basic argument is that this frame plays a crucial role in making critique possible—it has an enabling function (see Strunin-Kremer, this volume). In fact, it makes critique a duty. Methodologically, I advance this argument through an approach that emphasizes the constitutive power of language and relies on a logic that reads critique among friends as a *Freundschaftsdienst*, an act of friendship done out of concern or care for the other.

The chapter focuses on how the concept of friendship is employed by German intellectuals and politicians over a period of five years (2012–17) to enable critique of Israeli policies and practices in three issue areas: possible military action against Iran, settlements in the occupied territories, and the stigmatization of left-wing nongovernmental organizations (NGOs). While language can be indicative of identity, this analysis is primarily concerned with tracing how the friendship frame is used in these contexts. That is, it understands language to be performative but does not try to explore whether bilateral relations between Germany and Israel actually constitute a friendship. With that in mind, the discussion proceeds as follows: after outlining the "special" context of the empirical case and the methodological approach, the main part presents the empirical analysis of German critique of Israeli practices on three topics: Iran, settlements, and NGOs. The conclusion wraps up.

Critique in the Shadow of the Holocaust

Relations between Germany and Israel were born and remain in the shadow of the Holocaust. The memory of the Holocaust is recognized on both sides as the foundation of the relationship, as the element that makes German-Israeli relations "special." As German chancellor Angela Merkel put it in her first speech to the Knesset in 2008: "Germany and Israel are and will always remain linked in a special way by the memory of the Shoah" (Merkel 2008). This, and the joint commitment to keeping this memory alive, means that the historical roles of victim (Israel) and perpetrator (Germany) remain part of the relationship. Still, observers and political leaders on both sides have noted that German-Israeli relations have undergone a remarkable process of rapprochement, if not reconciliation. Central to this process is the German government's acceptance of the state's historical responsibility for the systematic mass murder of six million Jews, accompanied by a "nonnegotiable" commitment for the security of Israel. German governments have underlined this through financial and military support of Israel since the 1950s, as well as solidarity in the diplomatic arena (Gardner Feldman 2012, chap. 4; Weingardt 2002; Wittstock 2016).

Yet, critical attitudes in Germany toward Israel have been on the rise since the late 1970s (Wolffsohn 1988, 84; Oz 2005, 46; Stein 2011, 62ff). The militarization of Israel's state[2] and society and the occupation of Palestinian land deemed illegal under international law are difficult to reconcile with the pacifist identity of the "new" Germany and its status as a "civilian power," creating a normative dissonance between the two.[3] Dissonance does not necessarily generate criticism. As understood in this chapter, critique (or criticism) starts with disagreement between A and B but goes beyond that; it involves A saying to B, "I think you are (doing this) wrong" and, adding a constructive component, "I think you should do things differently." When critique is voiced, the question is not so much whether it is justified or valid, as content and premises can always be contested, but who expresses it, how, and why. The actions of B may be open to critique by a variety of actors in international society who think that B has violated an agreed logic of appropriateness. What matters, however, is A's identity and intention(s), especially how they are formed and conveyed in relation to B. Thus, critique is understood here as a phenomenon expressed in a particular relationship, and its political nature and effect depend on the character of this relationship.

Given the historical context, German critique of Israeli practices is highly sensitive terrain, and the questions of whether, to what extent, and how Germans can or should voice criticism toward Israel have been subject to repeated discussions in the public and political discourse. The perennial problem is that critique can drift into an undifferentiated anti-Israel stance grounded in stereotypes and, ultimately, anti-Semitism. And telling these apart is not always straightforward. In fact, voicing "valid critique" can be used to hide anti-Semitism, just as accusing someone of the latter can be used to silence critique (what is known in Germany as "swinging the Holocaust club"). And notwithstanding necessary and often sound efforts to establish clear criteria to distinguish between the two, drawing the line between "valid critique" of Israeli policies and anti-Semitism is also, unfortunately, a political act. Thus, while officials both in Germany and in Israel hold that it is legitimate and acceptable for Germans to voice factual (*sachliche*) critique of Israeli policies and practices (Stein 2011, 64; Author's interviews), it is equally clear that doing so always occurs against the backdrop of history and the continuous presence of anti-Semitism (Baumann and Meggle 2009, 275; TAZ 2012; Stein and Zimmermann 2017; Posener 2017). Prior to the interventions discussed below, the most prominent example in post-1990 Germany's political discourse was the debate in 2002 over statements by the politician Jürgen Möllemann (Free Democratic Party), whose criticism of then prime minister Ariel Sharon caused great domestic controversy and continues to haunt his party (*Frankfurter Allgemeine Zeitung* 2002; *Die Zeit* 2009; *Frankfurter Allgemeine Zeitung* 2012a). Thus, policy makers and diplomats are very careful what they say when it comes to expressing disagreements with Israel out of concern that statements may be construed or perceived as anti-Israeli or anti-Semitic.[4] The headline given to a 2017 interview with the outgoing Israeli ambassador to Germany conveys this cautionary stance: "Mr. Ambassador, How Does One Criticize Israel—and How Not?" (*Euronews* 2017).

Generally speaking, there are three ways, or steps, of practicing critique in international relations. The first is to voice disagreement behind closed doors and restrict any critique to a "private" setting. The second is a consequential act in public, such as canceling meetings and withholding support without explicitly referring to the disagreement though assuming that the message is understood on the other side. The third step is to voice disagreement and express criticism openly through public speeches, interviews, or press conferences. When German officials have expressed disagreement with Israeli policies in the past they usually have chosen the first and, at times, the second option. According to German diplomats interviewed, conversations with Israeli counterparts in private or confidential settings tend to be open and frank.[5] Yet despite the government's commitment to avoid open confrontation, its willingness to criticize the Israeli government in public has increased in recent years. In fact, and somewhat in contrast to the aforementioned caution, among diplomats there is now a sense that voicing disagreements and critique is "normal." As the German ambassador to Israel noted in 2015 while visiting an exhibition on the shared history of diplomatic relations:

> Naturally we also have different views [*Auffassungen*], and it is completely normal that we express these views; this criticism . . . is possible without problem *because it is carried by mutual solidarity*. For us the limit of critique clearly is that Israel's existence cannot be questioned and that the border to anti-Semitism can never be crossed.[6] (emphasis added)

This chapter probes the ambassador's suggestion that critique is made possible on the basis of friendship, gestured here in terms of "mutual solidarity." While the use of friendship language by German officials has become quite common when publicly addressing Israeli audiences, I argue that it takes on a particularly important function in instances of critique because it automatically rules out anti-Semitic motivation. In fact, it renders critique an act of solidarity. To illuminate this, the next section takes a closer look at how friendship relates to the practice of critique and outlines the logic that makes criticism a *Freundschaftsdienst*.

Approach and Framework

The analytical approach employed in this chapter is informed by the general insight that language matters in international relations. The "linguistic turn" in the social sciences has brought attention to the fact that language not merely is a means of communication but frames (social) reality and gives it meaning. As such, it also has a constitutive effect on how we relate to the world and to others. Frames provide an interpretation of something by placing it in a particular meaning context. It is a tool for speakers to influence not only what the audience sees and hears but also how a statement is being understood. Concepts are such frames that gain their meaning in part from their place in a "semantic field," loosely understood as a group of terms and symbols—a web of associated concepts—that relate to each other in a particular linguistic structure. Yet to understand how concepts gain meaning and how they work, we need to look beyond the purely semantic context. This is especially the case for "basic concepts" (*Grundbegriffe*), which, following Reinhart Koselleck, are fundamental features of a sociopolitical system. They are terms with a prominent place in a political discourse, and analysts trying to grasp their meaning and effect must pay attention to how they are used and understood within a particular sociopolitical environment and with what consequences.[7] Whereas some frames have become so dominant that they are taken for granted in everyday life,[8] others come into play when meanings are not settled. In the latter instance, a frame, or basic concept, is mobilized deliberately to advance one particular reading of an act, and the motivation behind it, instead of another. This is by no means an academic insight. Political practitioners are well aware that language matters, that certain words are used (or not used) to convey a particular message, and that the way state representatives talk to each other, in public and in private, has an impact on their relationship. And German and Israeli diplomats affirm that, in this bilateral relationship, especially, officials choose their words very carefully and pay close attention to what the other side is saying (Author's interviews; Stein 2011, 13).

Against this backdrop, this chapter takes the view that friendship language is employed purposefully in public and private encounters between political leaders and when engaging domestic audiences. In fact, a basic concept like "friendship" can be integral to the interaction between political actors and to the social contract between the political communities they represent. As Evgeny Roshchin (2017) has shown, friendship discourses can be used to frame and facilitate legal contracts and cooperative agreements, indeed, to constitute agreements between two parties; they can order relations among them and create a connection not limited to and exceeding formal ties and treaties. This is because, as Piki Ish-Shalom writes in the introduction to this volume, a basic concept is infused with a range of normative commitments and guides political action. Thus, consistent and emphatic use of friendship language is not simply a generic diplomatic trope. While the ontology of friendship cannot be reduced to language, the use of the concept directs attention to all the aspects that make such a relationship meaningful—trust, honesty, solidarity, and so on. It mobilizes these associations and attaches them to the practices in the context of which the concept is employed. This is particularly relevant if the practice is critique.

Because friends care about each other and their friendship,[9] they support one other. One central feature of this is solidarity, or loyalty—namely, standing by the friend's side and lending support in times of need—expressed not only in words but also in deed, that is, through material contribution. Practices of solidarity or loyalty can take many forms, all the way to self-sacrifice, and because they usually are costly, they cannot be explained solely with instrumental security or economic interests. At the same time, because solidarity or loyalty is integral to the ontology of friendship, such practices also are not expressions of altruism. That is, they are not simply an instance of "Other-help" (Wendt) but an affirmation of, and investment in, the friendship and a contribution to the shared project. At the same time, solidarity among friends is not about blind agreement. Indeed, friends' care for each other may also result in and, indeed, *require* criticism of the friend's views and/or actions, if they think that these views or actions are misguided and harmful to the friend and to the shared project. Because such critique is grounded in sympathy and care, it also is a form of support, even loyalty.

The reasoning behind this claim is grounded in the Aristotelian reading of true friendship as "the friendship of good people similar in virtue" (Aristotle 1999, Book VIII, 1, 2, 3), which broadly speaking is about finding an intermediate between excess and deficiency, about expressing feelings and acting in an appropriate and measured way (Book II, 6). Virtuous behavior, then, is understood as pursuing the "right" ends and employing the "right" means. Importantly, for Aristotle, virtue is not a fixed property or acquired naturally but, rather, obtained primarily through activity with friends. That is, friends not only choose each other on the basis of a shared "sense of . . . commitment and ends, and a sense of what we take to be ultimately good"; they also develop their moral capacities together over time. From this perspective, "the virtuous agent continues to grow, and . . . friendship is the most congenial context for such moral growth" (Sherman

1993 97–99). This reading of friends contributing to each other's moral growth highlights friendship as a creative or productive relationship. One central aspect of this is that friends learn from each other by honestly sharing their respective views, experiences, and concerns, by listening to and working through them together. This is expressed in friends giving counsel and providing privileged access to private information, considerations, and motivation that are closed off to others. They draw on each other for advice and confide in each other, offering insights into the "real" reasons for doing something, which are not revealed to others. And when their views differ, friends not only "respect and take an interest in one another's perspectives" (Friedman 1993, 189) but also are open to adjusting their views accordingly and recognizing the productive benefits that arise from doing so.

In their commitment to share and contribute to each other's "good life," friends do not want to see the other being harmed or undertaking harmful actions, understood in both a moral and a physical sense. As a generator of the moral space in and through which both sides unfold, friends also have the unique task or role to serve as "moral witnesses" to each other. So if friend A acts in ways that friend B considers morally wrong, or that B thinks will cause physical harm to A, then it is B's duty to intervene and attempt to keep A from undertaking that action. To be sure, friends expect sympathy and empathy, or "epistemic partiality" (Stroud 2006), from each other. That is, in the words of Simon Keller (2007, 31), friends should expect from each other to "make a special effort to see value in your friends' project before you decide (and say) that you think them misguided." But once B believes that A is about to make a great mistake, that A's thinking or behavior is fundamentally misguided, B must voice disapproval in an attempt to "save the friend from themselves" and bring them back to the right path.[10] In such a case, the friend not only is allowed but is expected to voice critique. One might even say that it is the friend's duty. Conversely, the recipient—the friend being criticized—can be expected to be open to the friend's view and listen to criticism. After all, friends are not looking for pretended approval but want the friend to be honest and their support to be genuine. Rather than a sign of distancing, critique motivated by goodwill or care for the other, then, is still about siding with the friend and, as such, a form of loyalty. It is not just an attempt to protect or save one's friend "from oneself" but also an investment in the friendship. In short, critique from a friend is a *Freundschaftsdienst*.

Empirical Discussion

Having laid out my approach, the remainder of the chapter examines how powerful German voices—intellectuals, government officials, and media outlets—employ the concept of friendship when criticizing Israeli policies or practices in public with regard to three issue areas: (1) military action against Lebanon and Iran, (2) settlements in the occupied territories, and (3) the stigmatization of particular NGOs. The speakers chosen here are recognized as authorities or formal representatives of the state and/or society and are aware that they speak from that position; hence, their words are more than private expressions of individuals.[11] That said, the analysis does not treat them as reifications of the state or society and also conveys some of the pluralism that exists within the political discourse.

Critique I: Military Action

In November 2006, a programmatic text entitled "Friendship and Critique: Why the 'Special Relationship' between Germany and Israel Needs to Be Rethought," signed by a group of twenty-five German academics,[12] was published in the German newspaper *Frankfurter Rundschau* ("Manifest der 25" 2006). The "manifesto" was written in the wake of Israel's war with Lebanon a few months earlier, in July and August 2006, and grappled with how a German government committed to supporting Israel's existence, as well as to fighting anti-Semitism, should react when the Israeli government undertakes disproportionate military action. The authors did not simply cite a dissonance with pacifist principles but noted concern with what they saw as potentially "catastrophic worldwide consequences" of such action in two ways: first, the risk of escalation into a wider war in the region that also involves the United States and Iran, feeding the antagonistic identities underpinning the "war on terror," which, second, would exacerbate a rift in the German public between supporters and critics of Israel and fuel anti-Semitic attitudes. The underlying message thus was that the military operation in Lebanon was counterproductive for creating a more secure environment for Israel and for Jews more generally. Arguing that Germany bears a historical responsibility for the well-being of not only Jews but also the Palestinian people, the manifesto suggested that the German government should do more to solve the Israeli-Palestinian conflict, including by scrutinizing the German provision of arms to Israel and taking a more critical attitude toward Israeli military practices ("Manifest der 25" 2006; see also Baumann and Meggle 2009).

As signaled by the title, these arguments were made through the friendship frame. The manifesto starts with a statement by Israeli foreign minister Zipi Liwni during her visit to Berlin on 31 August 2006, in which she characterized German-Israeli relations as "special and friendly." Noting that friendship between political collectives is possible, the authors emphasized that "a sustainable friendship" is characterized by trying to prevent the other from making mistakes out of care for each other's well-being, "even more so when much is at stake for both sides" ("Manifest der 25" 2006, 1). The authors did not seem to be convinced that such a friendship existed between Germany and Israel. Instead, the manifesto diagnosed a "problematic Philo-Semitism" among German elites that in combination with "unspoken prohibition of open criticism of Israeli decisions . . . strengthens anti-Semitism in Germany rather than weakens it." Against this, the manifesto argued that it would be an advantage for both sides to develop a friendship that is able to withstand stress (*belastungsfähige Freundschaft*) and "in which critique intended to be supportive, not derogatory, has its place" ("Manifest der 25" 2006, 1–2).

While the twenty-five signatories did not explicitly declare themselves friends of Israel in the text, the framing implies that the manifesto was written and should be understood in this spirit. The importance of this frame showed in the debate that ensued.[13] Next to discussions about factual claims and logics, the most stinging critique of the manifesto questioned the sincerity of the friendship frame. Micha Brumlik in his, at times, polemic response in the *Frankfurter Rundschau* called the signatories' affirmations of friendship towards the state of Israel "unbearable" and a "new German responsibility imperialism", adding "with friends like that, [Israel/Jews] do not need enemies" (2007). The implied suggestion that the friendship frame was used instrumentally was vehemently rejected by the authors of the manifesto, who emphasized their genuine concern for Israel and the Jewish people and their commitment to German-Israeli friend-ship, pointing to their efforts of engaging in constructive dialogue with critics and their willingness to acknowledge weaknesses in their text and to learn.[14]

The debate reappeared in a slightly different and more prominent form six years later. In April 2012 the *Süddeutsche Zeitung* published on its front page a poem by Günter Grass, winner of the Nobel Prize for literature and at the time one of Germany's most respected living novelists, entitled "What Must Be Said" ("Was gesagt werden muss").[15] The poem critically addressed the possibility of an Israeli attack on Iran's nuclear facilities and warned about Germany's role in this configuration. Specifically, Grass claimed that by playing with the idea of a preemptive military strike on Iran, Israel was endangering "world peace." And he criticized a Western double standard in quietly tolerating Israel's nuclear arsenal while disallowing it to other states in the region. His main target was the silence (or so he claimed) in Germany over these issues, which he argued was sustained by historical guilt that generated a felt obliga-tion to unconditionally support Israel and to avoid critique as not to be accused of anti-Semitism. Grass warned that because Germany supplied Israel with submarines capable of launching nuclear warheads, an Israeli attack on Iran would make Germany complicit in a crime. The poem concluded with a call for countering Israeli plans to attack Iran and to place both Israeli and Iranian nuclear potential under international con-trol regimes (Grass 2012; *Guardian* 2012).

While Grass gave the poem a personal tone, it was clear that he saw himself speaking as a public intellectual. Yet although he was not alone in voicing concern about a possible Israeli attack on Iran,[16] the poem caused an intense debate in Germany and received strong reactions from some Israeli officials. Most of the responses condemned the poem's con-tent, its form, the author, and his intentions. Grass was accused of anti-Semitism and an anti-Israeli sentiment (*Süddeutsche Zeitung* 2012a; Joffe 2012; Brumlik 2012; Broder 2012; Meotti and Weinthal 2012), with the Israeli interior minister declaring Grass a persona non grata (*New York Times* 2012), and the chairman of the Central Council of Jews in Germany saw him as an enemy of the Jews (*Berliner Morgenpost* 2012). An important factor in this regard was Grass's personal biography, which personified the complicated history of an entire generation of Germans. Born in 1927, he was known for his literary works dealing with the German experience and legacy of World War II; tackling difficult themes of destruction, discrimination, victims, and guilt; and probing unpopular ethical questions. Positioned on the left of the political spectrum and active in the peace movement in the 1980s, Grass caused controversy when he revealed in 2006 that as a teenager he had been drafted into the Waffen-SS during the last months of the war. For his critics, the latter aspect rendered Grass a "highly unsuitable critic of the Jewish state" (*Financial Times* 2012).

Despite the backlash, Grass stuck to his words and countered his critics by noting that he had written as a friend of Israel. The poem itself merely states that he is attached (*verbunden*) to Israel. It is the discursive moves following the publication to clarify his critique and the position from which he wanted it to be heard that are of interest here. To start with, Grass noted that he meant to criticize the current Israeli government, not Israel *as such* (*Süddeutsche Zeitung* 2012b).[17] This distinction is crucial because it allowed him to argue that the poem expressed disagreement with particular political agendas and practices and that anyone who cares about Israel had the duty to try and prevent its government from embarking on a self-destructive path through "a politics that creates more and more enemies for Israel" (*Süddeutsche Zeitung* 2012c). Grass then used the friendship frame to argue that true friends must have the courage to speak up and must be listened to.[18] In a conversation on German state television, he proclaimed that he was "worried about Israel . . . just like many Israelis worry about their country" and that shying away from criticizing policies that stand in the way to a peaceful region would come close to *Nibelungentreue*, namely, absolute and unquestioning loyalty, which he states "is the worst one can do to Israel." Thus, Grass notes, "I wish that many, out of friendship with Israel and also concern for Israel, would break this taboo" and express "valid critique" (ARD 2012). In another interview in October 2012, Grass doubled down on his critics:

> I think the best one can permit oneself to do as a friend of Israel— the state of Israel and its people, and I see myself as a friend of Israel—is to criticize it. The denied/refused critique, an uncritical, quasi philo-Semitic stance, is for me a new form of anti-Semitism! (NTV 2012)

To suggest that the silence of those who claim to be pro-Israel not only risks strengthening anti-Semitism, as the manifesto had argued, but is *itself* a form of anti-Semitism is, of course, problematic. But it exemplifies the force of the logic Grass employed—that it is the duty of the friend to voice critique—to defend his intervention. It also is a reminder that the primary target of his intervention was the German government for what he saw as solidarity gone wrong.

There are few signs that Grass convinced his critics that he spoke as a "friend of Israel." The newspaper *Die Welt*, which had been a prominent voice in accusing Grass of anti-Semitism, cast doubt on this claim by noting that, reportedly, Grass visited Israel only twice, in 1967 and 1971, thus implying that his practices did not match his words (*Die Welt* 2012a). Even one of the signatories of the "Manifest der 25" thought Grass was using the friendship framework in opportunistic ways "to project his own burdens" and not in the sense of a *Freundschaftsdienst*.[19] Yet there also were voices in Germany and elsewhere that came to Grass's defense and accused his critics of overreacting (see *Süddeutsche Zeitung 2012c*; Lau 2012; Grosser 2012). In either case, the debate affirmed the importance of the concept of friendship for the semantic field within which acceptable criticism had to move and raised the difficult question of whether the concept is employed sincerely or opportunistically.

When German president Joachim Gauck visited Israel less than two months after the publication of Grass's poem, one aim was to defuse the heated debate and to emphasize Germany's solidarity with Israel, making the official motto of his visit "We Germans stand on your side" (*Süddeutsche Zeitung* 2012d). In interviews, Gauck sought to take the weight off Grass's words by noting they were the author's personal opinion, while at the same time voicing his concern over polls showing a critical attitude among a majority of Germans toward Israel. And he noted, "We Germans, in particular, should ask ourselves critically: in which spirit do we judge Israeli politics? Please only in the spirit of friendship. There is also place for critique, absolutely, but not for prejudice" (*Frankfurter Allgemeine Zeitung* 2012b). This reflexive move appeared to be aimed at a German audience, but it also was meant to convey the position from which Gauck was speaking—that of a friend. The frame was affirmed by his counterpart, Shimon Peres, who, when welcoming Gauck, emphasized the "close friendship" between Germany and Israel (*Deutsche Welle* 2012). Notably, Gauck also stated that Merkel's declaration of Israel's security as Germany's raison d'etat could bring her into political difficulties in the event of an Israeli war with Iran. Widely reported as a carefully worded taming of Merkel's commitment, it was an implicit warning that Israel could not expect absolute loyalty—the *Nibelungentreue* Grass had criticized—from Germany.[20] Most German commentators considered this a "realistic assessment" coming from a friend (*Die Zeit* 2012c; *Die Welt* 2012c). So did Avi Primor, the former Israeli ambassador to Germany, who saw Gauck's visit and his critique as positive, noting "a friendship must be based on openness and honesty. President Gauck has found the right tone" (*Die Zeit* 2012a). Similar assessments were given by the chairs of the German-Israeli Society, the German-Israeli Parliamentary Committee, and the Central Council of Jews in Germany, who had accompanied Gauck to Israel. The latter, Dieter Graumann, who had called Grass's poem "an aggressive pamphlet of agitation," thought that Gauck had "highlighted the special friendship" and found "wonderful words" for German-Israeli relations (*Die Welt* 2012b).

Critique 2: Settlements

The second area of contention is the consensus among Germany's political leadership that solving the conflict between Israel and the Palestinians requires the creation of an independent Palestinian state. The commitment to a "two-state solution" has been a long-standing German position reiterated by Chancellor Merkel in her 2008 Knesset speech (Merkel 2008), and German officials see Israel's territorial expansion and occupation of Palestinian land through settlements that are illegal under international law as the biggest hurdle to this goal (*Deutsche Welle* 2014; *Frankfurter Allgemeine Zeitung* 2014a). However, the "two states" vision is not shared by the Netanyahu government, which appears to prefer the status quo and the expansion of the state beyond the 1967 borders through settlements, to the dismay of Berlin (Asseburg and Busse 2016; *Der Spiegel* 2015a, 2016; Author's Interviews). So there are fundamental disagreements between the two sides regarding Israel's settlement policies and practices. The German side voices its position on a regular basis, though it prefers to address contentious issues behind closed doors and ensures that it is accompanied by affirmations of friendship. When it was reported that President Gauck in private meetings with Israeli leaders had noted disagreement with Israel's settlement practices and the importance of upholding the rights of Palestinian people, he was quick to emphasize that all his statements were an "expression of a stable friendship" (*Die Welt* 2012b; *Süddeutsche Zeitung* 2012e; *Die Zeit* 2012a). The government also carefully signaled disagreement in public by changing its stance in areas where it has traditionally supported Israel. For instance, on 29 November 2012, Germany abstained in a vote in the UN General Assembly to grant Palestinians "non-member observer state" status, which Israeli leaders had expected Germany to vote against. When meeting with Netanyahu in Berlin a week later, Merkel appeared eager "to assure that the two are still friends" (*Christian Science Monitor* 2012) yet at their joint press conference affirmed the position through the remark, "When it comes to the question of settlements, we agree to disagree" (*Haaretz* 2012).

Merkel's reluctance to be more direct and open in her criticism prompted voices in the German media to call on the government to be more vocal in its critique of Israeli policies and practices and to put greater pressure on the Netanyahu government to change course. These calls were consistently made through the friendship frame and often included voices from within Israel to guard against possible accusations that the authors and message were anti-Israeli or anti-Semitic in orientation. Their tenor was that a healthy and strong friendship with Israel not only allowed but asked for more critique (Lau 2012). In the run-up to the 2014 joint cabinet meeting, *Der Spiegel* ran an article entitled "Silence among Friends" ("Schweigen unter Freunden"), which also quoted the Israeli director Dror Moreh saying that Germany, as one of Israel's closest friends, should voice more "targeted criticism" because "when you see your best friend speeding towards a wall you need to grab the steering wheel" (*Der Spiegel* 2014b). The same day, a commentary in the *Süddeutsche Zeitung* reiterated that German solidarity with Israel should not entail "unconditional support of every Israeli government," pointing out that many people in Israel "hope that Israel's friends . . . apply pressure from the outside to move . . . the leadership in Jerusalem to take positive steps in the peace process." Thus, "taking friendship seriously" requires facing the dispute over settlements (Münch 2014).

The Merkel government did become increasingly frustrated with what it considered Netanyahu's lack of sincerity in advancing the peace process. When in January 2014 the Israeli government announced new settlement constructions in the occupied territories, media on both sides reported significant tensions in German-Israeli relations and a growing antagonism between Merkel and Netanyahu (*Der Spiegel* 2014a; *Frankfurter Allgemeine Zeitung* 2014a; *Deutsche Welle* 2014; Ravid 2014). *Der Spiegel* noted that Merkel was eager to use the upcoming joint cabinet meeting in Jerusalem to defuse the tensions but also noted that both she and Foreign Minister Frank-Walter Steinmeier "believe that Israeli's settlement policy represents a decisive barrier to the peace process" and that they would not shy away from saying so in public (*Der Spiegel* 2014a). With Israeli media reporting that Steinmeier had "heaped tough criticism on Israeli settlement policy" prior to flying to Israel, Merkel upon arrival mobilized the friendship frame to set the tone. Speaking to journalists, she explained the unprecedented visit of fifteen ministers, representing almost the entire German government, by saying, "We wanted to show you in this way that this is indeed a very strong friendship" (*Ynetnews* 2014a, 2014b; *Haaretz* 2014b; *Süddeutsche Zeitung* 2014; *Frankfurter Allgemeine Zeitung* 2014b).[21]

The importance of embedding critical remarks in such language had just been displayed two weeks earlier when the president of the European Parliament, Martin Schulz, a German national, had in his otherwise "pro-Israel" speech in the Knesset implicitly criticized the Israeli blockade of Gaza. His point that Palestinians had less access to water than Israelis was heavily criticized by some in the Israeli government who argued that Schulz had his facts wrong. Netanyahu accused Schultz of "selective hearing" and "accept[ing] any attack on Israel without checking it," with several ministers going even further and accusing Schulz of "lies," with then Economy Minister Naftali Bennett storming out in protest during the speech (*Guardian* 2014; *Ynetnews* 2014c). However, Schulz was defended by other Israeli politicians who considered the harsh reactions as inappropriate and noted that Schulz was a "close friend" (Burg 2014) and a friend of Israel (*Haaretz* 2014a). While Schulz did not use the friendship frame in his speech, he had done so in a conversation with journalists just beforehand. Thus, when the *Times of Israel* reported the harsh reactions, it also noted that Schultz was "surprised and affected" by them and that he had presented himself a "staunch supporter of Israel." And after reporting that Schulz had been candid in saying that Israel's settlements in the West Bank were illegal and an obstacle to peace, the article pointedly closed with a quote of Schulz assuring that the EU is committed to friendship with Israel and that "an exchange of different views is not a break of friendship" (*Times of Israel* 2014). A similar tone was struck in other reports, and the controversy lost its edge. This episode demonstrated that the friendship concept can be effectively used by "insiders" to defend a speaker's motivation or message and, even more so, to criticize the reaction by warning that hurtling anti-Semitism accusations at friends is offensive.

German media continued to encourage Merkel to exercise her voice. One commentator noted that "a true friendship thrives on the courage to give criticism—and on the ability to accept it" and then argues that using "dubious Holocaust comparisons" to attack Germans who appear to take a critical stand runs the risk of alienating "true friends" of Israel (Schult 2015). In May 2015, in the context of the celebrations of fifty years of diplomatic relations between Germany and Israel, *Der Spiegel* published a widely noted article entitled "The Difficult Friend" ("Der schwierige Freund"), in which "outspoken friends of Israel"—former diplomats, high-ranking German politicians, and the Israeli historian Tom Segev—called for a tougher stance by Merkel toward the Israeli government regarding settlements (*Der Spiegel* 2015a). And in February 2016 the *Süddeutsche Zeitung* ran another commentary arguing that "Germany must dare more critique of Israel" ("Deutschland muss mehr Kritik an Israel wagen"), as otherwise the friendship stands on shaky ground (Münch 2016).

Critique 3: Democracy

The third and most recent area in which German politicians criticize Israeli policies and practices is democracy (see also Strunin-Kremer, this volume). Specifically, the issue is the attempt by members of the Israeli government and pro-settler organizations such as Im Tirtzu to delegitimize Israeli human rights organizations that are critical of government practices, such as Breaking the Silence, B'Tselem, or Peace Now, by accusing them of being "pro-Palestinian" and "anti-Zionist" and by stigmatizing them "as agents of foreign powers" (*+972 Magazine* 2016). The targeting of these and other left-wing organizations was formalized in July 2016 when the Knesset passed the controversial "transparency law," which requires them to declare their reliance on funding from foreign governments while, at the same time, excluding right-wing pro-settlement NGOs that tend to rely on private donations (*Guardian* 2016). While Prime Minister Netanyahu maintained that the law would "strengthen democracy" (*Guardian* 2016), it was strongly criticized within Israel and from the outside as undermining Israel's democracy.[22] Such critique also came from Germany, not least because German *Stiftungen* and the EU provide funding to these organizations and cooperate with them for projects within Israel. In February 2016, the chair of the German-Israeli Parliamentary Group, Volker Beck, described the law as an attempt to target the critical spectrum of civil society, calling it a "chicane" and "a big problem," and expected the German government to clearly address the issue with their Israeli counterparts during the joint cabinet meeting. At the same time, Beck noted that it was important to show "that we stand for friendship with Israel" and express understanding for Israeli security concerns, "as only then will our concrete critique of the current government be credible" (*Deutschlandfunk* 2016a).

Merkel's critique during the joint cabinet meetings in Berlin remained behind closed doors, and any controversial issues were left out of the official joint communiqué published afterward.[23] However, the issue came to a head a year later, when the Israeli government invited the newly appointed foreign minister, Sigmar Gabriel, to visit Israel in April 2017 for Holocaust Memorial Day. Five years earlier, then party leader Gabriel had caused a stir when during a visit to Hebron he called what he witnessed there an "Apartheid regime" (*Die Welt* 2012c), and during the 2013 election campaign he had called for Germany to be a "critical and demanding partner" toward Israel (*Jüdische Allgemeine* 2013). When asked about the incident on the eve of Gabriel's 2017 visit, the Israeli ambassador to Germany, Yakob Hadas-Handelsman, assured people that "this is resolved. Gabriel is a friend of Israel" (*Sächsische Zeitung* 2017). However, during the visit, Gabriel decided to also meet with Breaking the Silence and B'Tselem, despite Netanyahu's late objection, which prompted Netanyahu to cancel his planned meeting with the foreign minister. This was widely reported as an *Eklat,* an open fallout (*Frankfurter Allgemeine Zeitung* 2017; *Süddeutsche Zeitung* 2017a). While Gabriel appeared surprised by Netanyahu's move, as other German leaders had met with these organizations during earlier visits (*Süddeutsche Zeitung* 2017b), his decision not to comply with Netanyahu's objection was a signal in support of these organizations and of the critical discourse in Israel more generally. To cushion the fallout, Gabriel assured Israeli president Rivlin during a meeting that "you can absolutely be sure we are committed to the friendship, the partnership and the special relationship with Israel and nothing will change this" (*Haaretz* 2017b). In an interview with a German newspaper, Gabriel made a point of the "very friendly" and long meeting he had with Rivlin and emphasized his close personal connection to the country (*Hamburger Abendblatt*

2017). This resonated with support from a former Israeli diplomat and outspoken Netanyahu critic, who wrote a piece in the *Süddeutsche Zeitung* entitled "Thank You, Sigmar Gabriel," stating "your love of Israel, just like mine or that of my friends, is not in question" and endorsing the decision to meet with organizations like Breaking the Silence and B'Tselem as one that "strengthens the democratic structures" in Israel (Liel 2017).

When Gabriel's predecessor and now president of Germany, Frank-Walter Steinmeier, visited Israel a month later, he also mobilized the friendship frame to both calm the waters and reiterate the German government's position (*Süddeutsche Zeitung* 2017c). Steinmeier spoke with prominent intellectuals known as critical voices within Israel, and he openly expressed his disagreement with Netanyahu's cancellation of the meeting with Gabriel. His ability to embed this in an emphasis on German-Israeli friendship was on full display in a speech he gave to students at Hebrew University on 11 May 2017 (*Der Spiegel* 2017). Steinmeier began the speech by noting the "miracle of German-Israeli friendship" and then spoke extensively about the importance of democratic principles. Recalling the long and difficult path both Israel and Germany had traveled to establish themselves as democracies, he applauded "the spirit of dissent and the passion for the democratic dispute" as the "vital core of Israeli democracy." And then, claiming that in Jewish culture one likes to argue with friends and family, Steinmeier pleaded, "This is exactly how, namely as friends, we Germans want to participate in the argument!" In this spirit, he encouraged his audience to "let us talk about the challenges to democracy honestly and without prohibition of speech," to address the disagreements between the two governments regarding settlements and the two state-solution. Thus, Steinmeier made the double move of reminding his audience that open debate and criticism among friends are both necessary and normal, especially when they claim to be democrats (Steinmeier 2017).

Conclusion

This chapter sought to demonstrate that the concept of friendship matters in international relations, specifically German-Israeli relations. It might have been more intuitive to show how the concept is used to justify and guide practices of cooperation. However, tracing the use of friendship language in the context of criticism reveals an intriguing connection between solidarity/loyalty and critique and, thus, directs attention to critique as a *Freundschaftsdienst*. It shows the wide field in which the friendship concept performs in political discourse and highlights the need for more careful empirical and theoretical work on when and how critique and solidarity go hand in hand—and under what conditions tensions exist between them. Furthermore, because the historical context within which German-Israeli relations are situated makes acts of criticism particularly sensitive, the friendship frame takes on extra significance.

The discussion showed that the concept of friendship was employed by German intellectuals and political leaders on various occasions to legitimize their criticism of Israeli policies and practices, *as well as* by actors in civil society and the media to call on the German government to be more vocal in its criticism. Specifically, the empirical discussion revealed three patterns: First, and most importantly, the friendship frame was used to *enable* German disagreement with and critique of Israeli policies and practices. Second, it was used by speakers and others to *defend* their critical statements against accusations of anti-Semitism. Third, and slightly different, it was used to *demand* criticism as a duty from which friends should not shy away. As noted, the study assumes that in each of these instances the concept was employed deliberately, because the speakers were deeply aware that words matter. Did they mobilize the concept for instrumental reasons, that is, for the purpose of making critique safe, or was it a genuine concern for Israel, for a friend, that prompted criticism of Israeli policies and practices? The answer probably varies from case to case but in the cases looked at is likely to be a bit of both.

While the analysis did not systematically assess whether or to what extent Israeli audiences accepted the critique and the friendship frame through which it was delivered, it did indicate that reactions varied. A more careful assessment of this variation and a substantive discussion on what explains it were beyond the scope of this chapter. However, it points to three central questions that future research may want to tackle: First, what does friendship mean to the speaker who uses the term, and what connotation does it have for the audience? Second, even if they agree on the meaning, what makes the use of the friendship frame credible or persuasive? Third, when it is accepted that a political actor is speaking from the position of a friend, is this position limited to the individual or understood to represent a broader political collective? One aspect shining through the cases analyzed in this chapter but not further explored is the importance of the biography of the speaker and their ability to create a personal connection to the Jewish experience and to Israel. Such a biographical connection establishes a sense of "closeness" and signals empathy, which is strongly associated with the concept of friendship. It thus may be fruitful to take a closer look at the biographical narratives of the speakers, as perceived by the audience, and their effort to make a connection, as well as instances where that fails.

The chapter also pointed to instances when Israelis used the concept of friendship to accept critique from particular German speakers and/or to defend them from accusations of anti-Semitism. Statements such as that by Israeli president Rivlin, who in an interview to German television in 2015 noted that both states "can accept, as friends, that we do not always share an opinion" (*Der Spiegel* 2015b), are not uncommon. However, critique among friends involves more than allowing the other side to voice their opinion; it is also about taking criticism seriously and "on board." Rather than an isolated act, critique is an interactive process in which A not only shares their concern but also tries to make B understand it and change course. Conversely, B may convince A that their concern is groundless. As such, critique among friends is part of a conversation involving reflection and productive engagement—it is a process of mutual learning. So if we are wondering whether a friendship has developed between Germany and Israel, we may want to trace this process and assess whether and how such learning is taking place.

Notes

1. For various examples, see the official website of the jubilee at https://www.de50il.org/.

2. See also Beaulieu-Brossard, this volume.

3. Some argue that Germany feels (or should feel) responsible also for the well-being of Palestinians ("Manifest der 25" 2006). Others hold that (economic) ties with Arab countries generate anti-Israeli stances (Wolffsohn 1988, 174ff).

4. According to Moshe Zimmermann (2016, 46), "It is no secret that . . . the tactics of warding off any criticism of Israel's policies by Germany has become standard procedure for the Israeli government." See also *Haaretz* (2015). Author's interviews with German diplomats.

5. Author's interview with German diplomat, Berlin, 25 July 2017.

6. Phoenix "Forum Demokratie," 8 November 2015, https://www.youtube.com/watch?v=JpEFycHAZ_0.

7. See Ish-Shalom, this volume. For an extensive discussion, see Berenskötter (2017).

8. Erving Goffman (1974) in his influential analysis talks about "primary frameworks."

9. The question of what exactly friends care about requires a deeper discussion of the ontology of friendship, which lies beyond this chapter. For an attempt in IR, see Berenskötter (2007, 2014).

10. Aristotle differentiates between virtue of thought and of character, the former acquired through "teaching" and the latter through "habit" (Aristotle 1999, Book II). Criticism has an element of teaching.

11. An exception of sort is Martin Schulz, who at that time spoke in his function as a EU representative.

12. Most of them were political scientists, part of the '68 generation, and associated with the peace movement.

13. The manifesto generated a range of critical reactions, from noting that "it was never forbidden to criticize Israel" (Weingardt 2006) to discarding the argument that Germany had a historical responsibility vis-à-vis Palestinians (Brumlik 2007). For a comprehensive compilation, see Steinweg (2007).

14. See the unpublished open letter to Brumlik by Tilman Evers in Steinweg (2007, 70–72); Krell (2008); Baumann and Meggle (2009); correspondence of the author with Gert Krell, 3 February 2018.

15. The poem was published simultaneously in *La Repubblica* and in *El Pais*.

16. The military option had little to no support in the US administration and was criticized inside Israel (Remnick 2012). The German minister of defense also expressed strong concern. More broadly, Grass wrote in the context of a deterioration of Israel's image in the German public and an increasing frustration with the Netanyahu government among German politicians (Lau 2011; *Frankfurter Rundschau* 2012; *Frankfurter Allgemeine Zeitung* 2012a).

17. Grass even changed the verse when the poem was reprinted later that year in his book *Eintagsfliegen*.

18. Grass already made this point in an interview with *Der Spiegel* in October 2001. In the context of criticizing US military action in Afghanistan, he stated that "friendship also requires to try and hinder the friend from acting when he threatens to make a mistake. . . . for me such open criticism is part of loyalty." At the end of the interview he briefly touched on the issue of Israeli settlements, noting that "it is an evidence of friendship towards Israel when I allow myself to criticize the country—because I want to help it. . . . To criticize such critique—we must stop doing that" (*Der Spiegel* 2001).

19. Correspondence of the author with Gert Krell, 3 February 2018. See also Krell and Mueller (2012).

20. Rather than proclaiming eternal support, Gauck emphasized that "Germany should be the very last country that revokes its friendship and solidarity to Israel" (*Die Zeit* 2012b).

21. Given this, Merkel's decision to cancel the joint cabinet meeting planned for May 2017 in Jerusalem is particularly noteworthy. It is widely understood that she did so after the Israeli parliament passed a law legalizing a large number of controversial

settlements in the occupied territories, a move that "deeply disappointed" the German government (*Die Zeit* 2017; *Haaretz* 2017a).

22. A front cover article in *Le Monde Diplomatique* on the issue was headed "Israel Loses Its Grip on Democracy." The European Commission condemned the law for threatening to undermine Israel's democracy, and Israeli opposition leader Isaac Herzog called it an indicator of "fascism creeping into Israeli society" (*Guardian* 2016). See also Shalev (2015).

23. Interview, Berlin, 25 July 2017.

References

ARD. 2012. "Günter Grass im Gespräch mit Tom Buhrow." *Tagesschau.de*, 5 April. http://www.tagesschau.de/multimedia/video/video1093224.html

Aristotle. 1999. *Nichomachean Ethics*. Trans. Terence Irwin. 2nd ed. Indianapolis: Hackett.

Asseburg, Muriel. 2015. "50 Jahre deutsch-israelische Beziehungen." *SWP-Aktuell* 40 (April).

Asseburg, Muriel, and Jan Busse. 2016. "Das Ende der Zweistaatenregelung? *SWP–Aktuell* 27 (April).

Author's Interviews with German diplomats involved in conducting relations with Israel, Berlin, 7–8 July 2016, 24–25 July 2017, and 19 July 2019.

Baumann, Marcel, and Georg Meggle. 2009. "Jenseits von Denkverboten und Kritiklosigkeit. Das 'Manifest der 25' und seine Folgen." In *Friedensforschung und Friedenspraxis: Ermutigung zur Arbeit an der Utopie*, ed. Marcel Baumann et al., 275–87. Frankfurt/Main: Brandes & Apsel.

Belkin, Paul. 2007. *Germany's Relations with Israel: Background and Implications for German Middle East Policy*. CRS Report for Congress, 19 January.

Berliner Morgenpost. 2012. "Ist der alte Deutsche plötzlich zurückgekehrt?." 7 April.

Berenskötter, Felix. 2007. "Friends, There Are No Friends? An Intimate Reframing of the International." *Millennium: Journal of International Studies* 35 (3): 647–76.

Berenskötter, Felix. 2017. "Approaches to Concept Analysis." *Millennium: Journal of International Studies* (45) 2: 151–73.

Berenskötter, Felix, and Bastian Giegerich. 2010. "From NATO to ESDP: A Social Constructivist Analysis of German Strategic Adjustment after the End of the Cold War." *Security Studies* 19 (3): 407–52.

Broder, Henryk. 2012. "Günter Grass—Nicht ganz dicht, aber ein Dichter." *Die Welt*, 4 April.

Brumlik, Micha. 2007. "Wie der Bau der Bagdad-Bahn." *Frankfurter Rundschau*, 7 February.

Brumlik, Micha. 2012. "Der an seiner Schuld würgt." *Taz.de*, 4 April.

Burg, Avram. 2014. "Say a Big 'Thank You' to Martin Schulz." *Haaretz*, 14 February.

Christian Science Monitor. 2012. "Merkel Meets Netanyahu as Israel and Germany Hit Rocky Patch." 6 December.

Christian Science Monitor. 2015. "Fifty Years On, Practical Lessons from German-Israeli Friendship." 12 May.

Dempsey, Judy. 2010. "Embracing Israel Costs Merkel Clout." *New York Times*, 21 January.

Der Spiegel. 2001. Interview mit Günter Grass, "Amerikanische Politik muss Gegenstand der Kritik bleiben." 10 October.

Der Spiegel. 2014a. "Tensions Flare in German-Israeli Relations." *Spiegel Online*, 18 February.

Der Spiegel. 2014b. "Schweigen unter Freunden." *Spiegel Online*, 24 February.

Der Spiegel. 2014c. "Das lächelnde Bollwerk." *Spiegel Online*, 25 February.

Der Spiegel. 2015a. "Der schwierige Freund." 19/2015, 36–38. English translation published as "Critics Want Tougher Berlin Stance against Israel." *Spiegel Online*, 5 June.

Der Spiegel. 2015b. "Wir können akzeptieren, nicht immer einer Meinung zu sein." *Spiegel Online*, 10 May.

Der Spiegel. 2016. "Fremder Freund." 18/2016, 28–29. English translation published as "Scepticism of German-Israeli Friendship Growing in Berlin." *Spiegel Online*, 29 April.

Der Spiegel. 2017. "Steinmeier kritisiert Netanjahu's 'Sprechverbot.'" *Spiegel Online*, 7 May.

Deutsche Welle. 2012. "Bundespräsident Gauck betont Freundschaft der Deutschen zu Israel." 29 May.

Deutsche Welle. 2014. "A Turning Point in German-Israeli Relations." 24 February.

Deutschlandfunk. 2016a. "Die Bundesregierung muss kein Blatt vor den Mund nehmen" Interview with Volker Beck, 16 February.

Deutschlandfunk. 2016b. "Die grösste Bedrohung für Israel ist der Iran." Interview with Yakov Hadas-Handelsman, 13 March.

Die Welt. 2012a. "Nur zweimal in Israel." 11 April.

Die Welt. 2012b. "Gauck und der Kampf der Worte, der keiner sein soll." 30 May.

Die Welt. 2012c. "Gabriel nennt Israel 'Apartheid Regime.'" 15 March.

Die Zeit. 2009. "Westerwelle begegnet seiner Vergangenheit." *Zeit Online*, 24 November.

Die Zeit. 2012a. "Gauck in Israel: Kritische Töne in Freundschaft." *Zeit Online*, 30 May.

Die Zeit. 2012b. "Gauck distanziert sich von Merkels Haltung zu Israel." *Zeit Online*, 30 May.

Die Zeit. 2012c. "Presseschau: 'Gauck hat das richtige gesagt, aber nicht genug.'" *Zeit Online*, 30 May.

Die Zeit. 2017. "Merkel sagt Gespräche mit Netanyahu ab." *ZEIT Online*, 13 February.

The Economist. 2008. "Friends in High Places." 19 March.

The Economist. 2015. "A Very Special Relationship." 31 January.

Euronews. 2017. "Herr Botschafter, wie kritisiert man Israel—und wie nicht?" 17 January. http://de.euronews.com/2017/01/17/antisemitismus-betrifft-die-ganze-gesellschaft-gespraech-mit-israels

Eznack, Lucile. 2011. "Crises as Signals of Strength: The Significance of Affect in Close Allies' Relationships." *Security Studies* 20 (2): 238–65.

Financial Times. 2012. "Grass Poetry Sparks Israeli Rage." 9 April.

Frankfurter Allgemeine Zeitung. 2002. "Möllemann holt den Israel-Hammer wieder raus." 18 September.
Frankfurter Allgemeine Zeitung. 2012a. "Möllemanns Erben." 20 March.
Frankfurter Allgemeine Zeitung. 2012b. "Kritik bitte nur im Geist der Freundschaft." *FAZ.NET*, 29 May.
Frankfurter Allgemeine Zeitung. 2014a. "Reparaturarbeiten an einer entgleisten Beziehung." 24 February.
Frankfurter Allgemeine Zeitung. 2014b. "Trotz Siedlungsstreit eine 'treue Freundin.'" *FAZ.NET*, 25 February.
Frankfurter Allgemeine Zeitung. 2015. "Merkels Versprechen für Israels Sicherheit." 11 May.
Frankfurter Allgemeine Zeitung. 2017. "Eklat mit Ansage." 25 April.
Frankfurter Rundschau. 2012. "De Maiziere warnt vor Krieg mit dem Iran." 27 March.
Friedman, Marilyn. 1993. *What are friends for?: feminist perspectives on personal relationships and moral theory.* Ithaca: Cornell University Press.
Gardner Feldman, Lily. 1984. *The Special Relationship between West Germany and Israel.* Boston: Allen & Unwin.
Gardner Feldman, Lily. 2012. *Germany's Foreign Policy of Reconciliation: From Enmity to Amity.* Lanham: Rowman & Littlefield.
Gardner Feldman, Lily. 2016. "Defining Dualities: Context, Content and Comparison in German-Israeli Relations in the Framework of Europeanization." In *Rapprochement, Change, Perception and Shaping the Future*, ed. Alfred Wittstock, 195–205. Berlin: Frank & Timme.
Gerster, Johannes. 2015. "Vierzig Jahre deutsch-israelische Beziehungen." *Die Politsche Meinung*, no. 426 (May): 56–60.
Goffman, Erving. [1974]. 1986. *Frame Analysis: An Essay on the Organization of Experience.* Boston: Northeastern University Press.
Grass, Günter. 2012. "Was gesagt werden muss." *Süddeutsche Zeitung*, 4 April.
Grosser, Alfred. 2012. *"Grass hat etwas Vernünftiges gesagt."* Interview in *Süddeutsche Zeitung*, 11 April.
The Guardian. 2012. "Günter Grass's Israel Poem Provokes Outrage." 5 April.
The Guardian. 2014. "Israeli Rightwingers Walk Out during President of EU Parliament's Speech." 12 February.
The Guardian. 2016. "Israel Passes Law to Force NGOs to Reveal Foreign Funding." 12 July.
Haaretz. 2011. "Merkel Chides Netanyahu for Failing to Make 'a Single Step to Advance Peace.'" 25 February.
Haaretz. 2012. "Merkel after Netanyahu Meet: 'We've Agreed to Disagree on Settlement Construction.'" 6 December.
Haaretz. 2014a. "Knesset Walkout During EU Parliament Chief's Speech Is a New Low for Israel." 13 February.
Haaretz. 2014b. "Merkel Arrives in Israel to Talk Peace." 24 February.
Haaretz. 2015. "Israeli Diplomat in Berlin: Maintaining German Guilt about Holocaust Helps Israel." 25 June.
Haaretz. 2017a. "Germany's Merkel Cancels Summit with Israel in Wake of Palestinian Land-Grab Law." 13 February.

Haaretz. 2017b. "Netanyahu Cancels Meeting after German FM Refuses to Snub Israeli Leftist NGOs." 25 April.

Hafner-Burton, Emilie. 2008. "Sticks and Stones: Naming and Shaming the Human Rights Enforcement Problem." *International Organization* 62 (4): 689–716.

Hamburger Abendblatt. 2017. "Gabriel umgarnt Hamburger: Ihr seid Welt-Versteher." Interview. 28 April.

Handelsblatt. 2017. "Die Bundesregierung macht ernst mit Netanjahu." *Handelsblatt,* 26 April.

Joffe, Josef. 2012. "Der Antisemitismus will raus." *ZEIT Online,* 4 April.

Jüdische Allgemeine. 2013. "Wir sind ein fordernder Partner Israels." Interview. 23 May.

Keller, Simon. 2007. *The Limits of Loyalty.* Cambridge: Cambridge University Press.

Krell, Gert. 2008. "Deutschland, Israel und die Schatten der Vergangenheit: ein persönlich-politischer Reisebericht." Unpublished manuscript.

Krell, Gert, and Harald Mueller. 2012. *Noch ein Krieg im Nahen Osten?* HSFK-Report No. 2/2012.

Lau, Jörg. 2011. "An den Grenzen der Freundschaft." *Die Zeit,* no. 46, 10 November.

Lau, Jörg. 2012. "Feigheit vor dem Freund."*Die Zeit,* no. 16, 13 April.

Liel, Alon. 2017. "Danke, Sigmar Gabriel." *Süddeutsche Zeitung,* 5 May.

"Manifest der 25." 2006. "Freundschaft und Kritik. Warum die 'besonderen Beziehungen' zwischen Deutschland und Israel überdacht werden müssen. Das 'Manifest der 25.'" *Frankfurter Rundschau,* 15 November.

Meotti, Giulio, and Benjamin Weinthal. 2012. "Something Rotten in Germany." *Ynet Opinion,* 5 April.

Merkel, Angela. 2008. "Rede von Bundeskanzlerin Dr. Angela Merkel vor der Knesset am 18. März in Jerusalem." *Die Bundesregierung.*

Münch, Peter. 2014. "Wundersame Beziehungen." *Süddeutsche Zeitung,* 24 February.

Münch, Peter. 2016. "Deutschland muss mehr Kritik an Israel wagen." *Süddeutsche Zeitung,* 16 February.

New York Times. 2012. "Israel Bars German Laureate Grass over Poem." 8 April.

+972 Magazine. 2016. "Everything You Need to Know about Israel's 'NGO Law.'" *+972 Blog,* 12 July.

NTV. 2012. "'Eine notwendige Torheit' Grass erneuert Israel Kritik." *n-tv.de,* 15 October.

Oz, Amos. 2005. *Israel und Deutschland. Vierzig Jahre nach Aufnahme diplomatischer Beziehungen,* Frankfurt a. M.: Suhrkamp.

Posener, Alan. 2017. "An allem schuld." *Jüdische Allgemeine,* 16 May.

Ravid, Barak. 2014. "Israel and Germany, Milk That Has Soured. *Haaretz,* 24 February.

Remnick, David. 2012. "The Vegetarian." Letter from Tel Aviv. *New Yorker,* 3 September.

Roshchin, Evgeny. 2017. *Friendship among Nations: History of a Concept.* Manchester: Manchester University Press.

Sächsische Zeitung. 2017. "Beziehungen zu Deutschland nicht belastet." *SZ-online. de,* 24 April.

Schult. 2015. "Polemics Have No Place in True Friendships." *Spiegel Online,* 12 November.

Shalev, Chemi. 2015. "Im Tirtzu and the Proto-facsist Plot to Destroy Israeli Democracy." *Haaretz*, 16 December.
Sherman, Nancy. 1993. "Aristotle and the Shared Life." In *Friendship*, ed. N. Kapur Badhwar, 91–107. Ithaca, NY: Cornell University Press.
Stein, Shimon. 2011. *Israel, Deutschland und der Nahe Osten*. Wallstein Verlag.
Stein, Shimon, and Moshe Zimmermann. 2017. "Dieser Feind steht rechts." *ZEIT Online*, 26 June. http://www.zeit.de/gesellschaft/zeitgeschehen/2017–06/antisemitismus-deutschland-dokumentation-israelkritik/komplettansicht
Steinmeier, Frank-Walter. 2017. "Rede von Bundespräsident Dr. Frank-Walter Steinmeier beim Antrittsbesuch im Staat Israel und in den Palästinensischen Gebieten an der Hebräischen Universität am 7. Mai 2017 in Jerusalem." *Bulletin der Bundesregierung*, no. 51–1.
Steinweg, Rainer, ed. 2007. *Dokumentation: Das Manifest der 25 "Freundschaft und Kritik" und die darauf folgende Debatte*. Vol. 1. Forum Crisis Prevention e. V. http://www.crisis-prevention.info/wp-content/uploads/2014/03/doku_manifest_d_25_Bd1.pdf
Strenger, Carlo. 2012. "Estranged Friends? A View on Israel from Western Europe." *Haaretz*, 22 February.
Strenger, Carlo. 2016. "Germany, Israel, and Normality: From Tragic History to Complex Present." In *Rapprochement, Change, Perception and Shaping the Future: 50 Years of German-Israeli and Israeli-German Diplomatic Relations*, ed. Alfred Wittstock, 147–56. Berlin: Frank & Timme.
Stroud, Sarah. 2006. "Epistemic Partiality in Friendship." *Ethics* 116 (3): 498–524.
Süddeutsche Zeitung. 2012a. "Ist der alte Deutsche plötzlich zurückgekehrt?." 6 April.
Süddeutsche Zeitung. 2012b. "Grass präzisiert Kritik an Israel." 6 April.
Süddeutsche Zeitung. 2012c. "Grass beklagt Kampagne gegen sich." 6 April.
Süddeutsche Zeitung. 2012d. "Gauck will ein Zeichen der Solidarität setzen." 29 May.
Süddeutsche Zeitung. 2012e. "Kritik als Ausdruck einer stabilen Freundschaft." *Süddeutsche.de*, 30 May.
Süddeutsche Zeitung. 2014. "Merkel und 13 Minister zu Gesprächen in Israel." *Süddeutsche.de*, 24 February.
Süddeutsche Zeitung. 2017a. "Wie es zum Eklat mit Israel kommen konnte." 27 April.
Süddeutsche Zeitung. 2017b. "Aussenminister Gabriel: 'Ich habe gar nichts eskaliert.'" *Süddeutsche.de*, 29 April.
Süddeutsche Zeitung. 2017c. "Steinmeier bringt klare Botschaft nach Israel." 8 May.
TAZ. 2012. "Auszeichnung für Antisemitismus." *taz.de*, 29 December.
Times of Israel. 2014. "Harsh Reaction to Knesset Speech Surprises EU Leader." 13 February.
Weingardt, Markus. 2002. *Deutsche Israel- und Nahostpolitik*. Frankfurt a. M.: Campus Verlag.
Weingardt, Markus. 2006. "Israel zu kritisieren war nie verboten." *Frankfurter Rundschau*, 25 November.
Wittstock, Alfred, ed. 2016. *Rapprochement, Change, Perception and Shaping the Future: 50 Years of German-Israeli and Israeli-German Diplomatic Relations*. Berlin: Frank & Timme.

Wolffsohn, Michael. 1988. *Ewige Schuld? 40 Jahre Deutsch-Jüdisch-Israelische Beziehungen*. München: Piper.

Ynetnews. 2014a. "Top German Diplomat Criticizes Israeli Policy." 24 February.

Ynetnews. 2014b. "Merkel: Two-State Solution Is Essential to Israel's Security." 24 February.

Ynetnews. 2014c. "Bennett: Criticism Is Legitimate, Lies Are Not." 12 February.

Zimmermann, Moshe. 2016. "The Arab-Israeli Conflict as a Challenge to German-Israeli Relations." In *Rapprochement, Change, Perception and Shaping the Future*, ed. Alfred Wittstock, 43–54. Berlin: Frank & Timme.

CHAPTER 9

The Conceptual Virtues of the International Community

Mor Mitrani

> This is how the international community is supposed to work—
> nations standing together for the sake of peace and security, and
> individuals claiming their rights.[1]

In his 2011 speech to the UN General Assembly (UNGA), American president Barack Obama delineated how the international community is supposed to work. The saying is related to a specific context, as Obama took pride in the role of the coalition of Western states in freeing Libya and reopening the American embassy there in the very same week as the annual convention of the UNGA in New York took place. According to Obama, the involvement in Libya is an exemplar for the operation of the international community, as it demonstrates joint actions of states in a pursuit of peace and the advancement of individual rights. As such, Obama's statement enfolds three basic premises: first, that there is an international community; second, that it is capable of working and operating; and third, that there is a repertoire of goals and actions that infuses normative meaning to it, namely, that sets how it is supposed to work. All three premises are somewhat equivocal, mainly since it is not clear who or what is the international community.

The concept of *international community* is widely used by scholars, practitioners, and international political leaders and is an integral part of the common vocabulary of to world politics. Obama's reference to the

185

international community was in no way special or unique. In fact, it is the second most common phrase (two words or more), in states' speeches in the UNGA, right after the phrase "United Nations." Nonetheless, despite the great presence of the concept in the international discourse, it seems like international relations (IR) scholars find limited interest in exploring the international community either as a subject on its own right, namely, as an analytical category (but see, as an exception, Addis 2008; Brown 1995; Buzan and Gonzalez-Pelaez 2005; Ellis 2009), or as a prevalent concept in the international discourse, namely, as a discursive practice (but see, as an exception, Bliesemann de Guevara and Kühn 2011; Tsagourias 2006). This is especially puzzling given the notion that the power and sphere of influence of the international community are not sustained by any concrete material factor, and thus its authority—if it exists—stems from the mere usage of the term and from assigning it with specific practical and normative substances, just as Obama did in 2011 to justify the intervention in Libya and to frame it as successful.

This chapter aims at understanding the conceptual virtues of the "international community" and assessing the sociopolitical functions that it may serve in international discourse. The purpose, therefore, is not to suggest an ontological answer to the question of who is the international community or to provide a normative account of the international community's desired values and goals. The focus is rather on analyzing the role of the concept itself as a common discursive construct in international politics. The main argument is that while often the concept is dismissed by scholars as being loose and empty (Bliesemann de Guevara and Kühn 2011) or a political myth (Kaczmarska 2016), and thus treated as a pure (and redundant) rhetorical device (Tsagourias 2006), these features are exactly what renders it as a significant political concept.

The chapter contends that the intrinsic vagueness and emptiness of the concept and the absence of a specific signified serve as an epistemological basis to construct states as a "Self" in a greater collective as well as to establish normative and practical foundations of relations among states. Therefore, the tendency of states to affiliate themselves as an international community, attribute it with practices and norms, and use it to legitimize political concept, political phenomena, and political agents can tell a story about the social relations between states and especially about the urge of state agents to identify themselves with a greater "We" of states. The chapter proceeds as follows. The first section briefly surveys the ontological aspects of the international community as an analytical category and discusses the tension between its rhetorical and discursive traits. The second section argues that, conceptually, the international community is an empty signifier that allows it to develop and consolidate as established discursive practice. The third and last section analyzes the sociopolitical virtues of the concept as they arguably stem from its lack of content and signification.

The International Community: An Analytical Category or a Rhetorical Device?

Essentially, any attempt to theorize the international community requires a wider analysis of the conditions under which states may convene social relations that can form a community. Following the seminal distinction made by Ferdinand Tonnies ([1887] 1963) between a community and a society, a community is often seen as a form of association that is established by will and is based on real and organic kinship relationships. At the international level, the theoretical condition of real and organic kinship relations seems infeasible both as a political phenomenon and as an analytical category. Indeed, IR literature, confined to premises in the anarchical international system, hardly refers to the idea of the international community and depicts it as extrinsic to conventional assertions regarding the nature of international relations.

The most explicit references to the international community—either to the possibility of its existence or to its normative and practical modes of operation—reside in theoretical accounts on international law. The rationale is straightforward. Since law as a legal system essentially requires some sort of legal community that would be committed to both formulate the law and comply with it, an international community is a prerequisite to the operation of international law (Paulus 2003) as the foundation to which states are committed to and hence comply with international law (Franck 1990, 1995). The international community is portrayed not only as regulated by international law but also as constituted by it, and especially by customary international law (Nardin 1999) or the UN Charter (Dupuy 1997; e.g., Fassbender 1998). The existence and scope of operation of the legal community depend on the extent to which states conceive of themselves as part of a rule-governed realm and thus as members in a voluntary association of those who accept the rules (Mapel and Nardin 1999; Whelan 1999).

Nonetheless, there are two main caveats to the discussion of international community in the context of international law. First, it is somehow circular. International law is conceptualized as both the indicator and the originator of the international community (Simma and Paulus 1998), and the international community is both setting the operating systems of international law (Diehl, Ku, and Zamora 2003) and embodying them. Second, and not very surprisingly, it is highly normative. The international community is cast as the framework of international law, but the literature rarely doubts the existence of the international community or explores the processes through which it is constituted or operating. While the discussion is often situated in greater debates on states' commitment to and compliance with international law, on the one hand (Franck 1995; Kumm 2004), and on the legitimacy of international law, on the other (Koh 1997), the discussion on the international community essentially lacks a political angle (Koskenniemi 2004). The international community is acknowledged for its role in the international political arena and used to suggest a sociolegal framework to the phenomenon of international law, but it is not envisaged as a political phenomenon of its own.

From a political perspective, it seems natural to focus on the English school of international relations as a framework for theorizing the international community (or the possibility of an international community) as a political phenomenon. According to Hedley Bull (1977, 13), an international society exists "when a group of states, conscious of certain common interests and common values, form a society in the sense that they conceive themselves to be bound by a common set of rules in their relations with one another and share the working of common institutions." However, despite the affinity between the theoretical concept of international society and the concept of the international community, the latter is not very common among English school scholars, and only a few accounts have attempted to theorize the commonalities and linkages between the international society and the international community. Chris Brown (1995), for example, completely dismisses the possibility of an international community, arguing that any conception of a community at the international level stands in contradiction to the main ordering principle of the international society— sovereignty. On the other hand, Buzan and Gonzales-Pelaez (2005) portray the international community as a specific type of international society in its most solidarist form. For them, an international community can exist at the subglobal level as smaller hubs within an international society in which one can find a "tighter net of states within international society that share a higher degree of integration defined by a strong common identity" (Buzan and Gonzalez-Pelaez 2005, 38). This net, ties single actors via a greater (though not necessarily global) external environment in which they seek to act, serving thus as "a political function for those who act in its name" (Buzan and Gonzalez-Pelaez 2005, 31).

Nonetheless, if the ontological possibility of an international community is conditioned by very specific circumstances, which are quite rare in international politics, what stands beyond the great rhetorical presence of the international community? Especially, as in most cases, when both state leaders and academics refer to the international community, they tend to do so in a universal and inclusive way that is not confined to a specific ethos or region.

References to the rhetorical qualities of the international community are often made in conjunction with a greater discussion in regard to the gap between reality and talk in international politics and as part of an attempt to "peel off the mask" of the international community. The primary argument in this respect is that the international community is not real and cannot be real. That this is a loose concept, essentially ambivalent, used ubiquitously for empty signaling (Bliesemann de Guevara and Kühn 2011) through which actors frame political and legal claims (Koskenniemi 2004) justifies and legitimizes actions and clears up their moral consciousness in light of growing atrocities.

From a rhetorical perspective, the international community is a code word—an instinctive answer for all international crises and problems that its contents and contexts are open for political manipulation (similar to Strunin-Kremer's analysis of the concept of cyber, this volume), a rhetorical device infused by a high degree of euphemism that allows hegemonic actors to enforce their power and interests in a disguise of an overarching international community (Tsagourias 2006). This is accomplished either by strategically framing and embedding an "international community doctrine" (see Fairclough 2005 on Tony Blair's international community doctrine) into the normative vocabulary of international discourse or as a means to push responsibility away and to legitimize inaction by loosely attributing agency to a nonexistent international community (Bliesemann de Guevara and Kühn 2011, 148). Along these lines of argument, the international community is portrayed as an appropriated concept, a political myth that serves as an instant and fictitious model of cooperation and problem solving in contemporary world politics (Kaczmarska 2016; Kritsiotis 2002) but has no standing in the real world. However, even if the international community is nothing more than a loose rhetorical device, what is the purpose of the facade? Why do states—powerful or not—even bother to adopt such a discourse that is arguably nothing more than a mere charade? The main problem with reducing the notion of the international community to rhetorical usages is that it disregards that a concept, by definition, cannot be purely selective or preprogrammed. It depends on acceptance and credibility and hence is contingent upon constant discussion and shared understandings among all types of states.

If a community "exists in the eye of the beholder" (Koskenniemi, Ratner, and Rittberger 2003, 91), and precisely because there is no organic community at the international level, to understand the concept of the international community we must shift from a rhetorical approach to a discursive one. This requires adopting a reflexive approach that is focused more on the role of the speakers and of the content they infuse into the concept than on its analytical compatibilities with IR theory (Bigo 2011, 232). The international community is more than a rhetorical device that political leaders use for political purposes just to maximize self-interest and legitimize (in)action. It is a form of text and talk that is constituted and expressed by agents and should thus be seen as a discursive construct that materializes only once agents talk about it, refer to it, and attribute to it certain values, rules, and virtues. The question thus is not whether references to the international community are real or sincere but rather what we can learn about international relations from the ways through which the international community is discursively constructed. The contents that infuse and construct the concept of the international community can be the lens for further scrutiny of elements of common ethos and collective identity among states. Moreover, it can be a lens for understating the social foundations of international relations in their most literal meaning, as changes in the ways the international community is being recognized and conceptualized may reflect changes in how states position and see themselves as individual members of the wider social realm of the "international."

Here, I argue, lies the main puzzle of the international community and its role as a discursive practice. On the one hand, its frequent presence in the international discourse suggests that the vast majority of states (and other agents and actors) constantly refer to the existence and operation of the international community in general and to specific issues in particular. Hence, that agents can use the concept as an identification mechanism through which they relate to other states and to world affairs as well as a presentation mechanism through which they locate themselves publicly in the international realm. On the other hand, the international community is neither harmonious nor homogenous but rather loaded with notions of politics and power. It hosts political entities with various, and contradicting, interests and preferences that often interact and argue over the ways to maintain stability and define rightful conduct. Furthermore, as the international community lacks any concrete ontological existence, the contents and substances that construct it as a common ethos are essentially dynamic, contested, and open for interpretation.

The Conceptual Virtues of the International Community

Concepts play social and political functions in shaping behavior and actions through linguistic and nonlinguistic practices, but the attempt to understand these functions is first entailed in preliminary questions of representation and signification. Eventually, as concepts serve as the ideational-linguistic infrastructure to the operation of our socio-cognitive reality, all concepts are signifiers in essence, thus, not only asking ""What are we talking about?" but also discussing to what extent the concept enjoys a solid signification system, what it represents and for whom, and who loads it with meanings and contents. These are important questions in the quest to understand political concepts in general and concepts in relations in particular, not only because they can illuminate latent features that shape the extent to which a concept can function in the political sphere but also since political concepts evolve through sociopolitical struggles over signification, and thus attempts to reconstruct a concept may stem from redesigning its fluid and dynamic signification features.

Essentially, the fundamental semiotic model of Ferdinand de Saussure asserts that a sign is composed by two elements—a signified (the mental object) and a signifier (the material object). As language is a system of signs that are constituted through difference, its operation is conditioned first by a definite and known pairing of the signifier and the signified as well as by the relational positions among signifiers that define the limits and borders of signs. In this respect, signs are shaped both by an internal signification system and by their external relations with other signs. This is the prerequisite for a sociolinguistic space that is characterized by differentiation and clarity and hence allows a sense of objective identity.

However, not all signs are composed by a clear-cut match between the two components but might rather hold an ambiguous representation that requires instilling meaning by relating to a certain "currency" (Laclau 1996, 36). Political concepts—for example, "freedom," "peace," and "democracy"—which are often challenged in terms of differentiation and consolidation (Sartori 1970), are understood as floating signifiers that acquire differentiated meanings by placing other signifiers on a categorical spectrum, which allows (in a specific discursive framework) the ability to account more what a certain signifier is not than what it is.

The radical case of a discrepancy between the signifier and the signified is the case in which a signifier is void of any meaning and is thus empty. According to Ernesto Laclau (1996, 36–39), an empty signifier is a signifier that lacks not only a specific or a particular signified but also any signified object and is possible when "there is a structural im-possibility in signification as such, and only if this impossibility can signify itself as an interruption (subversion, distortion, etcetera) of the structure of the sign" (37). The absence of a signified and signification is therefore exactly where its (political) logic and significance stem from.

As opposed to floating signifiers, whose meaning may be ambiguous across discourses but can still be fixed within a specific discourse based on a relational measurement, an empty signifier operates like a sponge. It absorbs meanings from other signifiers (rather than a signified) through what Laclau and Mouffe term a "chain of equivalence" (Laclau 1995; Laclau and Mouffe 1985). Conversely, though, due to the lack of a signified and of a fixed meaning, there is an essentially endless attempt to fill its lack of meanings simply by welcoming any addition to the chain of equivalence. Thus, contrary to "regular" hegemonic struggles between political powers that aim to impose meanings on specific concepts by exclusion and differentiation (see Ish-Shalom, this volume), the inability to negate an empty signifier renders it open and inviting to any content. In the absence of content, there is no content to challenge or contest. This is, according to Laclau (1996, 40–46), the basic manifestation of hegemony, as creation and maintenance of absence precludes any contestation and enables political powers to constantly fill the concept but without limiting it. Thus, the intrinsic emptiness allows the empty signifier to operate as a pseudo-stable political concept that may provide deferential identity, due to its hegemonic role and despite its being empty of content.

To a great extent, Laclau's conceptualization of empty signifier is very relevant for understating the concept of the "international community." The gap between its popularity in the international political discourse and the fact that it is not really clear what or who is the international community suggests that it may function as an empty signifier. I argue that he emptiness of the international community and the ability to instill it with any content render it a useful discursive practice for states that may use it to normalize and regulate social relations between and among states. As an empty signifier, the concept is endowed with the ability to act as an identification and participation mechanism by casting a sense of communal equality in a nonequal setting and of a normative order in a power-based environment. As I demonstrate in the following section, this is not necessarily a pure hegemonic construction but rather a "democratic" device. Any state—strong or weak, developed or deprived—has both an opportunity and an incentive to participate in the discursive making and sustaining of the international community in order to both legitimize themselves as actors and establish normative standards of operation.

Below I suggest a reflexive reading of the concept as an empty signifier in light of its usage by states and political leaders in the day-to-day international arena. I argue that the discursive construct of the international community plays two main roles. First, based on Laclau's concept of the "chain of equivalence," as an empty signifier the international community is part of hegemonic struggles over other floating signifiers, like democracy, freedom, and development. It serves as a means to make them relational and to legitimize them by anchoring them to the international community, which in return may devalue and empty their ideological tangibility. Second, it perpetuates a false sense of equality in an unequal setting and reinforces identification with the unique class of states.

Conceptualizing the International Community as a Discursive Practice

The concept of the international community plays a performative role through which states can establish an I-We interplay but, more importantly, can charge it with content and construct what it means "to be a state" and "act as a state." The international community in this regard is a discursive practice through which "signifiers, meanings and identities are brought together to form a particular understanding of the world" (Solomon 2009, 5). As a discursive practice, the concept of the international community is a conduit for states to present themselves as a Self in the day-to-day political sphere and to establish themselves as an "I within a We," manifesting relations that cannot exist outside of the discursive construct of the international community. As such, the international community transcends beyond its conceptual barriers. It is not only a concept that is used to describe or reflect a certain condition but also a practice through which agents develop a sense of identification, define themselves vis-à-vis fellow states, and subscribe to normative and practical sets of conduct (see also Bueger, this volume, on the evolvement of the practice of "blue economy"). As a discursive practice, the international community operates at two intertwined levels—the social, by defining a framework for relations between states and for participation in world politics; and the political, by defining a framework for political action and conduct in world politics. Thus, while the international community has no material existence, like any other discursive practice it is as real as it can get, first, since it is constituted over and over through text and talk, and second, since it is entangled with both material and nonmaterial effects (Arnold 2004, 84–86). An analysis of the speeches of heads of state in the opening session of the UNGA between 1992 and 2014 (n = 4,246) reveals that the phrase "international community" is mentioned 15,122 times. It is the second most frequent phrase in these speeches (after "United Nations"), and it appears in 87.35 percent of the speeches (3,709 out of 4,246 speeches, with an average of 3.5 mentions per speech). The dominancy of the concept suggests that in general, states are widely attended to the notion of the international community.[2] Interestingly, there is hardly any variance in the usage patterns across years (see fig. 1) and a more apparent but not substantive variance across states.

Seventy percent of states (136 out of 196) mentioned the term in at least 87 percent of their speeches and thus have met or exceeded the average value of references. Thirty-six states mentioned the phrase in all of their UN speeches. Only seven states have referred to the phrase in less than 60 percent of their speeches (Brunei Darussalam, 35 percent; Venezuela, 35 percent; Andorra, 48 percent; Singapore, 48 percent; Norway, 57 percent; Tonga, 57 percent; and the United States, 57 percent).

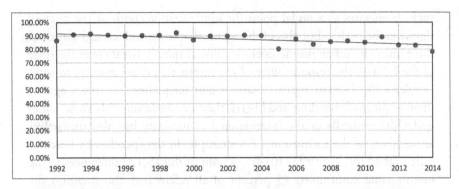

Figure 1. International community across years: The figure shows the percentage of speeches in the UNGA in a given year in which the term "international community" was mentioned (n = 4,264; 1992–2014).

That usage of the phrase is so prevalent in the UNGA discourse and at the same time is also hardly affected by factors of time or type of agents suggests that the discursive practice of "international community" is in fact an empty signifier. On the one hand, it is used ubiquitously by states, leaders, practitioners, and media outlets that never really question its existence, operation, or normative foundations. On the other hand, it lacks any specific signified. It has no ontological meaning or manifestation and no clear demarcations to set its internal/external borders or to determine who is in and who is out of them. It cannot be conceptualized as a floating signifier as it cannot be located on any relational spectrum—we cannot tell what it is as much as we cannot tell what it is not. Consequently, there is no explicit challenge to the concept itself or to its status in the international discourse and no debate over its intrinsic fragility or the paradox that it is embedded in, namely, that it cannot exist.

The emptiness of the concept is—however—its greatest virtue. An empty signifier serves in the framework of Laclau as a discursive nodal point around which differential elements create a discourse and is used to signify the discourse as a whole. Therefore, at the level of content, the prevalence of the international community as a dominant concept in international discourse demonstrates its ability to serve as an anchor to fix the meaning and make sense of central floating signifiers, such as freedom, democracy, and so forth, as part of the chain of equivalences (see also Wolff, this volume, on the concept of self-determination), and therefore the phrase is a discursive device to place other concepts in relation. As such, it operates as a nodal point for legitimization, both of the floating signifiers themselves but also of the agents that re-reproduce and construct these linkages. When nondemocratic illiberal states reiterate over the stage of the UNGA the responsibility of the international community to solve problems like human rights violations and inequality and to act against them to promote freedom and liberty, they legitimize not only these values under the umbrella of the international community but also themselves as members of the community. For example, in the speeches by heads of state in the UNGA (1992–2014), 745 out of the 15,122 references to the international community (5 percent of all references) also mention the concept of democracy; 499 sentences (3.5 percent) contain references to "human rights."[3] In both examples, the connection between the international community and notions of democracy and human rights is made by the majority of state members in the UNGA (85 percent in the case of democracy; 77 percent in the case of human rights). Many of these states that so naturally link the international community with democracy and human rights are far from being democratic or human rights advocates.

Thus, one might find perplexing the saying of Pak Kil Yon, vice minister for foreign affairs of the Democratic People's Republic of Korea, in his speech at the UNGA in 2009: "Today, the General Assembly is the only place in the United Nations where the views of the international community can be properly reflected and democracy ensured"; or that of China in 2006: "The Council should give greater attention to massive and gross violations of human rights caused by armed conflicts and should support the international community in its efforts to prevent conflicts, restore peace and combat terrorism in all its forms and manifestations." These are just anecdotal examples, but they suggest that the concept of international community functions as a means to tie both floating signifiers in a chain of equivalence and agents to a notion of a greater We of states.

At the level of agents, the concept of the international community projects on the social nature of relations among states as a class. It allows them to depict and identify themselves as a Self within a We—a Self that is infused not only from particular national or state-level characteristics like culture, religion, and power resources but also from the identity of being a state. Therefore, a state's identity is confined not only to internal sources or even to regional identity features but also to elements of identity that stem from being a state, from its deferential identity. The concept of the international community as an empty signifier accords states to maintain and reinforce such identity, since once a state refers to the international community, it—at least as a by-product—not only reinforces its own belongingness to the community but also accredits itself with the right to make claims in regard to the content of the international community, namely, to what it means to be a state and act as a state. For example, when Israel in its speech in the 2004 UNGA session says, "And the international community now realizes that terror and tyranny are the twin enemies of the individual freedoms and human rights—including the right to life itself—which define our humanity," it uses both the notion of the international community and its linkage to issues of freedom and human rights to legitimize its own (disputed) measures against terrorism in the context of the Israeli-Palestinian conflict. Since any state can affiliate itself with the international community and instill content into it, the concept can easily create a false sense of equality and universality in an environment that is constructed by power and interests. The universality of the concept, both in its name and in its widespread usage, echoes the connection that Laclau makes between hegemony, empty signifiers, and the universal/particular tension, as to him any claim to universality is a hegemonic maneuver of a particular entity to emit a "universal" status (see Fairclough 2005, 51).

However, as noted above, the international community is not necessarily a pure hegemonic concept that is used by powerful states to cast a spurious pretense of peace and equality. If this was the case, we couldn't explain the necessity of such a facade or its implications. The case of the international community reveals the need of the actor to be part of a community and to participate in the process of identifying the We and of identifying the I as a member of the We. As a discursive construct, the international community is more than the (maybe hegemonic) norms and practices that the concept carries. It is also a hub through which actors position, participate, and affiliate themselves with the rules of the international game. Thus, while actors do not challenge the notion of the international community or expose its emptiness, they use it to have voice, to be heard, and to legitimize themselves as members and to claim their role in the dynamic processes of meanings fixation. Moreover, since the discursive construction of the concept is accessible to all actors, as it spreads in the discourse it also accumulates some measure of accountability and credibility. Thus, although the international community is all and nothing at the same time, the more states rely on it when they talk with each other about each other and about the world they aim to govern, the more their relations—and the content of their relations—become contingent upon the international community.

Conclusion: Is the International Community a Fantasy?

The political life is surrounded by concepts. We use concepts to articulate reality and to signify representations of our world but also to share inter-subjective understandings of what life is, to infuse it with sense, meaning, and practical trajectories. As such, concepts play both informative and per-formative roles; they both define a phenomenon and inform actions that stem from it. The concept of the international community is especially intriguing in this respect. I argue throughout the chapter that although it is extremely popular in the public political discourse, the concept has no specific signified or meaning, and thus instead of defining a phenomenon, the concept itself is a political phenomenon in its own right. Importantly, I am not implying that it is not a significant concept. On the contrary, it is an extremely significant concept, exactly because it has loose and vague signification.

Indeed, an ontological existence of the international community stands in great contradiction to IR theory, and any attempt to theorize it is likely—quite justly—to meet rolling eyes and skeptical looks. Although IR schol-ars often refer to its existence, they hardly explore or discuss its ontological traits or functions in world politics. Indeed, the international community is not a very useful concept when it comes to theorizing world politics. There is no way to ontologically define or demarcate it, and thus its argu-ably inherent redundancy renders it profoundly challenging to integrate with IR paradigmatic frameworks, even with social constructivism. Even when the notion of community at the international level is theorized, it is used to explain other phenomena like peace or international law. The rare accounts in the international community itself usually focus on its norma-tive traits and depict it as "a community of morals, ethics, and common identities" (Ellis 2009, 5) and assess its normative functionality mainly as a desired end goal (Bliesemann de Guevara and Kühn 2011, 137–39; Buzan and Gonzalez-Pelaez 2005).

Yet, the virtues of the international community and its political signifi-cance lie not in the ontological questions of whether it exists or in what the conditions are that generate or maintain it. Rather, they lie in the popularity of the concept and thus in its epistemological qualities—in the tendency of political leaders, practitioners, academics, media reports, and laymen to talk about it. We name the international community; refer to its existence; attribute it with values, norms, and moral responsibility; and assign it agential capacities to act and respond in international event. These usages insinuate that it is not the international community itself that has a political function but rather the concept of the international community and the ways it is being used in international interactions and discourse. Thus, while it may seem useless or redundant to IR theorists, it must play a role in the political field itself and in the construction of international relations between and among states. This is the tension between the difficulty to theorize the international community and its prevalent presence in the day-to-day international discourse, thus between the international community as a theoretical construct and as a political concept.

At the political level, the international community is a discursive construct. It exists only once agents refer to it, attribute meaning to it, and construct it through common interactions. The discursive construction of the international community is, of course, intersubjective and contingent upon common and shared understanding and knowledge, but in the absence of (a fixated) ontological anchor it has no borders of signification. As such, the concept of the international community is almost the ultimate example of an empty signifier. It enjoys a surplus of meanings and usages, on the one hand, but has no fixated signifier or distinction between what it is and what it is not, on the other hand. Then, the question is what we can learn of the international sphere via the political phenomenon of constructing the international community as an empty signifier.

The international community serves as a nodal point for familiarizing and legitimizing both political phenomena and agents and as such may constitute international discourse as common, shared, and coherent— even when it cannot be. It allows identification as a means of order and stability, as it perpetuate the continuity of the (nonexisting) community through an endless cycle of nonmeaning. States may use the international community to (artificially) determine who is in and who is out, but since there is no significance of being out and since states cannot be excluded from acting internationally, such convictions cannot in practice construct who is the international We. The content that is attached to the international community cannot turn it into, a community, but only can create relations between other signifiers, agents, and the wider sphere in which they identify themselves, as an I within a greater We.

The constant reproduction of the international community by political agents is the process through which the empty signifier is being filled and emptied at the same time. In this respect, the political agents themselves treat the international community as a container that can be infused with any meaning that is relevant to their political goals. Laclau accentuates that filling empty signifiers with meaning is an illusionary process, as an empty signifier has an open structure that cannot hold specific meaning. Agents may attribute it with various, even contradicting, signifiers—but the imaginary existence of the international community is taken for granted. Against the prevailing popularity of the concept, no one shouts that the emperor has no clothes or even asks, "What are you talking about"? As long as agents do not question or contest the international community, they are in fact hindering its establishment and preventing any struggle over the meanings that may be attached with it. In this regard, the international community plays a fantastical role in international discourse, a constant reminder of what is missing and may ever be missing in international politics.

Notes

1. Barack Obama, "Address to the United Nations General Assembly," 21 September 2011.

2. "We" is one of the most frequently used words in the UNGA speeches, but it is problematic to distinguish between "We the states" and other references to "We," although in many cases states do refer to a collective "We" of states.

3. Note that although these seem like relatively low rates, in fact, such rates are quite high if we think about the probabilities that a certain word will appear in the same sentence with a certain phrase. Out of all the words that appear in "international community" sentences, "democracy" and "human rights" are among the top one hundred coinciding words.

References

Addis, Adeno. 2008. "Imagining the International Community: The Constitutive Dimension of Universal Jurisdiction." *Human Rights Quarterly* 31 (1): 129–62.

Arnold, Samantha L. 2004. "'The Language of Respectability' and the (Re) Constitution of Muslim Selves in Colonial Bengal." In *Identity and Global Politics*, ed. Patricia M. Goff and Kevin C. Dunn, 83–102. New York: Palgrave.

Bigo, Didier. 2011. "Pierre Bourdieu and International Relations: Power of Practices, Practices of Power." *International Political Sociology* 5 (3): 225–58.

Bliesemann de Guevara, Berit, and Florian P. Kühn. 2011. "'The International Community Needs to Act': Loose Use and Empty Signalling of a Hackneyed Concept." *International Peacekeeping* 18 (2): 135–51.

Brown, Chris. 1995. "International Theory and International Society: The Viability of the Middle Way?" *International Relations* 21 (2): 183–96.

Bull, Hedley. 1977. *The Anarchical Society*. New York: Columbia University Press.

Buzan, Barry, and Ana Gonzalez-Pelaez. 2005. "'International Community' after Iraq." *International Affairs* 81 (1): 31–52.

Diehl, Paul F., Charlotte Ku, and Daniel Zamora. 2003. "The Dynamics of International Law: The Interaction of Normative and Operating Systems." *International Organization* 57 (1): 43–75.

Dupuy, P. M. 1997. "The Constitutional Dimension of the Charter of the United Nations Revisited." *Max Planck Yearbook of United Nations Law* 1:1–33.

Ellis, David C. 2009. "On the Possibility of 'International Community.'" *International Studies Review* 11 (1): 1–26.

Fairclough, Norman L. 2005. "Blair's Contribution to Elaborating a New 'Doctrine of International Community.'" *Journal of Language and Politics* 4 (1): 41–63.

Fassbender, Bardo. 1998. "The United Nations Charter as Constitution of the International Community." *Columbia Journal Transnational Law* 36:529–620.

Franck, Thomas M. 1990. *The Power of Legitimacy among Nations*. Oxford: Oxford University Press.

Franck, Thomas M. 1995. *Fairness in International Law and Institutions*. Oxford: Calrendon Press.

Kaczmarska, Katarzyna. 2016. "The Powerful Myth of International Community and the Imperative to Build States." In *Myths and International Politics: Mythographical Approaches to the Study of IR*, ed. Berit Bliesemann de Guevara, 209–28. New York: Palgrave Macmillan.

Koh, Harold Hongju. 1997. "Why Do Nations Obey International Law ?" *Yale Law Journal* 106 (8): 2599–659.

Koskenniemi, Martti. 2004. "International Law and Hegemony: A Reconfiguration." *Cambridge Review of International Affairs* 17 (2): 197–218.

Koskenniemi, Martti, Steven Ratner, and Volker Rittberger. 2003. "Comments to Chapter 2 and 3." In *United States Hegemony and the Foundations of International Law*, ed. Michael Byers and Georg Nolte, 91–115. Cambridge: Cambridge University Press.

Kritsiotis, Dino. 2002. "Imagining the International Community." *European Journal of International Law* 13 (4): 962–92.

Kumm, Mattias. 2004. "The Legitimacy of International Law: A Constitutionalist Framework of Analysis." *European Journal of International Law* 15 (5): 907–31.

Laclau, Ernesto. 1995. "Subject of Politics, Politics of the Subject." *Differences: A Journal of Feminist Cultural Studies* 7 (1): 146.

Laclau, Ernesto. 1996. *Emancipation(s)*. London: Verso.

Laclau, Ernesto, and Chantal Mouffe. 1985. *Hegemony and Socialist Strategy*. London: Verso.

Mapel, David R., and Terry Nardin. 1999. *International Society: Diverse Ethical Perspectives*. Princeton, NJ: Princeton University Press.

Nardin, Terry. 1999. "Legl Positivism as a Theory of International Society." In *International Society: Diverse Ethical Perspectives*, ed. David R. Mapel and Terry Nardin, 17–35. Princeton: Princeton University Press.

Paulus, Andreas. 2003. "The Influence of the United States on the Concept of the 'International Community.'" In *United States Hegemony and the Foundations of International Law*, ed. Michael Byers and Georg Nolte, 266–77. Cambridge: Cambridge University Press.

Sartori, Giovanni. 1970. "Concept Misformation in Comparative Politics." *American Political Science Review* 64 (4): 1033–53.

Simma, Bruno, and A. L. Paulus. 1998. "The 'International Community': Facing the Challenge of Globalization." *European Journal of International Law* 9 (2): 266–77.

Solomon, T. 2009. "Social Logics and Normalisation in the War on Terror." *Millennium: Journal of International Studies* 38 (2): 269–94.

Tonnies, Ferdinand. 1963. *Community and Society: Gemeinschaft und Gesellschaft*. New York: Harper and Row.

Tsagourias, N. 2006. "International Community, Recognition of States, and Political Cloning." In *Towards an "International Legal Community"? The Sovereignty of States and the Sovereignty of International Law*, ed. Stephen Warbrick and Colin Tierney, 211–40. London: British Institute of International and Comparative Law.

Whelan, Fredrick G. 1999. "Legal Positivism and International Society." In *International Society: Diverse Ethical Perspectives*, ed. David R. Mapel and Terry Nardin, 36–53. Princeton, NJ: Princeton University Press.

CHAPTER 10

Concluding Chapter: Concepts at Work in Global IR

Jan Wilkens and Oliver Kessler

Given that the linguistic turn and, with it, the so-called third debate were introduced into international relations (IR) theory more than twenty-five years ago, it is quite surprising that "concepts" have not attracted their deserved attention so far. Concepts are ideal "attractors" for an understanding of language that departs from the idea that a concept is like an invisible veil attached to things in the same way that price tags are attached to goods. Instead, concepts allow us to capture the linguistic turn's emphasis on the complexity, thickness, and opacity of linguistic entities. From this perspective, one would expect that a much larger debate would have already happened. However, it is only recently that a broader focus on concepts themselves has emerged (Diez, Bode, and da Costa 2011). It is only now that there is an acknowledged need for them to be further "unpacked" (Berenskoetter 2016, 2017; Ish-Shalom 2019). Of course, we do not want to argue that concepts have just been "discovered," as if now they are here and previously they were not. There were always occasional references to "conceptual analysis" (Baldwin 1997, 6)[1] and "conceptual history" (Kratochwil 1995; Onuf 1991; Guzzini 2005). However, IR is a latecomer when it comes to the analysis of concepts.

It is eventually quite important to remember that the Copenhagen School already from early onward had pointed out that security has to be understood as a *concept* rather than as a "state of affairs." However, it is quite telling that its *conceptual dimension* did not gain much attraction. Instead, the focus was rather on its recourse to speech act theory and the possible limits that come with it. Hence, today we see numerous studies that wonder whether there are conditions that foster the acceptability of the speech act and search for some criteria and their "empirical evidence." Further, we now have also seen a significant number of analyses that ask whether the speech act allows us to understand the processes not only of securitization but also of *de*-securitization? We certainly do not want to criticize these attempts and discussions, but only point out that the link to "concepts" was for a long time not regarded as being somehow "problematic."

Given that concepts only move slowly to the fore, this volume is thus a timely and necessary step toward a better understanding about the status, use, and politics of concepts. What all chapters in the volume indeed show is that concepts *are* central for *understanding* and *producing* social reality. Concepts are not merely, as Max Weber once stated, "one of the great tools of all scientific knowledge" (qtd. in Gerth and Mills 1946, 141), but have to be placed in the context of how we understand reality: questions about meaning, boundaries, practices, discourses, and other signifiers of social reality cannot be answered without the recourse to concepts. It is of little surprise that concepts are understood and developed depending on epistemological assumptions within given paradigms (cf. Goertz 2006; Collier, LaPorte, and Seawright 2012). In discursive practices, for example, concepts express and reproduce ontological assumptions about what constitutes an object or social phenomenon. This book's attempt to understand the meaning of concepts through their enactment substantially contributes to this critical engagement by shifting the perspective on social dynamics in which concepts are *at work*.

In these concluding remarks, we do not want to engage in a nuanced critique of the individual chapters and thereby identify some particular readings or misreadings of some of the masters of conceptual history and/or conceptual analysis. Neither are we interested in engaging in a debate on why one approach might be better suited rather than another to advance a particular agenda. We do not want to play intellectual soccer—where one master of conceptual history (like Koselleck, Collingwood, or Skinner) is then put in competition with another (like Gallie or Sartori). It would be almost preposterous to assume that an engagement of a—at least for IR—rather new topic does not come with shortcomings, biases, and misreadings. These shortcomings, biases, and misreadings are important and productive. What seems more important than a "true" reading of the classics is the need for those of us in IR to find our own way of "doing" conceptual analysis/history. This is where this book helps us to move the agenda forward. We cannot simply "translate" or "apply" an existing body of literature onto some problem and claim that we have therefore shown the right way. Moreover, almost every well-known philosopher has his or her own take on concepts.

It is simply an impossible task to describe the whole of past avenues. While it is true that conceptual history and analysis are both well-established fields in social theory, this does not mean that "concepts" cannot be new for IR and that finding our own way is a formidable task on its own. It is simply unproductive to already at this stage say "why have you" or "you should have," as if we who write the conclusion are on a higher moral or epistemic position. Instead, we want to use the discussion in these chapters to identify a couple of themes and anticipate some further questions ahead. This more thematic discussion starts with the move from "concepts" to "concepts-in-use." The aim of this concluding chapter is to discuss what a critical engagement and self-reflexive approach to concepts in IR entails. In the first part, we therefore explore the link between concepts, contingency, and power to highlight the different patterns of impact of concepts-in-use in the process of the construction of social reality. Analytically, we differentiate between single, double, and triple contingency to explore the different patterns of how concepts-in-use work. Since concepts are cultural and historical artifacts, that is, context specific in relation to the time and social space in which they have been developed and interpreted, a critical engagement with concepts-in-use within the discipline of IR means a reflection on their Eurocentrism. For that reason, the second part discusses what a reflexive approach to concept-in-use analysis could look like. Against this background, the chapter will connect the discussion about concepts to the recent call of Global IR (Acharya 2014, 2016; Hurrell 2016; Wiener 2018) to "better account of culturally diverse agents that act under plural conditions of engagement at different local sites in global society" (Wiener 2018, 1). To this end, the chapter puts the recent call of Global IR into conversation with concept analysis in IR to indicate an outlook and pathway for a critical engagement with concepts at work.

From Concepts to Concepts-*in-Use*: The Next Step in Conceptual Analysis?

Quite in line with the path laid out in the introduction to this volume, all contributions have shown how concepts-in-use shape practices and have, at the same time, changed over time. The chapters provided in-depth discussions of examples that show how the meaning of a concept emerged and how they have changed through discursive practices. Concepts and their meaning are, as the introduction highlights, constantly reshaped through their use in sociopolitical contexts. These shifts can evolve in relation to different geographical and temporal contexts (cf. Bueger, chap. 7). The meaning of concepts then changes when concepts "travel" and are used in different contexts. Further, changes unfold through the strategic use of concepts to legitimize a policy, which can occur through a narrow definition or, in contrast, the fuzziness and ambiguity of a concept (cf. Mitrani, chap. 9).

In this sense, concepts shape and limit our understanding of social phenomena, as they create certain images and produce an order through contextualizing the image within a narrative (cf. Beaulieu-Brossard, chap. 5). Scholars cannot "solve" the puzzle of concepts by some criteria of verification or falsification where concepts would be reduced to the status of variables. The use of concepts is not "false" in a logical sense. Rather, as the chapters have shown, concepts "do" something; they are enacted and performed and therefore inscribe themselves onto "reality" through all sorts of decisions and (speech) acts. In this representation, concepts are often imagined as an *outcome* of a process (as for example assumed in the claim "Israel is a democratic state"). In other cases, as the chapters have shown, concepts are meaningful within given contexts in which they describe *processes* themselves (i.e., "In modern nation-states, people participate in elections"). Thus, concepts are to be understood, as Onuf stated with reference to the concept of "society" as "a thing *and* a process" (1994, 1). Hence, practices of sense making through concepts have to be analyzed, as shown in the previous chapters, within a dynamic relationship between the *outcome* of social processes and the very *social practices* that produce them.

At the same time, the use of concepts is not detached from their context and is always subject to translations, interpretations, and modifications. This use of concepts, hence, is always linked to questions of continuities and discontinuities: their use is characterized by tensions, ruptures, and contingency rather than a continuous history of ideas. This emphasis on contingency highlights that "nature" (or any event, crisis, or "failure") does not determine the terms in which we identify, categorize, separate, put in relation, and so forth. Instead, the use of concepts always refers back to a political move in the sense that a given event, crisis, or failure could have been described in different terms: it makes a great difference whether something is analyzed in conceptual terms of inequality, market failure, or justice, for example.[2] This "could have been different" inevitably then also refers to the power of concepts-in-use: power refers to the performative processes whereby concepts are inscribed onto the world and create their own "condition of possibility."

In the following, we want to explore this link between concepts, contingency, and power by differentiating different kinds of contingency. Here, we use the terms "single contingency," "double contingency," and "triple contingency" to *analytically differentiate* between "discursive" positions that researchers on concepts-in-use implicitly or explicitly draw on: do we analyze the decision of a single actant, intersubjective processes, or a constellation of three actants? This analytical differentiation *does not* constitute different levels of analysis, a conceptualization of social reality in itself that assumes distinct systemic processes operating on each level.[3] In contrast, our differentiation aims at highlighting how the analysis of concepts-in-use is shaped by the discursive position that research focuses on—yet, that the different contingencies are neither structurally (or systemically) separate nor working according to distinct logics but rather are co-constitutive and shape the contingency of concepts at work. The differentiation is a methodological reflection that allows highlighting various approaches and focal points in the chapters of this volume. Hence, this is not about the creation of a hierarchy but a call to consider the various contingencies in future research on concepts at work in IR.

Single Contingency

Eventually the most famous frameworks for studying contingency are approaches that examine individual decisions: a given actor has to face an objective albeit contingent reality that she has to master. Approaches here may fall into "explanation" or "understanding" with eventually behavioral

208 Concepts at Work

approaches moving in between. In the context of concepts-in-use, we may here see how concepts are used *strategically* to either limit the range of possible arguments or impose specific meaning on certain actions or events. We may place the concepts of the "success" of war as outlined by Brent J. Steele and Luke Campbell in chapter 3 or place the use of "democracy" within both Israel (Beaulieu-Brossard, chap. 5) and democratic peace arguments (Geis, chap. 4). We may also, as Bueger (chap. 7) has outlined, follow concepts into different "contexts" and thereby highlight the contingency of their use, that is, highlight the agenda and aspired positionality of the actor who uses certain concepts. Already here, we can identify the political projects that inform the concepts-in-use and concede that every use of concepts is never just an empirical description of externally given facts.

Double Contingency

Another context emerges when we look at how concepts are negotiated among different actors. While we may assume that the meaning of concepts arises from their capacity to serve as mental representations of a certain social phenomena, the chapters also show how actors are involved in the dynamics of meaning making by "attaching meaning to concepts, [which] commits them and renders them useful vehicles of persuasion" (see Ish-Shalom, introduction). The vocabulary of understanding, persuasion, performance, and similar concepts cannot operate in a context where there is only one actor: there is speaking and there is listening, there is illocution and perlocution in speech acts.[4]

In this context, we find the question of the *contestation* of concepts that stresses the patterns in which concepts are undermined, reframed, or changed. Contestation is eventually a topic that is "present" in all chapters but that can certainly be developed in further detail. For example, the book introduces and touches upon different strategies in which concepts are used to maintain hegemonic structures or to legitimize specific policies. Based on a Gramscian understanding of hegemony, the (in)determinacy of meaning in regard to a concept allows to uphold or establish dominant structures. The concepts "security," "democracy," "blue economy," or "international community" do not work because actors simply know what they "are"; they work in light of their contextual contingency, which entails dynamics of reinterpretation at the same time. Thus, in most cases the interpretation of concepts is not a focused negotiation of one "correct" understanding in which rational actors interact with each other. In contrast, concepts are, as critical scholarship has also argued in regard to IR theories more generally, "crucial site[s] in which attempts to think otherwise about political possibilities are constrained by categories and assumptions that contemporary political analysis is encouraged to take for granted" (Walker 1993, 5). Quite in line with this, constructivists have pointed out that actors are rather driven by habits and embodied dispositions than abstract concepts such as national interests (McCourt 2016, 475).

Triple Contingency

A third context can be identified by drawing on discursive constructions of social reality. Here, concepts are not the result of some kind of "convention" or "agreement" among actors. Within the double contingency framework, there is no limit to what the actors "agree" on or what common sense is fabricated and manifested. The "relationality" among actors does not determine where the actors end up in their positions and relations. The introduction of the third position highlights that actors enter a (discursive) field that is already in the making and where the rules of the game already prefigure or "delimit" the range of possible interactions: when you enter a hospital, you do so in already established "roles": for example, as visitor, employee, or patient. The chance of renegotiating the concepts of "health" or "freedom" in these contexts is close to impossible. The securitization literature has, for example, shown that the "use" of a "successful" security speech act has performative consequences insofar as a certain temporality ("emergency"), forms of knowing (security experts, military), and "range of arguments" are already enacted (see security analysis in chapter two of Buzan, Waever, and Wilde 1998). The actors already, however, need to "know" what the "communication" of security actually implies: existential threat. The same can be said about the market: the actors may interact as customer, consumer, producer, salesperson, consultant, or whatever role they chose to take. Yet, the "context" of the market already limits the range of possible positions and ways of knowing about the position, interaction, and the rules of the game. Within security, the market, or law, we already have in mind a set of "valid" arguments that can be exchanged, a set of experts who "know" how the field works, and the kind of identities and "relations" that are formed.

Yet, security or the market does not work simply as a simple concept (or a range of concepts): but they are filled with images or metaphors that somehow influence the way concepts relate to each other. In the words of Charles Taylor, they can be described as "social imaginaries" that "now become so self-evident to us that we have trouble seeing [them] as [some] possible conception[s] among others" (2004, 2). The importance of concepts as social imaginaries helps actors to better grasp what a certain concept means as opposed to other concepts. That is, to define myself as a "democratic state" it is crucial to articulate who is a "barbaric state" or a "totalitarian regime." In this context, then, a concept is often embedded in a web of concepts that ultimately constructs specific visions of order as legitimate and often "naturalizes" them. According to Taylor, Western modernity is imagined through the interplay of concepts such as "the market economy, the public sphere, and the self-governing people, among others" (2004, 2). Hence, in both cases, concepts centrally contribute to the production of normativity and order.

Although this could be regarded as unproblematic within an imagined community, this concluding chapter proposes that this foregrounds normative problems. Given the characteristic and indeed constitutive diversity in Global IR, scholarship has to challenge the taken-for-grantedness not only in regard to a specific concept but within the hegemonic context in which a concept is meaningful. When a concept is at work, as Margaret Somers has argued, within "a deeply naturalized metanarrative, it cannot be destabilized by competing evidence or routine empirical investigation" (1995, 116). Somers's sociology of concept formation can provide an interesting avenue for future debates and constitutes a substantial ground to reflect on concepts in use within societal and political dynamics. Hence, in the following sections, this chapter seeks to highlight why it is key to advance a reflexive approach to concept analysis in Global IR. While the introduction and the different chapters have highlighted critical aspects of how specific concepts and patterns of conceptualization shape structures and practices of domination, this concluding chapter seeks to embed the critical reflection about concepts into the broader debate on contestation in Global IR (Acharya 2014, 2016; Wiener 2018). As a new perspective on researching IR and a political project, Global IR aims to engage with questions of who actually has access to contestation and who is excluded in IR in empirical and theoretical terms. As Mor Mitrani (chap. 9) argues in her contribution to this volume, "[P]olitical concepts evolve through sociopolitical struggles over signification,[. . .]". Hence, understanding a concept requires a scrutiny of the match between the concept as a signifier and the elements it is supposed to signify. This reminds us that, as summarized above and identified in this book, the different patterns in which concepts are actually in use have to be critically assessed. Yet, research on contestation in IR points out that it is also key to understand who actually has access to the sociopolitical struggles over signification and who has been excluded or neglected.

Where Do We Go from Here?

Continuing the discussion of contingency and concepts, then, we think that the book also points us to some important questions that will certainly be influential for future debate. First, we believe that three contexts identified above tell us about different problems of contestation and the "dialectics" of justification and critique. In the first context, critique and justification appear to be "limitedless": there is always a "plurality" of concepts (or different meanings inscribed in one concept) that one could use. Critique, then, is voiced by challenging the strategic use of some concept by pointing to another one (or by pointing out another meaning of that concept).

In the second context, concepts resulted from interactions are inscribed in or even constitutive of the very habits, conventions, and institutions that then guide further interactions. Critique and justification then manifest themselves in a change of the conceptual "basis" of habits or conventions. Critique seems almost impossible when it comes to "imaginaries" or "metaphors." How can one criticize the use of the market or security except by pointing to alternatives like "democracy"? While these debates certainly are part of our everyday readings of newspapers, they cannot be solved by empirical evidence. Such an argument would simply confuse the kind of contingency we deal with. Without engaging in these debates too much, as we simply cannot solve all questions within the given space limit, we rather want to point to two further questions that we think needs further unpacking for future contributions.

The "Situatedness" of Concepts and Reflectivism

Somers's approach is very insightful for the study of concepts in use because of her reflexive and relational perspective on how they "work." Particularly, to understand and dissect the hegemony of a concept and specific interpretation, her definition of concepts as "relational concepts" (Somers 1995, 134) offers a useful analytical perspective.

Her central observation is that specific concepts used within and beyond academia appear as impartial or natural because the meaning of concepts is "produced, constrained and contained by its embeddedness in [a] conceptual network," which "is a structured relational matrix of theoretical principles and conceptual assumptions" (Somers 1995, 134). Hence, concepts are not objects that evolved over time and within specific cultural and spatial contexts but social artifacts produced in *relation to* other concepts and social imaginaries. Their meaningfulness and hegemonic interpretation develop through their relation to the normative background in which concepts are at work and ontological connection to other concepts. "That is, concepts cannot be defined on their own as single ontological entities; rather, the meaning of one concept can be deciphered only in terms of its 'place' in relation to other concepts in its web" (Somers 1995, 136). This is not to suggest that this network develops one distinct internal logic in which only one specific rationality is meaningful. Even within imagined communities and with regard to specific conceptual networks, it is likely to encounter competing interpretations and concepts. Yet, "it suggests the influence of the Foucaultian notion of the historically contingent but nonetheless internal integrity of a cultural pattern or logic, such that pragmatic choices within this pattern are regulated by the pressures of meaningful consistency" (135). Thus, concepts are *historical and cultural* artifacts unfolding their power in cases where they appear as "natural objects" within a given community in which a definition of the concept seeks to reflect "most clearly the *concrete* reality they are trying to represent" (136). Hence, a critical engagement with hegemonic interpretations of concepts needs to entail the analysis of sensemaking dynamics and its normative background. Normativity is not limited to scholarship that explicitly promotes a particular project, for example, Kantian or Marxist envisioning a global order, but is also ingrained into many IR theories in an implicit manner. Notably, the epistemological and ontological conceptualization of many IR theories implies particular normative assumptions despite the claim of conducting impartial research. However, they, first, do not acknowledge that the production of a given academic community is embedded in historical developments (Guzzini 2000) and, second, tend to remain uncritical toward their Western background while marginalizing perspectives beyond the West (cf. Acharya 2011; Hobson 2012).

For example, state-centered approaches are grounded in the premise that the modern state system, consisting of independent and power-seeking units, began in 1648 (Havercroft 2012). However, their conceptualization poses problems on three levels. These approaches either remain ahistorical, describing the Westphalian system as given, or present a historical development starting with 1648, reinforcing the notion that only "European exceptionalism" was able to create a modern system. This perspective not only "consign[s] the pre-1948 era to the dustbin of history" (Hobson 2012, 2) but also ignores alternative political orders that were in place after 1648 in other parts of the world claiming universality. Eurocentric perceptions describe modernity in conceptual terms of progress and the sovereign states as natural units of social order. This discourse based on a network of normative concepts has shaped non-Western agency in contending patterns as it created resistance in different forms but also the desire, especially among political elites, "to recreate themselves as 'modern' states against a backdrop of an emerging international society of states" (Zarakol 2011, 38), which indicates the normative power of this discourse. Hence, among the "community of states," the concept of the state unfolds its power because it appears to be the best form of social order *in relation* to other "less modern" forms. It is, further, a *historical and cultural object* in the sense that it has evolved through interaction between and within Western and non-Western elites and other actors around the globe. Yet, if we acknowledge that social science concepts are objects "embedded in *symbolic and historically constructed cultural structures* and assigned meaning by their location of those structures" (Somers 1995, 137), then we need a critical conceptual analysis of the power of concepts. This is particularly relevant for IR, which needs to advance an inclusive agenda focusing on those actors who are affected by international structures but who have limited agency to shape or change them.

Reflexivism and Concept Analysis in IR

Critical scholarship is concerned with its own "scientific" knowledge production and how particular "subjective meanings *become* objective facticities" (Hamati-Ataya 2012, 679) within science itself (see also Amoureux and Steele 2015). Thus, *reflexivism,* first, emphasizes that knowledge and thought have to be historically contextualized and, second, acknowledges, therefore, that it entails normative connotations by default. However, these underpinnings cannot amount to a kind of "transcendental truth" but rather engage with the discursive production of historical meanings valid in a particular context (Hamati-Ataya 2011). Therefore, this approach is "emancipatory" as it seeks to account for the plurality of normative backgrounds and *situated* agency as well as due to its aim to explicitly articulate its own ethical commitments (Hamati-Ataya 2013). Hence, normative perceptions of how the world is or ought to be are constantly altered through interaction and social learning processes. In terms of academic engagement with concepts, reflexivism focuses on "why and how and to what effect have social scientists had the particular idea that the social world contains something significant" (Somers 1995, 135), which they described under the label of a particular concept. Many theories in IR (and beyond) draw on normative assumptions, which they do not reveal or reflect and thereby "tend not to notice the features of both the shared languages of description they employ and the practices of governance (legal and political institutions) they refer to that are imperial in a broader sense of the term" (Tully 2008, 129). Against this background, all chapters of this volume show that a hegemonic language evolving around concepts shapes public discussions and discursively underpins power relations. Whether we talk about "stabilizing operations" or "civilian powers" during war (cf. Geis, chap. 4), which aim to frame political dynamics in a particular way, or if we look at concepts such as "international community" (cf. Mitrani, chap. 9) as well as "self-determination" (cf. Wolff, chap. 2), which appear prima facie as natural concepts of international politics, the hegemonic language is based on and developed in relation to at least two interrelated *imperial* discourses.

First, these concepts draw on a "normative and juridical language of an international system of constitutional states" (Tully 2008, 143). The language is presented in a universal and impartial way that appears to represent the only possible and legitimate path to global order. Yet, its state-centric and Eurocentric normative structure, which developed over long episodes of colonial history, neither is reflected nor accepts other forms of "rightful order." These state-centric concepts develop their hegemony as they are presented as objects embedded in a historical and cultural narrative of progress. Thus, their power and hegemony are based on the dominant assumption in international politics that they are a moral duty and natural part of modernity that rational actors ought to implement or achieve.

Second, this is underpinned through a positivist social-scientific language. It deploys a discourse of progress and modernization dividing international politics between "us" and "them," "barbarians" and "civilized" peoples. Academic concepts such as the "clash of civilization" or "failed states" continue to shape public discourse and contextualize people into categories that are presented as universal but are based on Eurocentrism and serve hegemonic structures. The concept of self-determination, discussed by Jonas Wolff in chapter 2, is another vivid example of the imperial nature of concepts, which appear as impartial elements of global politics. The concept has been used by Western governments to justify its own position and interventions into other countries at the same time, as Wolff shows, until today. In periods of formal colonial rule, the right of self-determination has been acknowledged, yet merely with the argument that more advanced democratic states have the duty to actively help and support less-developed countries via military training, education of elites, and other forms of intervention. This form of "informal imperial rule" (Tully 2008, 153) seeks to vest its hegemony by maintaining "free trade" and Western-style democracy as central concepts of proper development in international politics.

Based on this conceptual critique, we hold that future scholarship needs to take more seriously a truly global perspective on IR and dissect instances of contestation of existing concepts and their meaning-in-use (compare Milliken 1999; Wiener 2008). If scholarship seeks to critically unpack hegemonic relations based on concepts-in-use, it has to depart from state- and Eurocentric assumptions. As concepts are embedded in historical and cultural contexts, scholars need to dissect who is in a position to define and shape the meaning-in-use of concepts and who is not? Who is able to advance new concepts in international politics and decide whether affected stakeholders, that is, those who are affected by a given concept-in-use, are able to intervene in the implementation (compare Wiener 2018, 53–56). Dominant concepts, and their interpretations, unfold through sense making in which relations to other concepts and meanings are established. As seen above in the context of state- and Eurocentric concepts, hegemony can be established when concepts are part of a powerful narrative, such as the narrative of modernity and progress. Thus, the question is, "Who is placed well enough to develop—and thereby change—the narrative?" (Wiener 2018, 54).

To this end, conceptual analysis in IR needs to advance tools that are open to analyze and engage with those actors who are affected by concepts and seek to change them. That is not merely an imperative to engage with the discipline's complicity with the state-centric interpretations and reproduction. Concept analysis needs to further develop reflexive methodologies that allow to dissect new or "hidden" concepts that are not yet regarded as relevant in IR and international politics. In a situation where concepts like sovereignty, self-determination, and international community are at work in the sense that they reproduce hegemonic power structures, scholars and practitioners alike face a normative challenge, which Carol Cohn identified three decades ago in the context of scholars and politicians operating in the nuclear defense industry. In the late 1980s, she summarized that "those of us who find U.S. nuclear policy desperately misguided appear to face a serious quandary. If we refuse to learn the language, we are virtually guaranteed that our voices will remain outside the 'politically relevant' spectrum of opinion. Yet, if we do learn and speak it, we not only severely limit what we can say but we also invite the transformation, the militarization, of our own thinking" (1987, 716). Thus, a challenge is not only to identify dominant interpretations of concepts and the consequences for affected actors. It also opens up the conceptual analysis to other discourses of subaltern actors, for example, nonstate actors, civil society, or indigenous people who may seek to implement alternative visions of order. In contrast to the state, as highlighted in the introduction, "not everyone is empowered or entitled to call things into being" (Guzzini 2013, 83) in international politics, yet this requires scholarship to shed light on *practices of contestation* that signify attempts to change interpretations or even advance new concepts.

Concepts-in-Use and Global IR

In this last section, we aim to draw on the critical insights formulated in the introduction to this volume and the different empirical cases throughout the subsequent chapters. We argue that a dialogue with scholarship on Global IR is a promising next step if scholars not merely are interested in uncovering power dynamics in and through concepts in use but also seek to develop a more inclusive and, in many cases, a decolonial approach to concepts in the discipline of IR. The chapters have in their own ways analyzed the political nature of concepts as the agency strongly varies between those who are authorized to name, categorize, or classify (cf. Ish-Shalom, introduction) and those actors whose agency seems to be shaped by the process of becoming a subject of politics by being assigned a "relevant" category. In IR, as the introduction has argued with reference to Pouliot and Mérand the "state, more than any other institution, possesses the power of appointment, of nomination", (2013, 39) and thereby possesses substantial power to create and (de-)legitimize subjects in international politics. However, an analysis of concepts at work needs to differentiate (a) which states are more powerful in this process and who ought to have access to contribute to nominate, categorize, and classify. Moving beyond the state-focused analysis of power, conceptual analysis needs, as the chapters in this book have shown, (b) an in-depth look at other (nonstate) actors who are affected and seek to gain access to processes of nominating and categorizing as to become equal subjects within international politics themselves.

Here, Global IR understood as a project and call for greater inclusiveness and diversity (Acharya 2014, 649) in the discipline, that is, not as an already narrow and substantial theory of IR, offers a way forward. Following Amitav Acharya's main concern within Global IR, main theories of IR and the concepts in use need to consider how regions have shaped and contributed to particular interpretations of concepts. As such, conceptual analysis has to acknowledge the agency and diversity of different regions when it comes to hegemonic interpretations of concepts. Again, the concept of the "war on terror" constitutes an important example, which state actors from different regions have used to justify certain policies toward nonstate actors. The international dimension of the concept has been developed (and used) not only by Western (i.e., the United states) but also by non-Western elites to legitimize violent and nondemocratic policies. Yet, of course, this also entails the acknowledgment that concepts such as the "responsibility to protect" have been interpreted in very different ways in non-Western contexts and that the "success" of concepts has always been highly contingent depending on the acceptance of a particular interpretation. Hence, as these examples and the empirical cases in this volume have shown, the interpretation of concepts-in-use is also very much related to the understanding, acceptance, and rejection of norms involved in these concepts. A Global IR–inspired perspective therefore focuses on the practices of contestation and contested meanings of concepts at work instead of assuming certain concepts and norms as given in international politics. This approach allows to further account for the agency of nonstate actors, as those who are affected by concepts are also seen as capable of changing or shaping dominant interpretations through implementation, rejection, or simply the act of ignoring. A recent case in point is the right-wing populists in Europe (and elsewhere), who formally constitute only a minority in many countries but are powerful in changing dominant interpretations of democracy through advancing alternative concepts such as "illiberal democracy."

Ultimately, this book highlights that the analysis of concepts-in-use has to be contextualized in normative and ethical debates of IR as well. The patterns in which concepts work in different contexts imply that scholars need to consider the normative basis of a concept, which either does or does not resonate with the cultural and social background of actors who are affected. This also applies the other way around, in cases where concepts are used in a local context but with a moral reference to the international dimension of a concept. In light of the concept of justice, Amartya Sen aptly notes, "Even though actual agitations for justice may be conducted locally, the ethical basis of the demands for justice must have some universal relevance. . . . We cannot have an adequate conceptual grip on fighting injustice if we confine our attention only to what we see locally, ignoring what happens in the rest of the world" (2017, 261).

Notes

1. David Baldwin draws extensively from Hempel (1952) and hence a more "analytic" approach to concepts.

2. See here the quite instructive Boltanski and Thévenot 2006.

3. Kenneth Waltz introduced the concept of "levels of analysis" to the discipline of IR in his seminal work (1959), while David Singer's (1961) text is equally central in terms of influencing the understanding of international politics according to three different levels and systems operating within them.

4. Scholarship on speech acts, most prominently from John Austin and John Searle, has distinguished locution, illocution, and perlocution to define what counts as a speech act. While illocution, broadly speaking, refers to making a speech act, locution refers to making meaningful sentences. Speech act theorists have discussed whether the latter already constitutes a speech act, as the question is whether there is what Austin called an *illocutionary force*. Austin's intention to use this concept, which he and later Searle tried to systematize, is to emphasize that "speech acts" have aims

and effects albeit without a clear determination about the kind of effects. The characteristic aims of speech acts, for example, in speech acts where actors seek to pursue someone else to do something, are described as *perlocution*. See, among others, Searle (1969) and Austin (1976).

References

Acharya, Amitav. 2011. "Dialogue and Discovery: In Search of International Relations Theories Beyond the West." *Millennium: Journal of International Studies* 39 (3): 619–37.

Acharya, Amitav. 2014. "Global International Relations (IR) and Regional Worlds: A New Agenda for International Studies." *International Studies Quarterly* 58 (4): 647–59.

Acharya, Amitav. 2016. "Advancing Global IR: Challenges, Contentions, and Contributions." *International Studies Review* 18 (1): 4–15.

Amoureux, Jack L., and Brent J. Steele. 2015. *Reflexivity and International Relations: Positionality, Critique, and Practice.* London: Routledge.

Austin, John L. 1976. *How to Do Things with Words.* Oxford: Oxford University Press.

Baldwin, David A. 1997. "The concept of security." *Review of International Studies* 23 (1): 5–26.

Berenskoetter, Felix. 2016. *Concepts in World Politics.* London: Sage.

Berenskoetter, Felix. 2017. "Approaches to Concept Analysis." *Millennium: Journal of International Studies* 45 (2): 151–73.

Boltanski, Luc, and Laurent Thévenot. 2006. *On Justification: Economies of Worth.* Princeton, NJ: Princeton University Press.

Buzan, Barry, Ole Waever, and Jaap de Wilde. 1998. *Security: A New Framework for Analysis.* Boulder, CO: Lynne Rienner.

Cohn, Carol. 1987. "Sex and Death in the Rational World of Defense Intellectuals." *Signs* 12 (4): 687–718.

Collier, David, Jody LaPorte, and Jason Seawright. 2012. "Putting Typologies to Work: Concept Formation, Measurement, and Analytic Rigor." *Political Research Quarterly* 65 (1): 217–32.

Diez, Thomas, Ingvild Bode, and Aleksandra Fernandes da Costa, eds. 2011. *Key Concepts in International Relations.* London: Sage.

Gerth, Hans H., and C. Wright Mills, eds. 1946. *From Max Weber: Essays in Sociology.* New York: Oxford University Press.

Goertz, Gary. 2006. *Social Science Concepts: A User's Guide.* Princeton, NJ: Princeton University Press.

Guzzini, Stefano. 2000. "A Reconstruction of Constructivism in International Relations." *European Journal of International Relations* 6 (2): 147–82.

Guzzini, Stefano. 2005. "The Concept of Power: A Constructivist Analysis." *Millennium: Journal of International Studies* 33 (3): 495–522.

Guzzini, Stefano. 2013. "Power: Bourdieu's Field Analysis of Relational Capital, Misrecognition and Domination." In *Bourdieu in International Relations: Rethinking Key Concepts in IR,* ed. Rebecca Adler-Nissen, 79–82. Abingdon: Routledge.

Hamati-Ataya, Inanna. 2011. "The 'Problem of Values' and International Relations Scholarship: From Applied Reflexivity to Reflexivism." *International Studies Review* 13 (2): 259–87.

Hamati-Ataya, Inanna. 2012. "Beyond (Post)Positivism: The Missed Promises of Systemic Pragmatism." *International Studies Quarterly* 56 (2): 291–305.

Hamati-Ataya, Inanna. 2013. "Reflectivity, Reflexivity, Reflexivism: IR's 'Reflexive Turn'—and Beyond." *European Journal of International Relations* 19 (4): 669–94.

Havercroft, Jonathan. 2012. "Was Westphalia 'All That'? Hobbes, Bellarmine, and the Norm of Non-intervention." *Global Constitutionalism* 1 (1): 120–40.

Hempel, G. 1952. *Fundamentals of Concept Formation in Empirical Science*. Chicago: University of Chicago Press.

Hobson, John M. 2012. *The Eurocentric Conception of World Politics: Western International Theory, 1760–2010*. Cambridge: Cambridge University Press.

Hurrell, Andrew. 2016. "Beyond Critique: How to Study Global IR?" *International Studies Review* 18 (1): 149–51.

Ish-Shalom, Piki. 2019. *Beyond the Veil of Knowledge: Triangulating Security, Democracy, and Academic Scholarship*. Ann Arbor: University of Michigan Press.

Kratochwil, Friedrich. 1995. "Sovereignty as Dominium? Is There a Right to Humanitarian Intervention?" In *Beyond Westphalia? State Sovereignty and International Intervention*, ed. Gene Martin Lyons and Michael Mastanduno, chap. 2. Baltimore, MD: Johns Hopkins University Press.

McCourt, David M. 2016. "Practice Theory and Relationalism as the New Constructivism." *International Studies Quarterly* 60 (3): 475–85.

Milliken, Jennifer. 1999. "The Study of Discourse in International Relations: A Critique of Research and Methods." *European Journal of International Relations* 5 (2): 225-254.

Onuf, Nicholas G. 1991. "Sovereignty—Outline of a Conceptual History." *Alternatives: Global, Local, Political* 16 (4): 425–46.

Onuf, Nicholas G. 1994. "The Constitution of International Society." *European Journal of International Law* 5 (1): 1–19.

Pouliot, Vincent, and Frédéric Mérand. 2013. "Bourdieu's Concepts." In *Bourdieu in International Relations: Rethinking Key Concepts in IR*, edited by Rebecca Adler-Nissen, 24–44. London: Routledge.

Searle, John R. 1969. *Speech Acts: An Essay in the Philosophy of Language*. Cambridge: Cambridge University Press.

Sen, Amartya. 2017. "Ethics and the Foundation of Global Justice." *Ethics & International Affairs* 31 (3): 261–70.

Singer, David. 1961. "The Level-of-Analysis Problem in International Relations." *World Politics*. 14 (1): 77–92.

Somers, Margaret. 1995. "What's Political or Cultural about Political Culture and the Public Sphere? Toward an Historical Sociology of Concept Formation." *Sociological Theory* 13 (2): 113–44.

Taylor, Charles. 2004. *Modern Social Imaginaries*. Durham, NC: Duke University Press.

Tully, James. 2008. *Public Philosophy in a New Key—Volume II: Imperialism and Civic Freedom*. Cambridge: Cambridge University Press.

Walker, R. B. J. 1993. *Inside/Outside: International Relations as Political Theory*. Cambridge: Cambridge University Press.

Waltz, Kenneth N. 1959. *Man, the State and War: A Theoretical Analysis*. New York: Columbia University Press.

Wiener, Antje. 2008. *The Invisible Constitution of Politics: Contested Norms and International Encounters*. Cambridge: Cambridge University Press.

Wiener, Antje. 2018. *Contestation and Constitution of Norms in Global International Relations*. Cambridge: Cambridge University Press.

Zarakol, Ayşe. 2011. *After Defeat: How the East Learned to Live with the West*. Cambridge: Cambridge University Press

Contributors

Piki Ish-Shalom is the A. Ephraim and Shirley Diamond Family Chair in International Relations and chair of the Department of International Relations at the Hebrew University of Jerusalem. He is the author of *Democratic Peace: A Political Biography* (2015) and *Beyond the Veil of Knowledge: Triangulating Security, Democracy, and Academic Scholarship* (2019), both with the University of Michigan Press.

Philippe Beaulieu-Brossard is assistant professor specializing in defense, security studies, and design thinking at Canadian Forces College. He is currently on leave as a Marie S. Curie Fellow at the Centre for Military Studies, University of Copenhagen. He is completing a book developing a sociology of military design thinking. For this project, he literally followed the footprints of design thinking from the Israel Defense Forces, the US Army, US Special Operations Forces, and Canadian Armed Forces in a first research phase between 2015 and 2017. He is currently pursuing fieldwork tracing design thinking in Europe as it is emerging in professional military education programs in Denmark, Sweden, Poland, France, and NATO. Beaulieu-Brossard has published in the *Review of International Studies*, *International Relations*, and the *Journal of Military and Strategic Studies*. He holds a PhD in international relations from the University of St Andrews in the United Kingdom.

Felix Berenskötter heads the Department of Politics and International Studies at SOAS, University of London. He specializes in international theory and concepts of friendship, identity, power, security, and space-time, with an empirical focus on European security, German foreign policy, and transatlantic relations. He has published widely on these topics and is currently working on a book on friendship and estrangement in international relations.

Christian Bueger is professor of international relations at the University of Copenhagen, honorary professor at the University of Seychelles, and a research fellow at the University of Stellenbosch. His areas of research include international practice theory, the sociology of expertise, ocean governance, and maritime security. Further information on his work is available at http://bueger.info.

Luke Campbell is assistant professor of political science at Northwest Missouri State University. His research interests include international theory, international ethics, memory, nostalgia, and Just War theory. He has published various book chapters and articles on these topics.

Dr. Anna Geis has been professor of international security and conflict studies at Helmut Schmidt University / University of the Federal Armed Forces Hamburg (Germany) since April 2016. Her research and teaching areas include the domestic and international legitimation of military interventions, theories of peace and war, German foreign and security policy, liberal world order, citizen participation in Western foreign and security policy, external relations of the European Union, African security governance (military missions of the African Union), private military and security companies, the (non)recognition of armed nonstate actors in violent conflicts, and international criminal justice / transitional justice.

Oliver Kessler is associate professor at the University of Erfurt, Germany. His research focuses on the intersection of international political economy, global social theory, and international theory of law and politics—with particular interest in the promises and limits of interdisciplinary research. It reconstructs the limits and boundaries of these fields by exploring the connectivities to economic sociology, social systems theory, heterodox economics, and the history of economic and political thought more generally and uses these inquiries to highlight conceptual shortcomings, disciplinary biases, and avenues for interdisciplinary research.

Mor Mitrani is lecturer in the Department of Political Studies at Bar-Ilan University Israel. Her research focuses on the role of international interactions in a globalized world, patterns of international discourse, and the discursive construction of the international community.

Brent J. Steele is the Francis D. Wormuth Presidential Chair, professor, and chair of the Department of Political Science at the University of Utah, where he teaches courses on US foreign policy, international security, international relations theory, and international ethics.

Neta Strunin-Kremer is a PhD candidate in the International Relations Department of the Hebrew University of Jerusalem.

Dr. Jan Wilkens earned his PhD in international relations from the University of Hamburg, where he works as a postdoc at the Chair of Political Science, especially Global Governance, and in the Cluster of Excellence "Climate, Climatic Change, and Society." His work focuses on norms and contentious politics in international relations. This interest is informed by bringing together constructivist and postcolonial scholarship in IR. Empirically, he focuses on the global politics of West Asia and North Africa (WANA).

Jonas Wolff is executive board member and head of the research department Intrastate Conflict at the Peace Research Institute Frankfurt. His research focuses on the transformation of political orders, contentious politics, international democracy promotion, and Latin American politics. Recent publications include *The Negotiation of Democracy Promotion* (special issue of *Democratization,* 2019, coedited with A. E. Poppe and J. Leininger), *Socioeconomic Protests in MENA and Latin America* (Palgrave Macmillan, 2020, coedited with I. Weipert-Fenner), and *Justice and Peace: The Role of Justice Claims in International Cooperation and Conflict* (Springer, 2019, coedited with C. Fehl, D. Peters, and S. Wisotzki).

Index